THE TIGER HEART CHRONICLES
a new history of Shakespeare

TIGER'S HEART IN WOMAN'S HIDE

BY

Fred Faulkes

THIS PRINT-ON-DEMAND ITEM
IS AVAILABLE FROM WWW.TRAFFORD.COM
AND WWW.TIGER-HEART.COM

© Copyright 2007 Fred Faulkes
All rights reserved. No part of this publication may be reproduced, stored in a retrieval system, or transmitted, in any form or by any means, electronic, mechanical, photocopying, recording, or otherwise, without the written prior permission of the author. Critics however, are welcome to quote brief passages by way of criticism and review.

Typeset by Jon Whipple MGDC
Cover art and line-drawing illustrations by Diane Kreme
Back cover photograph Sukie Kandola

Note for Librarians: A cataloguing record for this book is available from Library and Archives Canada at www.collectionscanada.ca/amicus/index-e.html
ISBN 1-4251-0739-7

Printed in Victoria, BC, Canada. Printed on paper with minimum 30% recycled fibre. Trafford's print shop runs on "green energy" from solar, wind and other environmentally-friendly power sources.

Offices in Canada, USA, Ireland and UK

Book sales for North America and international:
Trafford Publishing, 6E–2333 Government St.,
Victoria, BC V8T 4P4 CANADA
phone 250 383 6864 (toll-free 1 888 232 4444)
fax 250 383 6804; email to orders@trafford.com

Book sales in Europe:
Trafford Publishing (UK) Limited, 9 Park End Street, 2nd Floor
Oxford, UK OX1 1HH UNITED KINGDOM
phone +44 (0)1865 722 113 (local rate 0845 230 9601)
facsimile +44 (0)1865 722 868; info.uk@trafford.com

Order online at:
trafford.com/06-2497

10 9 8 7 6 5 4 3 2

THE TIGER HEART CHRONICLES

Volume 1

TIGER'S HEART IN WOMAN'S HIDE

PREFATORIAL ACKNOWLEDGMENTS

Many people have played key roles in originating, encouraging and aiding me in this project. I thank my friends Rachel and Roy, by whose conversations I first found myself staring at 'the question'; my father, Eddy, and brother, Ronald, for their support and encouragement throughout; my aunt Judith for her generous bequest; and my friends and colleagues Roy, Ron, Sophie, Ginger, Pat, and Martin for all their help as I went through the process of learning to write.

I acknowledge the help many individuals at the Vancouver Public Library, the University of British Columbia Library, Simon Fraser University Library, and the National Library of Canada extended as we waded through all the bibliographic minutiae. I thank the many university libraries throughout Canada and the United States who generously provided me with copies of rare holdings.

I acknowledge a special debt to Kevin Perley for his help editing the manuscript in the end run.

And I thank Angelina and Jeremy for putting up with their father's *folly* these past nine years!

This book is dedicated to you all.

THIS BOOK HAS BEEN PRINTED IN CANADIAN ENGLISH

CONTENTS

PROLOGUE
i

CHAPTER 1
A STRATFORD MYSTERY
1

CHAPTER 2
THE OLD ACTOR & THE LADY
17

CHAPTER 3
SIX PLAYWRIGHTS & A SONNET PIRACY
45

CHAPTER 4
DEFENDING HER HONOUR
76

CHAPTER 5
NASHE'S PADDLE & GREENE'S MONTH OF DYING
98

CHAPTER 6
IS IT MARY?
127

EPILOGUE
156

BIBLIOGRAPHY
159

INDEX
176

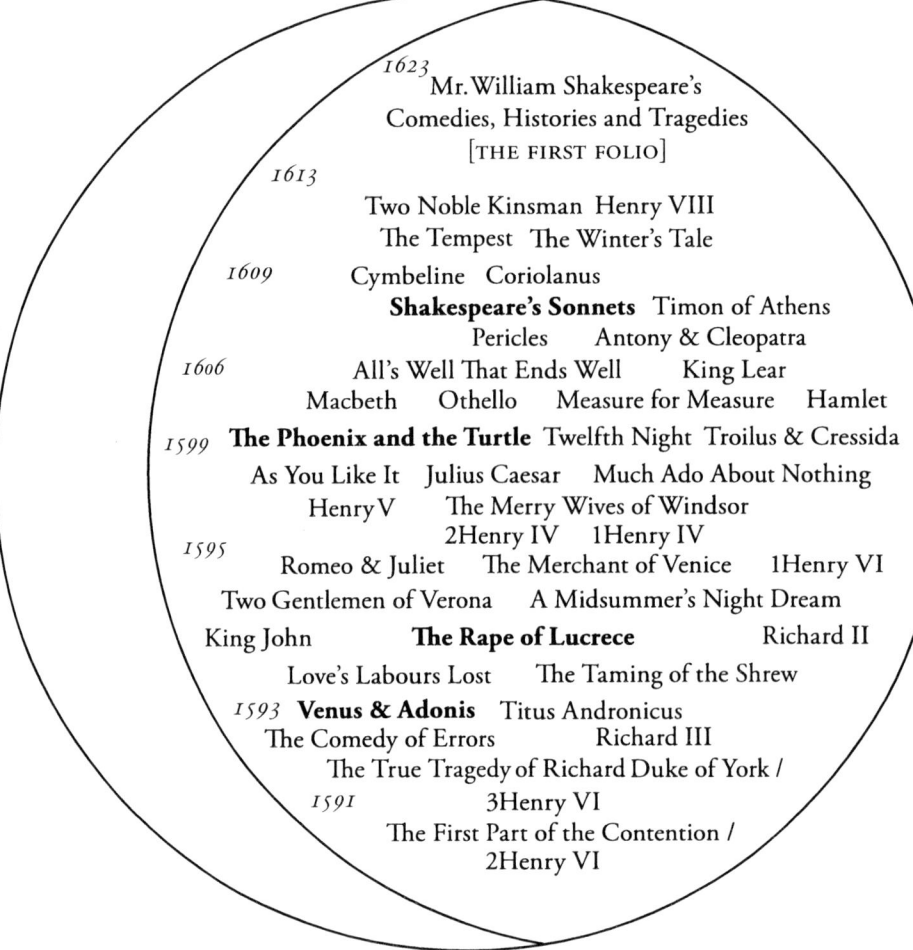

Shakespeare's works laid out in reconstructed chronological order (from bottom to top); the narrative poetry is highlighted.

PROLOGUE

Shakespeare's Detached Orb

In that Elizabethan galaxy of literary wits and worthies, no orb shines more brilliantly than Shakespeare's. It is the centrepiece jewel of a star cluster that appears as if out of a long, dreary literary night. For a couple of hundred years only Chaucer's orb and the few dim stars about it were visible in that English sky. But then from one generation born in the 1550's and 60's and reared in the full flush of 16th century humanism, there is again English literature worth the retelling. But of all that literature suddenly to appear, it is Shakespeare's body of work that truly captivates our attention.

A million words cover the pages that paper that body, immediately giving it outsized proportions. This is also true of the quality for every strand of words seems to ring and resonate with a considered life of its own. Even without understanding all the layered meaning, the sheer musicality entices us to draw closer. It is mostly a stage-play world we find, made up of some 37 different plays, some of which appear in variant versions. For the average student barge this can make for some tumultuous waters. But, like scattered isles, lie the pieces of narrative poetry where the poet would speak to us more distinctly in a single voice: *Venus & Adonis* (1593), *The Rape of Lucrece* (1594), and *The Phoenix and the Turtle* (1599).

And then in 1609, *Shakespeare's Sonnets* will draw back the curtain altogether and let the *I* step forward and tell us something about the self and why it had all been done. At the heart of these sonnets there is the painful yet empowering memory of a young man of high hope whom the poet loved very much but whose life had somehow been cut tragically short. The young man was also a poet, probably the 'EVER-LIVING POET' of the sonnets' cryptic dedication. For Shakespeare he remains a daily inspiration. A bittersweet mood speaking eloquently of love, loss, memory, fantasy and immortality cuts a wide swath through the heart of these sonnets. A swarthy woman rivals Shakespeare for the young man's affections. There is attendant another man, a 'rival poet'. But the 'loved one', around whom all their lives had revolved, had somehow died. For Shakespeare his monument casts a very long shadow, indeed. More buoyantly the sonnets elsewhere show the poet demonstrating a great deal of parental concern for a young man who has been identified with the *Mr. W.H.* found in the sonnets' dedication. Here Shakespeare would see him settled with wife so that he might beget an heir. But other than that, the poet's autobiography is almost entirely a blank. It is one reason I call the poet's orb detached.

For such a long-active poet as Shakespeare, this almost total lack of life story, even by the more modest standards of that day, is startling. It is as if silence was a conscious decision. But others alive at the time appear to have been far less reticent. Satirists such as Thomas Nashe, Robert Greene, Gabriel Harvey, William Covell, Henry Willobie, John Weever, and so on, right up to Ben Jonson laying Shakespeare to rest in 1623, leave us a series of strangely-worded news notices that sits like a long line of carnival mirrors beside Shakespeare's body of works as this came into being. The news they all impart is surprisingly consistent: in the matter of Shakespeare, there was an actor, yes, but behind him they describe 'a woman'. Several of the commentators will openly identify her. It appears that in the years that the Shakespeare chronicle came into being, the matter of who was authoring the works was something of an 'open secret'.

This series, THE TIGER HEART CHRONICLES, will endeavour to lay bare all the documentary remains to have any bearing on Shakespeare's history, including, for the first time, that prickly line of satirical notices the scholarship has acknowledged but generally ignored.

Although this study is founded first and foremost on the work of the best scholars in the field, I do admit to having boiled all these sources down to nothing but the hard, provable facts they contain. After some four years of gathering and an indescribable amount of sorting I had little more than a point-form description of all the items in the Shakespearean debris field covering the period 1591 – 1623.

I began the task of reading all those Elizabethan and Jacobean documents and texts in the order in which they appeared, following out the lives of their authors so that I might better understand them at those moments that really count in the search for Shakespeare. Making sense of large numbers of obscure renaissance texts is no easy matter, especially when little context immediately appears for any of them. In order to re-create that context I found myself having to sort the documents further.

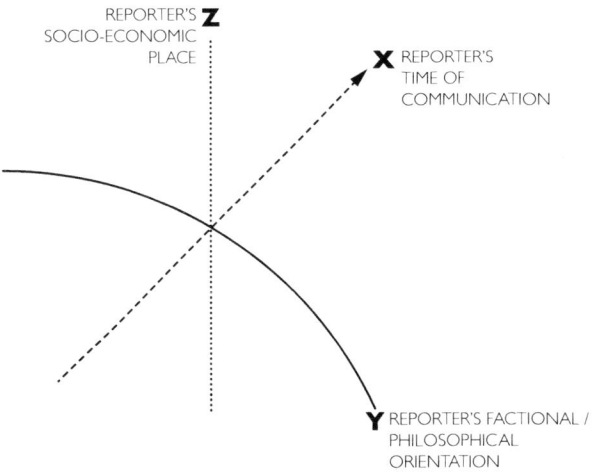

The tri-axial sorting that evolved allowed me to move beyond the one-dimensionality that chronology on its own produces. By sorting according to the factional allegiance (as well as the religious/ political/ philosophical outlooks of the various reporters) I was able to do an 'across-the-board' sort of the documentary remains, allowing each document to once again speak from the particular point of view it held in its time. (It was at this stage that it emerged some of the books were holding back-and-forth conversations through time.) Third, the reporter's place in the social/economic hierarchy was factored in so that the dynamics of the reporter's tone and intent, as well as the interplay of the texts, might be better understood. This tri-axial sorting creates a three-dimensionality in which each of the pertinent written, printed, inscribed, painted or etched remains can be given a place commensurate with that held in the original psycho-social space of the times. Such a reconstruction of Shakespeare's history has, to my knowledge, never before been attempted.

But it is a grinding thirty-two-year history, made up of several always-shifting tableaux of people, and it can all only be properly presented over the course of several volumes. Here in volume 1, I shall describe the particular confluence of people who make up the first year of Shakespeare's history. We shall discover from where they came, determine the roles they were playing in the enterprise, and how they interrelated at the time that Shakespeare's hand first appears.

Out of respect for the orthodoxy, chapter 1 begins with a re-examination of the early life of William Shakspere of Stratford from his birth in 1564 to his removal to the London stage, which is here placed in the 1591-92 season. Although the orthodox view is that Shakspere the actor is Shakespeare the poet, this series will contend that they were, in fact, two separate (though allied) individuals. (The spelling distinction in their names is therefore maintained throughout, not out of malice but for purposes of clarity.) And in this opening chapter we will meet the sheriff's son from just outside Stratford who will later claim to have played the 'master' in all this.

Chapter 2 follows with William Shakspere's new London employer, James Burbage, owner of the Theatre playhouse, and illustrates how allied they already were by their factional histories. We determine how the company of players with which Shakspere (and Shakespeare) will be associated, the Earl of Pembroke's Men, came to be established and meet the woman who will act as their patron, a countess by the name of Mary Sidney.

Chapter 3 introduces us to the playwrights (Marlowe, Kyd, Peele, Greene and Nashe) who first worked up the scripts for the Pembroke troupe. We will consider the rough-and-tumble history that already lay at back of their relations before going on to discover a daring act of literary piracy committed by one of them, Thomas Nashe, against their patron. This episode gives us our first mirror image of 'the company' as it stood in 1591 before the arrival of either Shakspere or Shakespeare.

Chapter 4 presents the company of writers who rush to the countess's defence in order to counter Nashe's assaults on her. They give us in the process a vivid look at this woman's literary agenda and the inherited role that was propelling her forward.

Chapter 5 brings us to summer 1592 and shows us Nashe under the guise of *Pierce Penniless* continuing his crusade against the countess, revealing why he could not possibly be patronized by her. August will be playwright Greene's last month of life and the letter he writes from his deathbed will alert the other playwrights that someone has been overwriting their plays. Greene will be the first to inform us that in the matter of authorship, there stood a womanly presence behind the actor.

Given all that will have come into view, we shall ask in chapter 6 if that woman, indeed, is their patron, Mary Sidney, and put her case to the same unforgiving scrutiny every other contender for Shakespeare's mantle has had to endure. But where others come up short in specific regards, we shall see that Mary Sidney's pre-Shakespearean life is a point-for-point fit with the learning, life experience and aspirations the poet Shakespeare will betray the moment the writing begins in 1592. The epilogue will indicate the new model that comes into view and suggest some directions for further study.

In my presentation all quotations are given in italics with no quotation marks used except where these are set off from the main body of the text. I have done this for the expedients of a clearer, cleaner presentation, especially as there is much original text to consider. Although I have mostly modernised the spelling, I have retained the original punctuation. Even though renaissance punctuation is no longer understood (and therefore sometimes modernised, as well), I believe we may retain it if we will treat it as musical, not grammatical, notation. The punctuation marks would then come to represent the following series of breath marks:

.	full stop	a pause roughly equivalent to the time it takes to fully fill the lungs with air
:	three-quarter stop	a pause that is three-quarters the length that given the full stop
;	half stop	a pause half the length that given the full stop
,	quarter stop	a pause a quarter the length that

_,_ eighth stop	given the full stop (where comma sits wedged in between two words) the shortest audible pause

As to the question mark (?) sometimes found in what are obviously declarative sentences, I propose this indicates the speaker's intonation is to rise step-wise over the course of the line as when, for example, becoming more and more concerned or more and more angry. I myself have found reading Elizabethan texts out loud giving the punctuation marks these values produces a smooth, cadenced and emotionally convincing read. (This is especially true of Shakespeare's works which tend to be punctuated rather more heavily and particularly than most.) If this proposition should come to be seen as true, we may find ourselves recovering many a poet's true original intentions with regards to how they wished to hear their works read out loud.

The Elizabethan and Jacobean bedrock, which the present series seeks to lay bare, brings into view a charming landscape but one very different from our own. English is spoken but it is very old-fashioned and often requires glossing. Here we find a society ruled by a generally mild but nonetheless absolute monarch and everything of import does pass by her. Around her are the several factions of nobles and churchmen who constantly rise and fall at her Majesty's discretion. Further down it is a highly stratified society and everyone holds some regulated place in it. Almost everybody is connected by family to some faction and we do well to come to terms with that social/political reality. We arrive at a time when people are deeply divided by religion and philosophy, some holding to the comforts of the Catholic-Aristotelian old, some trying to steer a middle course, while others would rush headlong into the Protestant new. As well, we shall find in our story a scientific vein though it is a science most of us will only vaguely recognise. Neo-Platonism was a synthesis of 'hard' sciences like mathematics, geometry, cartography, metallurgy and astronomy placed at the service of the 'divine' sciences – astrology and alchemy. Some of the people of our story will be heavily under those golden, starry influences. But what will perhaps most challenge us as we come to understand these people through their writings is that they lived in a 'closed society' in which one simply did not speak one's mind in matters affecting church, state or one's social superiors. If something of that sort had to be said openly, a coded language (called *fustian*) was used. Here any pertinent situation or event in the Bible, classical mythology, local folklore, history, literature, or whatever else was in circulation, was used as cover for that which could not be said openly. In order to understand these pre-plain-speaking people, we will have to develop the same ever-alert sensitivity to layers of meaning that for people living in closed societies is second nature.

CHAPTER I

A Stratford Mystery

In the immediate years up to 1623 there appeared two documents that seemed to fix the matter of who wrote the works of 'William Shakespeare' once and for all. There had, of course, been multiple editions of the poetry and some of the plays in the three decades leading up to 1623, but in all those little books there had ever only been the name, abbreviated to W.S. or written out as William Shakespeare or simply Shakespeare, with almost nothing outwardly to identify the author.

Martin Droeshout the Elder. Engraving for the First Folio, 1623.

It was only with the first publication of the collected plays of Shakespeare in 1623 that a very particular group of people headed by poet-playwright Ben Jonson would come forward and, for the first time in print, identify the author as having been William Shakspere of Stratford, Warwickshire, England. The volume included a somewhat odd engraving of the man [above], had some strangely worded things to say about him, and told of a monument that had been erected to his memory back in his hometown.

The monument, shown here as Sir Walter Dugdale drew it within decades of its installation, corroborates what the 1623 folio

after Sir Walter Dugdale's drawing of the Shakespeare monument.

edition claims. It is primarily these two substantial historical artefacts – the folio edition and the original monument – that establish the now orthodox view that the man from Stratford is the poet history identifies as William Shakespeare.

That is certainly how readers of the First Folio took matters and with these two beacons to guide them, began shortly to arrive in Stratford. But at Holy Trinity Church, where the monument had been installed, the pilgrims were in for something of a rude surprise. There in the floor in front of the monument lay the great stone slab covering the earthly remains of William Shakspere. The whole stone had been left blank except for a small verse he had had inscribed.

> Good friend for Jesus' sake forbear,
> To dig the dust enclosèd here:
> Blessed be the man that spares these stones,
> And cursed be he that moves my bones.

And the townsfolk were happy to usher the pilgrims just down the aisle to another similar epitaph this same poet had left. It was the verse emblazoned about the tomb of the man's friend, John Comb, a moneylender of Stratford, who had died three years before him.

> Ten in the Hundred here lieth engraved
> A hundred to ten his soul is now saved
> If any one ask who lieth in this Tomb
> Oh ho quoth the Divel, 'tis my John a Combe.

These two merry, country verses, with their earthy bravado in the face of death, came rudely and unexpectedly to the pilgrims. Were these truly the work of the same poet whose shimmering legacy of 100,000 lines of distinctive iambic pentameter verse had brought them here? Visitors murmured. And that curse on his tomb! It was so unexpected, so unnecessary and philosophically so alien to the spirit of the poet they had come to pay homage to. And why did he leave his stone mostly blank? Did he expect others to fill the spaces with verses such as those that ended up in the wall-mounted monument? Immediately people were forced to think up explanations that might pacify the uneasiness already setting in here between the man who lay under this stone and the poet, Shakespeare.

The pilgrims were reassuringly directed to the registry of the church. There it was recorded that *Guiliamus filius Johannes Shakspere* [WILLIAM, SON OF JOHN SHAKSPERE] was christened on 26 April 1564 and was buried 52 years later on 25 April 1616. William Shakspere's life then sits comfortably enough beside the Shakespeare chronology—1591-1623. But the centuries of searching for this man's life would reveal something quite unexpected. While he is in Stratford there is sufficient documentation for him and his family to draw out the broad contours of their lives. But at the supposed height of his career, what should have been the glory years in London, he becomes much more furtive, keeping out of sight.

The further surprise was that the story the records of Stratford tell of William Shakspere's early life fails to lay the right sort of foundation stones for the specific skills that Shakespeare the poet will need the moment the writing starts over the 1591-92 season.

But the records of Stratford do indicate that William Shakspere was born into a family of self-starters, mobilised to rise. His father, John Shakspere, had come from a farm north of town, served an apprenticeship in town and in the early 1550's become one of its proud (and free) citizens. He had learned the art of dressing leather hides and making gloves. He worked hard and began immediately to invest his profits into properties about Stratford, including the house on Henley Street where William would be born.

Some seven years before William's birth, John Shakspere married Mary Arden, a woman ten years his junior. She brought 50 acres, another house and £6 13 shillings 4 pence in the bargain. The records indicate neither she nor her husband could write, both signing their names throughout their lives with marks. But they appear to have been highly numerate, able to take nimble advantage of the new emerging capitalist order.

As John Shakspere thrived he was invited to take part in the responsibilities of the town government. At the time of his marriage he was already one of the town's watchdogs, ensuring the brewers and bakers offered fair measure and consistent quality. In 1558 he became one of Stratford's four constables. All merchants were expected to play roles of this sort for short terms.

In 1558 Catholic Queen Mary died and Princess Elizabeth came to the throne ready to return England to the Protestant fold. Warwickshire had been without an earl since Queen Mary beheaded John Dudley, the old Earl of Warwick. Old Warwick had played too keen a role in young King Edward's final will and testament that bypassed his two Tudor sisters in favour of the third in line, the more studiously Protestant Lady Jane Grey. But that reign would crumble after nine days. And though John Dudley lost his head, he had a couple of sons who survived him, one of whom, Robert, would over the course of the Protestant exile from court become the chief love interest of the Protestant Princess Elizabeth. The moment Elizabeth came to the throne she made the strong, dashing, intellectually-stimulating Robert Dudley her Master of the Horse while his older, stronger, and even more dashing brother, Ambrose, immediately became Master of the Armouries. And then on St. Stephen's day 1561 the queen made the older Ambrose the new Earl of Warwick.

Under Ambrose Dudley's influence the towns about Warwickshire felt the tug of the reforming spirit returned. When the change hit Stratford, it appears John Shakspere changed with it. The Shakspuses now began to pay their annual rent for the land on which their Henley Street house stood to the new earl. That year William's father, John, became one of the town's two chamberlains under whose auspices the religious images adorning the Guild Hall chapel were removed. (The suppression of religious images reflected the Protestant view that in the relationship between an individual and God, no icons need intercede.) The following year John Shakspere was made one of the thirteen Aldermen of the Stratford Council.

It was this council that voted to deny the now too Catholic vicar, Roger Dyos, his wages thereby forcing the man to resettle some forty miles south in Wiltshire. Dyos was replaced by Ambrose Dudley's choice of John Bretchgirdle (M.A., Oxford). This reflects another of the aspirations of the new Protestants at court, to have university-educated preaching clergy in all the congregations of the realm. The vicar's house received repairs. Meanwhile the schoolhouse that had been built only in the time of Edward VI a decade before was abandoned for a new classroom in the upper story of the Guild Hall. The reformed religion, humanist education and culture, and legally-sanctioned capitalism were the forces that would draw their society out of its backward state.

When William was four, his father was selected to serve as bailiff (mayor) for a year. Although the town had been incorporated in 1553, giving it a measure of self-government, the Earl of Warwick maintained the power of veto over the aldermen's choice of bailiff. But Ambrose Dudley appears to have had no problem with Shakspere's candidature and over 1568-69 John served his term.

It was during his mayoralty that troupes of actors visiting Stratford were first paid by the town council for public performances. This was in keeping with the Protestant reform agenda that would see secular theatre supplant the church-sponsored miracle and mystery plays that had marked the seasons for many centuries now. This, too, was part of the campaign to suppress religious icons. (Only the morality plays with their portrayals of sin leavened with satire and burlesque would survive this suppression.) Right from the beginning of her reign, Elizabeth had led the secular theatrical charge by becoming patron to her own troupe of players, the Queen's Men. When they first appeared at Stratford they received 9 shillings while the Earl of Worcester's Men later the same year earned only 1! This is not to say that her Majesty's players pleased the town fathers nine times better than did the Worcester company, only that the burghers would under no circumstances offend the person of the queen. (Troupes were paid according to the social standing of their respective patrons.) Soon the troupes the Dudley brothers had raised would visit Stratford as well.

As the town's bailiff, John Shakspere enjoyed the powers of a

Justice of the Peace, giving further indication of the sway he held in the town's affairs. It is no surprise then that at the end of his year as mayor the elder Shakspere applied to the college of heralds for a coat of arms. In his petition he described himself as Bailiff, Justice of the Peace, the Queen's Officer and Chief of the Town of Stratford. If his petition had succeeded, John Shakspere and his family would have joined the outer ring of what constituted the 'ruling class'. Throughout England there were perhaps some 50,000 families in that class, governing a population of some three and a half million. To be able to bear arms was a badge of great social distinction in an age that was hypersensitive to such things.

Although John Shakspere sometimes signed his name by drawing a pair of shears, it appears that much of his income over the course of his civic involvements came to be centred on wheeling and dealing in real estate and tradable commodities, and whatever he may have gotten through his official duties. (Systemic corruption was then very much more blatant than now.) Throughout this period John and Mary Shakspere's family grew apace. William was joined by siblings Gilbert in 1566, Joan in 1569, Anne in 1571, Richard in 1574 and Edmund in 1580. As one of the town's leading burghers, John Shakspere would have been permitted to send his sons to the grammar school as they came of age. Although there are no records, the townsfolk would later report that young William did attend. This was probably around 1571 when William was seven. The choice of the headmaster was again Ambrose Dudley's responsibility and he ensured that the town had university-trained instructors. The council was obliged to pay the headmaster the competitive annual wage of £20. A house was provided free.

The curriculum of the Elizabethan schoolhouse consisted mostly of the long, arduous grind of mastering the Latin language so that one might one day stand in the full glow of the more advanced classical and classically-inspired culture found within it. For the rest of the long school day it was religion, a little history and arithmetic, recess and the long break for the midday meal. Some teachers added foreign languages, music and other subjects according to their skill. In the case of the Stratford masters no records remain.

With the matter of his coat of arms pending and his wealth still less than stupendous, William's father was doing everything he could to improve the family's net standing. We find him lending money at interest rates that exceeded the legal limit of 10 percent per annum. In 1570 he was brought before the court of the Exchequer on charges of usury, lending money (in his case) at rates of 20 and 25 percent. The mood of the merchants' class was generally unsentimental where capital accumulation was concerned even if the pulpit and the pundits railed against reigning abuses.

By this time John had also begun to deal in large amounts of wool, an activity to which his trade of glover gave him no right. What appears to have grown up in the Midlands was a kind of squeeze play whereby unauthorized dealers, such as John, bought up large amounts of wool at source and, after withholding it to produce conditions of scarcity, then sold it to the Staple at Westminster at inflated prices. As the Staple was forced to sell it at more or less expected prices to their continental customers, the rise in price may have directly affected their profits. The wool trade contained a long history of these sorts of shenanigans and successive pieces of legislation had sought to stamp out the perpetual scamming. The Staple held the patents and the authorized wool traders the licenses and so the task for the government could only be to uproot the intruders. Twice John Shakspere found himself arraigned. Whatever his fines may have been, it appears he did not let up. One expects the profits were simply too tempting. Certainly none of these appearances before a judge interfered with his standing among the politicians of the town, who may have thrived in similarly quasi-legal ways. John's dexterity with numbers is borne out by the fact that he was the town's bookkeeper at this same time.

In 1575 Ambrose Dudley's brother, Robert, entertained her Majesty for three weeks at Kenilworth Castle, just fourteen miles up the road from Stratford. At Kenilworth the younger Dudley had laboured three years, spending the astronomical sum of £60,000 in preparing the grounds and buildings and the monumental series of extravaganzas with which he would entertain the queen. It was the last time Robert Dudley would do all within his power to persuade the queen to marry him. He had come close before but now he had left nothing to chance. For three weeks in July Lord Robert would woo the queen with musical and theatrical delights by night and day on land and water (for he had had an artificial lake made for the purpose). It was on a scale England had never seen before. Two accounts were published. And to help him stage this grand gesture, Robert Dudley had invited all the town leaders from around the shire to come and attend the outdoor events. Although no record remains, it is almost certain that John Shakspere and his family were invited, and quite probable that they went.

Although everything appeared to be going well for the Shaksperes, it was now all to come dramatically tumbling down. First there was word from Robert Cook, Clarenceux King-of-Arms, that John's 1569 application for a coat-of-arms had been denied. That left the Shaksperes respectably of yeomen stock and was perhaps to John a subtle reminder to get back to his trade and thrive by more legal ways. We may surmise that the rejection bruised the family's feelings, especially the father's. He had faithfully worked for the betterment of the town these past twenty years – far, far longer than was required by statute.

But this was only a forewarning of greater calamity to come. In November of 1576 her Majesty's Privy Council finally decided to bring the gauntlet down on illegal wool dealing and the entire trade was brought to a complete halt until everything could be sorted out. Bonds of surety were gathered from all authorized buyers and the unauthorized ones like John Shakspere were squeezed out. This unregulated quasi-futures market may have relied on lots of credit and John may have been holding a lot of debt when everything suddenly came crashing down. (With his financial standing suddenly a-wobble, we can only hope that John had not earlier this year gambled on Martin Frobisher's claim to have found gold in the Canadian Arctic. The scheme to extract the deposit was being heavily promoted by Ambrose Dudley's wife, Anne Russell, the Countess of Warwick. Despite promises of enormous returns, the shiploads of ore Frobisher eventually brought back turned out to be England's disheartening introduction to fool's gold.)

Wherever all the money went, it would be a full decade before the Shaksperes were financially back to where they had been, giving some indication of the extent of the damage. John stopped attending council meetings, but he did not lose the favour or support of his fellow councillors. The town council was not to fine him for his absenteeism, as was the usual practice. Protectively, they simply marked him absent for the next nine years! He also stopped going to church. The reason for all this appears to have been that in order to escape gaol (where his creditors no doubt wished to put him) John had gone into hiding and was running what was left of his business interests out of sight. Besides keeping him as one of their own, the town council further helped by excusing him certain taxes, while elsewhere cutting some of his fees.

With the onset of the family's problems, the townsfolk reported that William was taken out of school and made to work for his father. With five children to feed, it makes sense that John could no longer afford to keep William at his studies. The boy turned 13 in 1577. Some preschool followed by at most six years of elementary education, despite the long, harshly disciplined schooldays, would have provided William with only elementary literacy and learning. But with even these skills William would have been a tremendous boon to his father who could not write at all.

If he was in hiding, as appears, John would have needed a factotum – an agent who could deal with the people of the outer world on his behalf. And if he was broke, as appears, he would have immediately turned to his eldest son, William. Judging from the size of the man as portrayed in the later Chandos image of him, young Shakspere may already have been a stout lad at 13. His peculiar situation here would have offered the young man a measure of freedom most apprenticed sons who had to work under the ever-vigilant eyes of their fathers or masters would not have had.

And so it happened when he was 18 that William managed to impregnate a woman some eight years older than himself called Anne Hathaway who lived a mile and a half north of Stratford. There was what appears to have been a forced marriage away from the town's eyes and a daughter, Susanna Shakspere, was born some five months later. In late January of 1585 twins, christened Hamnet and Judith, were born. They appear to have been named after friends, Hamnet Sadler, a baker in High Street, and his wife, Judith Staunton. It appears the three generations of Shakspere lived together in the house on Henley Street. Although there was nothing unusual about this by the standards of the day, for William, at 21, to be the father of three, with limited formal education, and no profession other than wheeling and dealing, does not lay the right sort of foundation for what the poet Shakespeare will soon be ready to do. The next stage of William's life is no real help in this regard, either.

The story the people of Stratford told visitors was that in the years before his move to London, William Shakspere was in a butcher's apprenticeship. It appears that by 1586-7 enough debts had been paid to take John out of danger of imprisonment, and that he could operate freely again. The new choice of career for William makes impeccable sense from the family's point of view. John Shakspere was forced to buy his hides from the butchers, his trades of tanner and glover giving him no right to slaughter animals or sell meat. William's new trade would have permitted the Shakspere's, father and son, to process the whole animal from hide to hoofs! Apprenticeships usually lasted about seven years. If William started this about 1586, he would have been finished around 1593.

But before Shakspere reached the end he was caught poaching game out of a warren belonging to one of the local magnates, a fierce conservationist by the name of Sir Thomas Lucy. This was more than mere youthful hi-jinx. The fact is that William Shakspere was here acquiring those very commodities that fed his extended family's enterprise. For a family rebuilding its fortunes to get these raw materials for no more than their labours was, of course, all to the better.

Robert Dudley, who had been made Earl of Leicester in 1564 and through his brother had become the prime magnate in Warwickshire, had knighted Sir Thomas Lucy back in 1565. The Lucies were stalwart supporters of the Dudleys' Protestant agenda. But next to Catholics, the people Sir Thomas most fervently prosecuted were poachers. Enjoying the favour of the faction, he had been selected to sit in several Parliaments at Westminster as one of two members from Warwickshire. From parliamentary records we learn that one of his big issues was the preservation of wildlife in such forests and parks as still remained. He drew up a *Bill for the better preservation of grain and game* in 1584 whereby poaching would have been made a felony. Luckily for William Shakspere the bill did not pass! The townsfolk reported that the fiery knight had every intention of taking Shakspere to court, but that somehow William slipped away to the London stage before the matter could proceed.

With his coming to London William Shakspere needs now to be ready to be the poet, Shakespeare. The first work we have from the poet is a rewrite of a play first produced by a committee of professional playwrights working for a new troupe in town, the Earl of Pembroke's Men. As a team these playwrights represented the best educated, most talented, most experienced poet-playwrights then working in London. Shakespeare's first task, as we shall shortly discover, was to polish their work in matters of courtly protocol and etiquette, in how kings and queens ought to be made to speak, to eliminate the artificial and add more poetic substance, and above all, to bring the female characters to three-dimensional life. But what in William Shakspere's background would have specifically prepared him to take this substantial and highly particular task in hand?

A great unease set in over the course of the seventeenth and eighteenth centuries as students of Shakespeare became more and more aware of this second gulf here opening. The gathering storm was only averted by a quip that Ben Jonson had uttered in Shakespeare's 1623 folio about the Stratford man. There Jonson had written: *Who, as he was a happy imitator of Nature, was a most gentle expresser of it. His mind and hand went together: and what he thought, he uttered with that easiness that we have scarce received from him a blot in his papers.* All innuendo aside, to those gaping at the hole here in the biography of Shakspere-as-Shakespeare, Jonson's remarks appeared as a godsend. Though Jonson never said so much, the implication appeared to be that William Shakspere had not needed study, that all the words had simply appeared spontaneously in his brain from where they had flowed unerringly via his pen unto paper! By the time of the second edition of the Encyclopædia Britannica (1777-84) it could be safely reported that Shakspere(-as-Shakespeare) *was the only instance of a human being to whom learning was unnecessary; the favourite child of Nature, produced and educated entirely by herself; but so educated, that the pedant Art had nothing new to add.* But when we consider the poet's particular set of skills (which aside from the above also includes knowledge of foreign languages, the law, statecraft, and so on), we see this to be a myth for the simple reason that knowledge of such matters does not appear spontaneously in the brain. These are highly particular skills for which years of study and experience are required. And despite the many theories that have been advanced over the 19th and 20th centuries to explain how the Stratford man may have acquired that education and experience of life to be a fully-functioning Shakespeare by 1591-2, the story the people of Stratford told immediately after his death was that William went straight from his butcher's apprenticeship and predicament with Sir Thomas Lucy to the playhouse, with no intermediary steps in between.

Now the small metropolis of London was only a hundred miles away, but at this time more like a world apart. People still moved very, very little. Yeomen (especially ones under prosecution like William Shakspere) were not free to up and move wherever they pleased. William would have needed a passport from someone in authority to travel. (The first address we have for him at the London end shows him, remarkably, living inside the walls of the city. This is significant because London was much more strictly patrolled than its suburbs and people without permit were generally shown the gate at the end of the day.) People at the time (economics and social controls being what they were) did not make such moves unless there were people at the other end ready to take them in and offer them a livelihood.

Who might have bridged the gap, extricating Shakspere from his legal problems with Sir Thomas Lucy on the Stratford side, keeping those problems out of court, providing warrant for travel and residency within the city, and helping him to his new occupation as an employee of Master James Burbage of Shoreditch, owner of The Theatre playhouse, and as a player in that new troupe in town, the Earl of Pembroke's Men? It is here that I should tentatively like to place some remarks made in the next century by a quite remarkable man.

By the time Fulke Greville, Baron Brooke, made his remarks in the mid 1620's he had already been Clerk of the Council of Wales and Treasurer of the Navy under Queen Elizabeth and Chancellor of the Exchequer under King James. He was then living in retirement at Ambrose Dudley's former home of Warwick Castle, only eight miles up the road from Stratford. He made the remarks shortly after the appearance of the 1623 First Folio and the monument at Stratford just down the way. He was showing visitors around the castle when he was asked about the legacy he would leave. Greville replied that he hoped to be remembered *under no other notions than of Shakespeare's and Ben Jonson's Master, Chancellor Egerton's patron, Bishop Overal's Lord, and Sir Philip Sidney's friend.* This is as it was printed in David Lloyd's *Statesmen and Favourites of England since the Reformation* in 1679.

We know that Greville was a scrupulously honest, deeply moral (and guarded) man, who by these qualities won the trust of his monarchs. Greville appears here to encapsulate the five scenes out of his busy life that had personally given him the greatest satisfaction by the good they represented. The first four appear to show him in a superior position directing, pulling strings or greasing wheels, things of which he had done a great deal over the course of his long life, and of which other examples will surface as we proceed through the chronicle. Only the last–his years of friendship with the scholar-soldier-poet, Sir Philip Sidney–shows Greville describing a relationship of some equality. But for such a man as Greville to summarise his 70 years thus, placing his relationship with Shakespeare (notably, no first name or title given) in the first place but acknowledging Ben Jonson in the same breath, may betray much more than at first appears.

That Greville mentions Ben Jonson is significant for it was he who had prepared that prefatorial material for Shakespeare's First Folio of 1623. It was Jonson who had peppered the text with all sorts of quibbling allusions to the poet that have struck many commentators since as sinister and invidious. As we shall find at the end of this chronicle history, Jonson's quibbles were nothing but a comic layering-over (called 'fustian' at the time) that would hide the larger truths the present volume will already reveal. But that Greville had been Jonson's Master, too, opens up the possibility that the baron had played some role in overseeing the publication of the First Folio that has gone unrecognised to now.

That there was a great deal of interest in the poet Shakespeare's work at Warwick Castle at the time Greville made his remarks is attested to by his squire, a young man by the name of William D'Avenant. By the education Greville provided him, D'Avenant would leave Warwick Castle at the baron's death in 1628 already a full-fledged playwright very much out of the Shakespearean mould. Later D'Avenant would prove a major transmitter of the Shakespearean tradition to the generation after the Restoration of 1660. Greville would go to his death then having personally sewn some of the seeds that ensured Shakespeare's survival.

Fulke Greville was born 3 October 1554 at Beauchamp Court, seven miles west of Stratford, and was still living at home at the time William Shakspere was born down in the town 9½ years later. Like the Shakesperes, the Grevilles had been in Warwickshire for many generations but in the game of social climbing were about a century ahead. Fulke's great-grandparents had already done just those sorts of civic assignments that John Shakspere had been doing before his financial downfall.

Robert Dudley, the Earl of Leicester, had knighted Greville's father (also called Fulke Greville) at Kenilworth Castle in August of 1564. That October young Fulke had travelled north to attend school at Shrewsbury with Robert Dudley's nephew and heir, Philip Sidney, who impressed Greville terribly by his sweet-natured maturity.

The elder Sir Fulke Greville was, among other things, sheriff of Warwickshire. In Camden's additional notes to his later monumental *Britannia* he described the elder Greville as *a gentleman full of affability and courtesy, and much given to hospitality, which got the love of the whole country* [COUNTY]. Sir Fulke would personally have known the former alderman, bailiff and justice-of-the-peace of Stratford, John Shakspere, along with his son, William, and as the chief law enforcement officer of the shire, would have been drawn to take an interest in their predicament with Sir Thomas Lucy.

Fulke Greville the younger had employment of his own in the shire as well. During the Kenilworth celebrations of 1575, he had been formally presented to her Majesty by Robert Dudley, along with the earl's nephew Philip and niece Mary Sidney. Fulke, Philip and Mary were the first generation of offspring Lord Robert could offer for service to the queen. Fulke and Philip were then 21; Mary only 14. Although her Majesty felt a little miffed by the too-too-precocious Philip Sidney (who had been expected to shine here), she would take a rather genuine liking to his friend Fulke whom the queen told she would groom for higher office.

Among the kinds of tasks her Majesty had given Greville we hear that in 1590 he was appointed *to take the view and musters of the horsemen and footmen in co. Warwick, and put them in good array for the Queen's service.* These rolls required the names of all men between the ages of 16 and 60 fit for military service. William Shakspere, here 26, along with his brothers, Gilbert and Richard, and their father, John, would all have been eligible for that roll. All this indicates how close Fulke Greville the younger was to Stratford and the kind of leverage he could exercise there even on his own.

Both Grevilles, father and son, were on intimate terms with Sir Thomas Lucy, both families owing their allegiance to Robert Dudley, the Earl of Leicester. Sir Thomas and young Fulke had taken turns as members of parliament for Warwickshire, a seat Greville would continue to hold throughout the rest of Elizabeth's reign. The Lucies' manor of Charlecote lay just to the east of Stratford while the Grevilles' Beauchamp Court lay just to the west. But it was Sir Thomas and young Greville's overlapping responsibilities since 1590 that indicates their real day-to-day closeness.

Of all the posts her Majesty provided him, young Greville's most important employment at this time was in the new administration in Wales of Henry Herbert, the Earl of Pembroke. Herbert had been appointed Lord President of the Council of Wales upon the death in 1586 of his father-in-law, Sir Henry Sidney (the father of Philip and Mary Sidney). The Welsh governing body was one of several outlying councils that replicated what the government in London did for southern England. Fulke Greville was appointed Clerk to the council in 1590 while Sir Thomas Lucy was made a permanent member at the same time. Other people to come up in this story were simultaneously given other positions in Pembroke's administration.

This is important because of where William Shakspere will now go. When we first read of the man from Stratford in the capital in playwright Greene's deathbed letter of August 1592, he is clearly identified as one of the Earl of Pembroke's Men. This means then that in the timeframe of William Shakspere's first identification as one of his lordship's players, the Earl of Pembroke was the head of the council of which Greville and Lucy were both part. But Greville's ties to the House of Pembroke went much deeper than this.

Greville's bosom friend from early childhood had been Philip Sidney. Sidney's sister, Mary, had married Henry Herbert back in 1577 and had thereby become the current Countess of Pembroke. Greville had known her from early childhood and with her had gone through the excruciating pain caused by the death of Philip in 1586, a loss everyone took very hard though none harder than these two.

At the time of his dying, Philip Sidney had divided his literary remains between his friend Fulke and his sister Mary. Greville (with the help of two other editors) had prepared his portion and (with a few additional notes) set the material into print in 1590. But the effect of Philip's legacy on his sister, Mary, was to be altogether of a different order. For after nearly dying from grief, she would rebuild her life with those literary remains, learning to write as well as her brother so that she might complete all he had begun. By the time the Earl of Pembroke's Men was established in the summer of 1591, the countess had already developed some advanced notions as to which way English literature ought to proceed but had then suffered a public rebuke at the hands of one of the playwrights working for her company of actors.

It was with this trouble already brewing that William Shakspere would leave his butcher's apprenticeship and legal problems in Stratford and make his way to the London stage.

CHAPTER 2

The Old Actor & The Lady

Sketch of the Globe playhouse which was constructed with the timbers from the original Theatre playhouse

The place that would bring together the people surrounding the first appearance of the poetic hand we seek is the Theatre, a multi-sided playhouse in the northern London suburb of Shoreditch. The whole of the poet Shakespeare's dramatic corpus would first be performed between its timbers. In 1599 those timbers would be disassembled and moved to the Southbank where they would arise as the more famous Globe playhouse. They unfortunately burned to the ground during a performance of Shakespeare's last play, *Henry VIII*, in 1613. But out of ashes sometimes a phoenix appears!

The Theatre had been built in 1576 by a carpenter-turned-actor named James Burbage while under the patronage of the leader of the extreme Protestants, Robert Dudley, the Earl of Leicester. As his brother, Ambrose Dudley, was the Shakspares' landlord back in Stratford, it may reasonably be said that there was already some 'factional familiarity' between the two, James Burbage and William Shakspere, long before they first met.

While both Dudley brothers were keenly aware of the power of theatre in terms of promoting their overall political and religious goals, it was Robert who from the beginning made a point of patronizing only the best in everything, including players and poets.

It was his Leicester's Men who would rise to prominence over the 1560's and 70's, outshining all the other adult troupes.

In the first decade of the reign, the players were not yet so well off. Life in London over the winter (when the court sat there) was perhaps comfortable enough but in the summer when they had to go out and tour the countryside in search of an audience, they had to tramp about on foot carrying their playing things in packs on their backs. They found unwanted competition for the summertime crowds from roving bands of actors made up of masterless men whose repertoire appears to have consisted of old-fashioned biblical drama and lowbrow domestic tragedy and comedy. The courtly troupes would set a new standard of style which in drama would be more Senecan and in comedy more Italianate, matters of which their country cousins probably had as yet little inkling.

These roving bands of players were finally suppressed by royal order in 1572, their men forcibly returned to their towns of origin. Over the course of the next decade, the rights held by certain towns to perform seasonal cycles of religious miracle and mystery plays began, one by one, to also be suppressed. It was in such manner that our modern secular world was set into motion, and here at the turning point no noble family championed it more heartily than did the extended Dudley clan.

With these changes the troupes protected by the nobles started to thrive. They began to tour on horseback with a wagon to carry the props, costumes and musical instruments. With these developments they could now extend their geographical reach. In 1573 Robert Dudley was able to get Burbage and the rest of his actors a royal warrant whereby they could perform anywhere within the realm. With this passport the men whose livery coats bore Dudley's arms of 'the bear and ragged staff' criss-crossed England several times over the next decade. As payments from town councils to them were just below those paid to her Majesty's players, we can determine that Robert Dudley commanded great respect most everywhere in England his players went. With this accruing wealth, as well as the reputation of the company, its chief actor, James Burbage, decided to capitalise on their seasons in town by building England's first commercial playhouse.

It was in the immediate wake of the Kenilworth celebrations of 1575 that Burbage built the Theatre up at the north end of London. Given the number of designers that Robert Dudley had accumulated at Kenilworth to prepare the grounds and buildings for the queen's visit, we may wonder if some aspects of the playhouse's design came as a by-product of this intellectual gathering. Whoever its designer, it worked wonderfully well, and daily the money rolled in.

It was an economy made up of many pennies. The public who entered the playhouse paid a penny at the front gate and could then proceed to the ground surrounding the stage and there find a place to stand. Or one could mount the stairs and pay another penny to sit in the lower gallery, where there was tiered plank seating. If you had a further penny still, you could rise to the upper gallery where the tiered seating was cushioned. But if you would sit above everyone else, you will have to go by the actors' door and climb the stairs to the Lord's Room, (unusually) the balcony that sat high above the actors' main entrances onto the stage. From here you will see the backs of the players on stage below and the sea of faces about them. The cost of this privilege is 6 pence. (You will, however, need to dress to the nines!) Fruit, nuts, ale and the like were sold by roving concessionaires. There is a different play put on everyday out of a rotating repertoire of about 25 plays. Into this 'month of plays' something new is added every 4-6 weeks, even as the biggest money-loser is sloughed off. Entry prices are doubled at premières (to 2, 4, 6, and 12p), the performances where the patrons, no doubt at their impressive best, were most likely to occupy the Lord's Room.

Given the poverty that marred life in many quarters of the city and its environs, the rich face that the playhouse exuded began to arouse indignation. Stephen Gosson, who worked his way up from musician to playwright and finally to actor in the first years of the Theatre's existence, was eventually repulsed by the excess of it all and in 1579 converted to Puritanism. He wrote and published this year a book critical of his experiences at the Theatre, a generally anti-cultural diatribe called *The School of Abuse*.

From out of his rant we gather that he was well paid as a musician, better still as a playwright, but that the big money was in acting. The one figure he quotes is that extra actors earned 16p per day (this at a time when the London average was 8p, 4 in the country). As to how many people the Theatre (or the later Globe) held, there is no record. By my own reconstruction, I guesstimate approximately 2,000 with a daily average attendance of perhaps 1,000. If 600 of them mounted the stairs, there would be 1,600 pennies in the pot. If a third of these chose the cushioned seats, there would be 1,800 pence to split. Four in the Lord's Room would make it 1,824. The players appear to have received the receipts of the groundlings and half the galleries while the playhouse owner took the other half of the galleries and the concessions. Circumstances such as these would lead to a take of some 1,100 pennies for the actors.

The troupes had some forty mouths to feed. There were the boy apprentices, the extras [16p/day], and the supporting actors to be given their stipends and wages. There were also the musicians, the stage manager and his prompter and hands to be paid. Then there were the upfront as well as the ongoing maintenance costs of any production – script, music, costumes, accessories, and so on – and this for dozens of plays at a time. And then there were the six or so principal actors who stood above the rest. But after everyone had received their pay, most days there would have been somewhat left over to divide between the shareholders. The principal actors probably earned on the order of £60-70 per year. Many among them soon had sufficient to become gentlemen and buy fine houses of their own. James Burbage, as chief actor *and* playhouse owner, would have earned well above everyone else, though he was, for the time being, yoked by his mortgage and debts incurred building his playhouse.

Actors as a professional body took to dressing in the fine clothes of their noble patrons and Leicester's Men had an excellent model in Robert Dudley who always dressed as if he were already the queen's consort. This Gosson opposed. He was also offended by the actors' easy profanity and abhorred the way the playhouse was a magnet for all sorts of improper amorous liaisons, backstage as well as out front. But because of the *crocodiles* he would not *tell tales out of school*. The new playhouse audience did not include many of this persuasion, and the Puritan pamphlets would do little to thwart theatrical momentum. That would be done, in sort, by celestial events in 1583.

The great conjunction of Saturn and Jupiter slated for April of that year, an event that occurred only once every 960 years, was reckoned by contemporary Christian mathematician-astronomers to represent the seventh time this had occurred since the (biblical) creation of the world. Their astrology told them that a new world order was about to emerge and all Europe was abuzz, especially its royal courts. Whether this new order would appear slowly or cataclysmically depended entirely on which astrologer was consulted. Doctor John Dee, her Majesty's most trusted (though largely unrewarded) astrologer, correctly foretold of a benign passing during the event itself followed by improvement in England's international standing in the time to follow. Other astrologers' predictions were much more troubling and one can imagine the anticipatory pandemonium then reigning.

Her Majesty decided to stave off any destabilization and took steps to bring the nation's three broadcasters – pulpit, press and players – under much more centralised control. With regards to the actors, she instructed her chief of security, Sir Francis Walsingham, to gather the best actors from all the adult and children's companies and to amalgamate them into two 'super troupes' which would perform under her Majesty's exclusive patronage. Although some lords might choose to continue patronizing troupes of their own after her Majesty had had her pick of the best of their players, only those troupes under Elizabeth's protection would now appear before her court and enjoy that complete freedom of the realm. Seven weeks to the day before the dreaded event, Walsingham instructed Edmund Tilney, Master of the Revels, to make the choice as to which actors were to be included. Although some of the changes affected during the panic became permanent, her Majesty's theatrical resolve would only last a couple of years.

No troupe made a larger contribution of actors to the new Queen's Men than did the now disbanded Leicester's Men. But their leader, James Burbage (50-something years old now), was not one of them. With Robert Dudley's temporary retirement from theatrical patronage, Burbage appears to have established a patronage relationship with Henry Carey, a cousin to her Majesty, who became this same year the Lord Chamberlain. During this time, Burbage raised no new troupe and concentrated instead on featuring the new Queen's Men at his playhouse. In his wife, Ellen Brayne, he always had an able co-manager, one who had run the operation all those summers he was away on the road. And it was her rich brother who came in with a lot of the money that got the Theatre playhouse built. The two Burbages now had time to concentrate on the business while preparing their two sons to take over their roles. While the older Cuthbert Burbage, aged 16 in 1583, would learn the business of managing the playhouse, their younger son Richard, here about 12, would follow in his father's buskin footsteps onto the stage. This Richard arrests our attention for it is he who will become the chief mouthpiece for the entire Shakespearean theatrical corpus as this unfolds between his father's playhouse timbers from 1592 on.

In 1585, in anticipation of his military expedition to the Netherlands to fight the Spanish, Robert Dudley resurrected Leicester's Men and took them with him to boast of his 'Herculean strength' to the Dutch. Once done, the troupe returned to England and performed in the city, at court over Christmas, and continued touring the country. This troupe would perform until word reached them the Earl of Leicester had died in late September 1588.

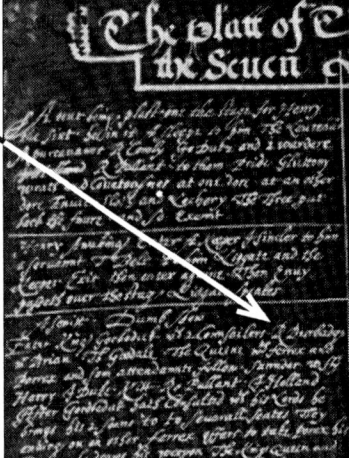

Plot outline for "The Seven Deadly Sins" identifying R. Burbadg as one of the actors.

It was after this final dissolution of Leicester's Men that young Richard Burbage's name begins to appear in surviving plot outlines of plays performed by the troupe patronized by Charles Howard, the Lord Admiral of England. Although Richard was never an Admiral's man himself, it may be surmised that his father struck a deal whereby they would perform at his Theatre and in return Richard would act with them.

The fact that James Burbage's patron, Henry Carey, was the father-in-law of the Lord Admiral may have abetted this somewhat unusual relationship. Further, we know that the Lord Admiral had been a close friend and ally of the recently deceased Robert Dudley, the Earl of Leicester.

This arrangement between the Burbages and the Admiral's company lasted until May of 1591. They had much going for them – the biggest and most popular playhouse in London, the most exciting playwrights in Marlowe, Peele and Kyd, and the best dramatic lead in Edward Alleyn. But it was all to be spoiled by a great dispute backstage over the *dividend money*. Others also accused James Burbage of dipping into the till before the receipts were counted and divided. But whenever any Burbage was challenged, all the members of the family would form one defiant, united front and, if necessary, physically beat off any would-be challengers.

In the actors' confrontation with Burbage, their star actor, Edward Alleyn, appears to have invoked the name of their patron for Burbage, in reply, swore *by a great oath, that he cared not for three of the best lords of them all*. This was the one utterance Edward Alleyn's brother, John, also an actor in the troupe, carefully committed verbatim to his diary, the one damning utterance that was reported back to the Lord Admiral and his father-in-law, the Lord Chamberlain. In their anger, the Alleyn brothers and their allies left Shoreditch, headed south across the river and amalgamated with Lord Strange's Men who were then performing at the Rose playhouse on the South Bank. Philip Henslowe had built his playhouse in 1587. (The first thing Henslowe had to do as a result of this sudden windfall was to enlarge his playhouse to accommodate the much bigger crowds that started to appear at his gate that first season, 1591-92.)

James Burbage had simultaneously burned his bridges with the Lord Admiral, the Lord Chamberlain, the best acting troupe of the moment, along with a string of hits by Marlowe, Kyd and Peele that those Alleyn brothers had presciently bought up and now taken with them to the Southbank. Burbage would have to start from scratch – obtain a new warrant from a new patron, build a new troupe, and get the writers to produce new repertory. Burbage had lost a true star in Edward Alleyn, considered the best dramatic lead England had produced within living memory. But perhaps that was to the good for now his twenty-one-year-old son, Richard Burbage, could step forward and learn to fill that breach.

Given Burbage's longstanding relationship with Robert Dudley, it would be natural that he look to that man's survivors for patronage.

Of those remaining, it was perhaps Dudley's niece, twenty-nine-year-old Mary Sidney, the Countess of Pembroke, who would have been the most open to such a request. At the time of Burbage's troubles, a number of notices had recently appeared that carried the countess's name or identity.

The year before, the countess had been the dedicatee of her brother Sir Philip Sidney's literary masterpiece, renamed in her honour, *The Countess of Pembroke's Arcadia*. This was Fulke Greville's portion of the legacy left him at the time of Sir Philip's death in 1586. Published by William Ponsonby, England's foremost bookseller to the courtier class, this *Arcadia* was to be one of the formative events of the English literary renaissance – to read it made everyone more of a poet.

Its letter of dedication was one Philip had written to his sister, Mary, back in 1580-81, at the time he completed the first version of *Arcadia*. His letter acknowledges that he had originally made it for her; Greville's naming the work after her then has some basis in fact. The particular circumstances surrounding its first creation carry within them the seeds of so much that is to come, that it is vital we momentarily look back.

After an adventurous early life spent in Wales and Ireland, with summers in Kent and Christmases at court, Mary Sidney was formally presented to her Majesty at the Kenilworth celebrations of 1575. For the next two years, she was one of the queen's maids-of-honour. But in the spring of 1577, the fifteen-year-old was wed to Henry Herbert, the forty-something-year-old, twice-married Earl of Pembroke. For the young noblewoman it was the sort of arrangement that required her to play the dutiful daughter, as most of the women in her family had already done. Mary Sidney's uncle, Robert Dudley, appears to have been the man with whom Pembroke negotiated the terms for her hand, while her father, Sir Henry Sidney, groaned under the £3,000 dowry required of him.

As he had done with his first two brides, Henry Herbert installed his new wife at his West Country manor of Wilton, just down the road from Salisbury. Herbert possessed a surrounding network of lesser manors about Wiltshire where the household could reside through the seasons. In the next century, the antiquarian John Aubrey would repeat some Wilton gossip about Herbert's father having put a great fear of cuckolding into young Henry, telling him to keep his brides well away from the temptations of the court. Though Henry Herbert's father had died seven years before his marriage here, the earl would follow the advice still.

Wilton House at the time of Mary Sidney's first coming.

Certainly there were things to assuage any possible resentment young Mary may have felt emotionally at being matched in this loveless way. She would now be a countess, which represented a considerable social leap for a knight's daughter. Wilton's was one of the loveliest pastoral settings in England. She was to bring her childhood nurse with her. Mary was given a large portfolio of properties throughout England and Wales that would give her a personal yearly income of £1,000. She could continue her education. There would be no childbearing until she was 18. While her own parents had been forced to live much closer to the bone, the estates belonging to her new husband produced the princely yearly income of some £35,000. This placed young Mary among the richest people in England. Wilton held armouries full of weapons and stables full of warhorses if she felt any insecurity.

Mary's brother Philip Sidney was away in Vienna and the German states at the time of the marriage, on the only embassy her Majesty ever awarded him. (The queen had even allowed his inseparable friend, Fulke Greville, to accompany him.) After their return, Philip debriefed at Westminster and then immediately left London and travelled to his sister's new home of Wilton. All through the next couple of years he often came to stay for extended periods, Wilton being his favourite home-away-from-home. Despite the seven-year gap in age between brother and sister, people remarked on their physical resemblance and similarity of intellectual prowess. Philip's frequent visits must have eased his sister's transition to her new life as the young mistress of Wilton.

And in these early years an extraordinary thing was to happen that would have very far-reaching consequences. Philip and Fulke Greville and an old friend of the faction, Sir Edward Dyer, none of whom had sufficient employment from her Majesty to make them completely busy, began a series of literary experiments by which they set out to determine what the real poetic potential of English might be. They agreed that old Father Chaucer in his antiquated manner had brought English poetry up to the mark but that, for the rest, their language offered only spare or quaint poetic pickings. They thought they could do better by mathematically working through every conceivable line and verse form until they found those that worked best under the peculiar conditions the English language imposed. From the beginning Mary Sidney was one of their eager listeners/readers and under the name of *Mira* or *Myra* also one of their poetic subjects. Being so close to this first budding forth on the part of her brother and his friends would already have given the isolated countess an emotional stake in the literary odyssey undertaken here. Through these first years there were many delightful little poetic victories that were as spring flowers but not one of the three succeeded in producing some great breakout work. This was a pressure that the precocious and ambitious Philip Sidney would have felt above the others. Events were, however, to conspire to bring him poetically out of himself and in this his sister would play a pivotal role.

1579 had been a very hard year for Philip Sidney. He had spoken out against the queen's proposed marriage to the French-Catholic Duc d'Alençon, circulating a letter in which he outlined the reasons for the Protestants' opposition to it. He had endured a heated exchange on the tennis court on account of it with the arrogant Earl of Oxford, a Catholic sympathizer. When the Queen heard of their proposed duel, she hauled Sidney before her and reminded him in no uncertain terms where he, the son of *mere gentry*, stood beside this earl who could trace his high noble lineage back seventeen generations! Although Sidney was at no time forbidden the court, his last place showing in Elizabeth's 1580 New Year's gift-list gives some indication of where he now stood. Her Majesty's remarks wounded the entire family very deeply.

1579 had been trying for Philip Sidney in other ways as well. That year Edmund Spenser, then one of the new secretaries to his uncle Robert Dudley, had set his exquisite little book of poetry, *The Shepherd's Calendar*, into print and dedicated it to Sidney. With it, Spenser had created a work immediately recognized as the best since the days of Chaucer. In it Spenser had propounded what he thought the shape of the new English poetics should be. Although Philip agreed with much of it, one matter did sit in his craw. In the need to build up the word-stock by which English might become a more expressive poetic force, where would the words for the finer concepts come from? Aside from their classical and contemporary European source-models, Spenser espoused dipping back into their English Chaucerian past and drawing from there what they could. (The French poets had done this.) This gave Spenser's language a neo-medieval sheen. This Sidney viscerally opposed, hoping the new English would have the sheen of classical Latin and Greek (as, in fact, it now does). But while Spenser had set his agenda into print, Sidney had yet to compose any sustained work where he might with some impact illustrate what he would do.

While this was on his mind, another dedication to him this year had a far more galling effect. Stephen Gosson, the author of that diatribe against the Theatre, *The School of Abuse*, had also dedicated his work to Philip Sidney, not to praise him but to embarrass him and his uncle Robert Dudley, whose troupe, Leicester's Men, Gosson appears to have laboured for these past couple of years. In the public mind this associated Sidney's name with the Puritan call to end all theatre, literature and music. These were among Sidney's great private passions. But how could he speak in the defence of poetry when he had not yet proven himself a poet? It was an axiom with young Sidney that study and contemplation had to be followed by right action.

Early in 1580 the frustrated twenty-five-year-old abandoned Elizabeth's court and (as he so often had) took the road west to Wilton. But he had come at an awkward time for his sister, Mary, was now in the third trimester of her first pregnancy. She, along with her court of ladies and female servants, had removed themselves to Clarendon House, a small lodge just north of Wilton, for the traditional last-trimester laying-in. Given that only women made up such maternity courts, Philip would have been unwelcome. But somehow he insinuated himself into their company (and one may wonder if he initially adopted the same cross-dressing strategies his fictional counterpart, *Pyrocles*, would adopt in his pursuit of female company in the *Arcadia*). Mary appears to have granted Philip visiting rights on the condition that when he come he have something new to read to them, presumably for their daily amusement. It was in this fashion that Philip's long poetic novel, *Arcadia*, was born.

Though he may have arrived with a troubled mind, the all-female company coupled with his sudden freedom from the constraints of court ignited a passion in Philip that would explode in his writing. He produced new material at breakneck speed but always at a level well above the mundane, daily presenting to his audience of ladies stories and poems that painted out the lively country adventures of an extended cast of escapees from a royal court set in the fabled country of Arcadia. In these stories the ladies (no doubt, to their great amusement) would have recognized themselves and him only too clearly.

Although the only indication comes from Philip's writings, it appears his flame of love for the lively, darkly handsome Penelope Devereux was ignited here at his sister's maternity court. Opposite his own character of *Pyrocles* (the man on fire!) stands the object of his affections, the lively, darkly handsome *Philoclea*. In the sonnets Philip would write the following year, this 'dark lady' would transmogrify into *Stella*. Philip himself would there in one place identify her positively as Penelope Devereux.

This sudden flowering of passion was not without that irony that Philip loved so well, though here it was turned on him. Only four years earlier he had refused the offer of Lady Penelope's hand given him by her father, the old Earl of Essex. The earl had written from his deathbed how much he still wished that Philip *might match with my daughter*. Essex had lovingly noted: *I call him son; he is so wise, virtuous and godly. If he go on in the course he hath begun, he will be as famous and worthy a gentleman as ever England bred.* Though Philip had rebuffed her then, now he was head over heels! And though he was ostensibly writing *Arcadia* for his sister, it appears this 'dark lady' was the real engine driving his pen! Mary Sidney may well have resented that dark lady who sought to steal away her brother's attention. (Although the full discussion must wait for a later volume, I find in this a perfect parallel with the story Shakespeare's sonnets will later tell.)

On the 8th of April 1580, Mary gave birth to a son. Her husband, who had been left childless by his two previous marriages, finally had an heir. Henry Herbert installed a tablet in St. Mary's Church, Wilton that fairly gushes with his contentment.

> Be it remembered that at the eighth day of April 1580 on Friday before twelve of the Clock at Night … was Born William Lord Herbert of Cardiff first Child of the noble Henry Herbert Earl of Pembroke By his most Dear Wife Mary … God bless with his Mother above named with prosperous Life in all Happiness … .

They named the babe William Herbert. (With this event other parallels with Shakespeare's sonnet story appear, for here was a boy a mother might indeed have called *'Master W.H.'* as in the sonnets' dedication.) At his christening on 28 May, Ambrose Dudley, the uncle Mary Sidney probably liked best, stood as godfather. His wife, Anne Russell, stood proxy for her Majesty as godmother, and Mary's brother Philip stood in for uncle Robert as second godfather. The whole parish was invited to the celebration. The family engaged Thomas Allen, the mathematician-astrologer, to produce the boy's nativity chart. Allen predicted what would turn out to be the exact day of William Herbert's death.

Philip Sidney stayed on all summer long, building up his physique by practicing his jousting in Wilton's tiltyard and his skill as a writer by continuing his great literary escapade. He often worked in his sister's presence. In the fourth eclogue, or pastoral dialogue, at the end of his Arcadian adventures, he evokes himself as *Philisides*, the melancholy shepherd (the 'dark lady' presumably had left by this time), and his sister, Mary, as *Mira*, the serving woman to two goddesses. The poem whose first line reads *Now was our heavenly vault deprivèd of all light*, begins with philosophical ruminations that are interrupted by the clamorous arrival of *Diana* and *Venus* and their serving woman. The noise is generated by an argument over which of the two goddesses should have the crown of amber fair. The young shepherd is forced to decide the matter but he chooses their serving-woman, *Mira*, whereupon the vengeful goddesses decree he shall suffer a fruitless, chaste passion for the young virgin ever thereafter! Indeed Philip should have been at court serving *Diana* (Queen Elizabeth) or at the court of love serving *Venus* (Lady Penelope), but instead he was here serving his sister (whose hair incidentally was already amber). Philip brought Mary from Clarendon back to Wilton House on 2 August. What might have been a time fraught with great anxiety for the young, first-time mother appears to have been made a time of triumph and joy, thanks in large part to all her older, brilliant brother had done. When Fulke Greville renamed *Arcadia* to *The Countess of Pembroke's Arcadia* for its publication in 1590, it appears he was mindful of the special place this book held in Mary Sidney's heart.

Besides this hefty tome, there were other publications in the time of Burbage's woes that may have alerted him to Mary Sidney's patronage potential. Earlier in 1591 the countess had been prominently featured in the leadoff piece of a cycle of poems called *Complaints* by England's now foremost living poet, Edmund Spenser. The poet had come over from Ireland the previous summer under the auspices of Sir Walter Ralegh and been successfully presented to the queen at court. *Complaints*, published in the spring of 1591while Spenser was still in England, is a poetic chronicle of the hard times that had befallen the Protestant faction these past several years.

Complaints begins with a lament called *The Ruins of Time* which Spenser dedicates to the *Noble and beautiful Lady Mary Countess of Pembroke*. In his prefatorial letter to her, Spenser assesses her brother

Philip's literary achievement as that of one whose possibilities *began in this life somewhat to bud forth: and to show themselves to him, as then in the weakness of their first spring: And would in their riper strength (had it pleased high God till then to draw out his days) [in]spired forth fruit of more perfection.*

In 1585, Robert Dudley was finally granted permission to launch an expeditionary force to aid the Netherlands in its war against Spain. Dudley would take along all his 'sons', who included Mary Sidney's three brothers – Philip, Robert and Thomas. This must already have had a worrying effect on Lady Mary's emotions. Then in May of 1586 came the shocking news that their beloved father, Sir Henry Sidney, had suddenly passed away after catching cold. Given how emotionally close the Sidney family was, this must have been a terrible blow to all of them. Two and a half months later their bereaved mother, Mary Dudley, (according to Molineux) with *such godly speeches, earnest and effectual persuasions to all those about her ... to exhort them to repentance and amendment of life*, also passed away. This second death struck Mary Sidney even harder and she became ill and took to her bed. Letters to her brothers in the Netherlands state there were fears for her recovery.

For Philip Sidney, the effect of the parents' deaths appears different. With the loss, he now threw himself into battle more heartily. And so foolishly he entered an attack on a Spanish supply train just outside of Zutphen without his knee and shin armour and on his third charge took a bullet in the knee. Edmund Molineux, writing in *Holinshed's Chronicles* published the following year, reported Philip received *hurt by a musket shot a little above the left knee, which so broke and rifted the bone, and so entered the thigh upward toward the body, as the bullet could not be found.* Although the surgeons were confident they could save his leg, this news could only have abetted Mary Sidney's gloom. She cared very deeply for her younger brothers, but the older Philip held a place they never could. Although there were several weeks of recovery, the wound would gangrene and Philip died 17 October 1586, one month shy of his 32nd birthday. With numbing irony the news of it would have reached Mary just in time for her 25th birthday on 27 October.

When Sidney died, he left his epic novel of *Arcadia* in an early, complete version as well as in a revised but unfinished form. There was also that beautifully crafted cycle of sonnets called *Astrophel and Stella* that Philip had completed around 1581. He had at some point metrified the first forty-three of the 150 psalms of David for a projected Psalter. There were bits of occasional poetry and playmaking as well as some poignant essays. The legacy was, as Spenser states, the first budding forth and had he lived beyond those first 31 years greater work may yet have been expected from him.

Spenser's *Ruins* paints a tableau that has as its central image the female personification of the town of *Verlame*, the second most important English town after Londinium in the later Roman Empire. Spenser's source information came from Camden's *Britannia*, as he acknowledges in his poem, but the ruins he paints are in fact not Roman at all, but the deaths that had encircled Mary Sidney these past five years. After the immediate calamities of 1586, the countess no longer knew if she wished to live or die. One of the poet-soldiers present in the Netherlands with Philip was Thomas Churchyard who in his short *Epitaph of Sir Philip Sidney Knight* writes, *His sister's life consumes away like Snow against the Sun.*

Though the worst was expected, Mary Sidney did not die. She already had a large household to support her, but into this, her dark night of the soul, would come a highly articulate young man who would help set her life on a whole new course. Until the tragic events in the Netherlands, Abraham Fraunce had been Sir Philip Sidney's squire. Fraunce hailed from Shrewsbury where Sidney and Fulke Greville had attended school in the mid 1560's. Philip Sidney, four years older than Fraunce, was taken by the boy's ability and personally paid for his education at St. John's College, Cambridge. Fraunce proved his worth by earning a fellowship. He wrote at least two popular Latin comedies for the student stage (in which he may have acted).

In 1583 he went on to the Inns of Court to study law. He began this year to draw up a comparative anatomy of the legal logic found in Ramus' *Dialectica* and Spenser's use thereof in *The Shepherd's Calendar*. He appears to have done this to help Philip Sidney when his master began to give legal consideration to what his characters had done in the enthusiasm of their first romp through Arcadia.

Sidney was two-thirds through his rewrite of *Arcadia*, leaving his manuscript mid-sentence at the start of Book III, when he died in October 1586.

Suddenly bereft of the patronage and support Sir Philip had afforded him, Fraunce made a plea to his sister, Mary, and her husband, the Earl of Pembroke, to take him in. Given Fraunce's closeness to Sir Philip, and how close Sidney had been to his sister and her husband throughout his life, we may with some safety surmise that Fraunce and the Pembrokes already knew one another. Although it would have been almost unthinkable for the Pembrokes to turn Fraunce away, given the patronage environment of the time, the highly articulate law student had some rather special skills by which he was able to give back immediately far in excess of whatever support the Pembrokes may have been able to offer him.

With the death of Sir Henry Sidney (followed by the immediate death of his oldest son, Sir Philip), her Majesty had bestowed the Lord Presidency of Wales on Henry Herbert, the Earl of Pembroke. Abraham Fraunce would spend a good part of 1587 anatomising the art of legal reasoning with the earl, a skill Herbert would need in his new role as chief magistrate of a rather large jurisdiction. All these lessons would end up in a great volume that Fraunce published the following year called *The Lawyer's Logic*. (This book will later be judged to sit at the heart of Shakespeare's legal reasoning.)

But Fraunce's main concern this first year would be with the countess and it is in this regard that his first Wilton work, *Amyntas*, must be considered. The story had started with Torquato Tasso's Italian pastoral tragedy, *Aminta* (1580), which told of how the strong and beautiful Alpine nymph, Sylvia, had aroused but scorned the love of a worthy shepherd named Aminta, leading to that young man's suicide. A few years later a highly cultured English agent by the name of Thomas Watson reversed matters and, in a Latin reply, had started with the death of the Sylvia-figure, now called *Phillis*, followed by a description of Amyntas' first ten days of mourning. Watson had published this narrative the year before Philip Sidney's death. It was this work that Abraham Fraunce now rendered into English.

The name of the deceased in Watson and Fraunce's story,

Phillis, given its proximity to the very recently deceased **Philip Sidney**, appears (in Fraunce's case, anyway) as a liability. But perhaps that was its greatest point of attraction, giving his text unavoidable real-life crackle. Fraunce couched the tragedy in lines of sweetly lilting hexameter verse, perfectly suited to lifting the atmosphere of mourning then overawing Wilton. But as bibliotherapy this would have been strong stuff. As listener and/or reader, Mary Sidney could certainly have identified with *Amyntas* as a companion-in-mourning. As Amyntas grieved the loss of his Phillis, the countess could grieve the loss of her Philip, tear for tear. But in her reception of the piece, Mary Sidney (as woman) could also have identified with the woman in the story, the fallen *Phillis*. This would have given her a very different perspective on the predicament at hand for now her point-of-view would have been that of the deceased. From that place what would she counsel the 'survivor' to do, wilt away and die or live to fight another day? However she would have Phillis counsel Amyntas was in effect to counsel herself.

Sir Philip Sidney's body was returned to England and in February 1587 he became the first non-royal in England's history to receive a state funeral. What Queen Elizabeth had denied while he was alive she would here in death quietly acknowledge – that there had been a rare and special quality of nobility in this young man. Mary Sidney's name does not appear in the rolls, possibly indicating she could not or would not attend the event. While Philip's command in the Netherlands passed to his younger brother, Robert, for Mary, the way out of the morass became to do what she could to finish Philip's broken literary legacy. She must have had in her possession a huge mound of paper containing most if not all of the stories, poems, essays and sketches Philip had written over the years, all unedited. Of all his started pieces, the one that perhaps lent itself most readily to continuation by a novice poet such as Mary Sidney was Philip's Psalter. Completing this became her first foray into the poetic arts.

But this presented problems. Despite the intensive training she had undergone throughout her growing-up years in learning languages and studying literature, she had ever only been taught to be the excellent reader, listener, translator, appreciator – but never the original maker. That was men's work, requiring training of a different sort. Rhetoric, in part the study of the literary forms and devices that give life to poetry and oratory, was one of the subject domains of the grammar schools and universities and there no women were as yet admitted.

But Abraham Fraunce was able to anatomise all this information and teach it to the countess in a clear, orderly fashion. At the same time as the appearance of *The Lawyer's Logic*, Fraunce also published *The Arcadian Rhetoric*. It is the key text to shape Mary Sidney's early poetics and will, in later centuries, come to be seen as the key text to have shaped Shakespeare's early poetic development as well. A consideration of its careful anatomy of concepts supported by hundreds of examples, gives us some insight into the nature of the conferences that must have passed between the two when Mary Sidney was just learning to write.

The whole scope of *The Arcadian Rhetoric* would indicate that, in following her brother, Mary Sidney would go the same distance he had, retrace his books and influences, in her own way relive his formative stages. Working from manuscript copies of Philip's works, Fraunce lay bare the techniques by which her brother had achieved his dazzling literary effects. These examples were complimented by ones from classical and modern authors who had helped blaze those pastoral, Arcadian pathways – Homer, Virgil, Horace, Ovid, Petrarch, Tasso, Du Bartas, Belleau, Boscan and Garcilasso, all presented in their original Greek, Latin, Italian, French or Spanish. It suggests that Fraunce and the countess's conferences were a far-ranging, polyglot affair. When Fraunce set the manual into print, he dedicated it to Mary Sidney with a short six-line verse that made equal use of all six languages. But that Philip's *Arcadia* is given pride of place in the examples indicates the special place that work held. Fraunce's wide academic experience, his brilliantly inventive and analytical mind, along with his school, stage and courtroom trained voice, would all have made of him a formidable teacher to both Pembrokes, husband and wife, here in 1587. That the law and rhetoric manuals that accrued over the year were set into print in 1588, both under Pembroke patronage, indicates, to a degree, a generosity of spirit on their parts not to withhold from general view that which was helping them.

As to what Philip left by way of example we may consider the first edge of his 43 finished psalms.

GENEVAN BIBLE	PHILIP SIDNEY'S METRIFIED VERSION
BEGINNING OF PSALM I	BEGINNING OF PSALM I 'BEATUS VIR'
Blessed is the man that doth not walk in the counsel of the wicked, nor stand in the way of sinners, nor sit in the seat of the scornful. But his delight is in the Law of the Lord, & in his Law doth he meditate day and night.	He blessed is who neither loosely treads The straying steps, as wicked counsel leads Ne for bad mates in way of sinning waiteth, Nor yet himself with idle scorners seateth. But on God's law his heart's delight doth bind Which night and day he calls to marking mind.

King David's book of Psalms contains 150 songs. The consoling, reaffirming, militantly uplifting messages David's psalms reiterate have always made them a restorative to the demoralized. In their ancient Hebraic versions these were songs but as the early Bible translators did not understand the poetic underlay, the poetry had been turned to prose. The would-be poet's task here was, as Philip's work demonstrates, to turn that prose back into poetry. Because the original poetic conventions were unknown, the poet was free to explore any conceivable line and verse form using any imaginable rhyme scheme. Mary Sidney made the most of the situation, making almost each one of her contributions unique in all regards. Though this does turn the Psalter from a vast heroic canvas to a more homely quilt, her approach indicates she would begin by exploring the entire range of poetic possibilities. As an opening apprenticeship work, this is already to take the measure of the entire horizon.

Like her brother, the countess worked from the very Protestant Genevan edition of the Bible. Outside the final copy versions of the 107 psalms that would sit beside Philip's to form the Sidney Psalter, there is a group of some 33 variants to survive that appear to represent her earliest work. One of these is her metrification of psalm 44, which the countess would have first placed next to where Philip's psalm 43 had left off. (Her work was left unpunctuated.)

GENEVAN BIBLE	MARY SIDNEY'S 1ST METRIFIED VERSION
PSALM 44	
We have heard with our ears, oh God: our fathers have told us the works, that thou hast done in their days, in the old time: How thou hast driven out the heathen with thine hand, and planted them : *how* thou hast destroyed the people, and caused them to grow. ... For they inherited not the land by their own sword, neither did their own arm save them : but thy right hand, & thine arm and the light of thy countenance, because thou didst favour them. ...	Our Fathers lord by hearing Have made us understand Thy works before their eyes appearing In time gone long ago How rooting nations, them thy hand Did plant and planted nourish The stock profane did leafless grow The faithful branch did flourish. Their sword did not procure them Possession of the land Nor more did their own arms assure them In doubtful time and place Thy arm it was, it was thy hand Thy favour passing measure Sent on them from thy lightsome face Why? only for thy pleasure ...

As one of the first 'keepers', this suggests that from the start Mary Sidney was working with some vigour. Of overarching significance is that she would immediately write in a voice that is sharper and more emotive than her brother's work might have suggested. The elaboration of the *planting* metaphor into *rooting, nourish, stock, leafless, branch,* and *flourish* indicates a mind alert to elaboration. There are moments of splendour as when a Genevan original such as *For they inherited not the land by their own sword* is turned into the more stately *Their sword did not procure them / Possession of the land*. In the exercise of using various kinds of repetition (one of the mainstays of Fraunce's poetic technique), we see the word *thy* used five times, the first three rising to a climax and the latter two falling in dramatic denouement.

And so it was that Edmund Spenser in *The Ruins* of 1591 could sing Sir Philip Sidney's praises as *the world's late wonder, and the heavens' new joy* and then acknowledge,

> …but who can better sing,
> Than thine own sister, peerless Lady bright,
> Which to thee sings with deep heart's sorrowing,
> Sorrowing tempered with dear delight,
> That her to hear I feel my feeble sprite
> Robbed of sense, and ravished with joy,
> O sad joy made of mourning and annoy.

Although the vast majority of people would have been completely ignorant of Mary Sidney's poetic development, it appears that Spenser, during his visit to England, had been in contact with her and that they had shared some of their poetic inventions with each other. Even as she had continued work on the Psalter, the countess had become engaged in translation exercises. Spenser's alluding to her as *Lady bright* appears to recall the opening line of a translation she had made of Petrarch's *The Triumph of Death*.

PETRARCH	MARY SIDNEY'S TRANSLATION
Quella leggiadra e gloriosa donna,	That gallant lady, gloriously bright
ch'è oggi ignudo spirto e poca terra	The stately pillar once of worthiness
e fu già di valor alta colonna,	And now, a little dust, a naked sprite:
tornava con onor da la sua guerra,	Turned from her wars a joyful conqueress;
allegra, avendo vinto il gran nemico,	Her wars, where she had foiled the mighty foe
che con suo' ingegni tutto 'l mondo atterra,	Whose wily stratagems the world distress.
non con altr'arme che col cor pudico	And foiled him, not with sword, with spear or bow,
e d'un bel viso e de' pensieri schivi,	
d'un parlar saggio e d'onestate amico.	But with chaste heart, fair visage, upright thought,
…	Wise speech, which did with honour linkéd go.
	… LINES 1-9 / 172

Aside from indicating a translator's knowledge of Italian, the work proves that by the end of the decade the countess possessed a maturing control over versifying. Petrarch had himself been surrounded by death in 1348 when he began writing the *Triumphs*. The Black Death had carried off several friends, of which the most lamentable loss was that of his beloved *Laura*. In the *Triumph of Death* the plague is allegorised as a windstorm toppling the laurel tree, which represents Laura as well as all poetry generally. But Laura returns from the dead to tell Petrarch that because of their chaste love, he would now have the power to continue being the poet he was while she yet lived. What Fraunce's *Phillis* may first have only suggested – the notion of the dead counselling the living to continue – is here by the countess's own hand given concrete form.

Although Mary Sidney's translation has been praised for its fidelity to the original, her small departures from the literal text again demonstrate the direction her voice would take if she were free to write *uncontrolled*. Everywhere what the Italian text would only suggest is turned into an English of a higher order. Hence, 'high column' becomes *stately pillar*, 'returned with honour' is now *a joyful conqueress*, 'a beautiful face' made *fair visage*. And in what will shortly become consequential, this work indicates that, by the end of the decade, all of Mary Sidney's poetic experiments were converging on mastering the iambic pentameter line, the line form that had come to dominate the stage.

In 1590 the countess completed a translation of one of Robert Garnier's Senecan five-act dramas, *Marc Antoine*, which she entitled *Antonius*. Designed (like all of Garnier's dramatic works) to be read aloud by a gathering of friends rather than acted from the stage, the play concerns Mark Antony and how his unlawful affair with Cleopatra brought about his downfall. It had appeared in Garnier's complete works as printed in 1585. What is of immediate interest is that Mary Sidney had taken Garnier's rhymed French alexandrine lines and turned them into a robust English iambic pentameter blank verse. According to her postscript, Mary finished *Antonius* on 26 November 1590 – four days before the 36th anniversary of Philip's birth, November 30, somehow a most attractive choice for the play's first reading.

A consideration of what Mary Sidney does with Garnier's text would again indicate her own inclination, if she were free to write, like a man, out of her own mind.

MARC ANTOINE BY ROBERT GARNIER	ANTONIVS TRANSLATED BY MARY SIDNEY
Puisque le ciel cruel encontre moi s'obstine	Since cruel Heav'ns against me obstinate,
Puisque tous les malheurs de la ronde machine	Since all misshapes of the round engine do
Conspirent contre moi; que les hommes, les Dieux,	Conspire my harm: since men, since powers divine
L'air, la terre, et la mer me sont injurieux,	Air, earth, and Sea are all injurious:
Et que ma Reine même en qui je soulois vivre,	And that my Queen herself, in whom I lived,
Idole de mon Coeur, s'est mise a me poursuivre,	The Idol of my heart doth me pursue;
Il me convient mourir. J'ai pour elle quitté	It's meet I die. For her have I forgone
Mon pays, et Cesar à la guerre incité	My Country, **Cæsar** unto war provoked
Vengeant l'injure faicte à sa Coeur mon épouse,	(For just revenge of Sister's wrong, my wife,
Dont Cleopatre estoit à mon malheur jalouse;	Who moved my Queen (ay me!) to jealousy)
J'ai mis pour l'amour d'elle, en ses blandices pris,	For love of her, in her allurements caught
Ma vie à l'abandon, mon honneur à mespris,	Abandoned life, I honor have despised,
Mes amis dedaignez, l'Empire venerable	Disdained my friends, and of the stately Rome
De ma grande Cité devestu miserable;	Despoiled the Empire of her best attire,
Dedaigné le pouvoir qui me rendoit si craint,	Contemned that power that made me so much feared,
Esclave devenu de son visage feint.	A slave become unto her feeble face.
Inhumaine traitresse, ingrate entre les femmes,	O cruel, traitorous, woman most unkind,
Tu trompes, parjurant, et ma vie et mes flames;	Thou dost, foresworn, my love and life betray:
Et me livres, mal-sage, à mes fiers ennemis,	And giv'st me up to rageful enemy,
Qui bientôt puniront ton parjure commis.	Which soon (ô fool!) will plague thy perjury
…	…

Despite the boundaries that translation work imposes upon a writer, a consideration of what the countess adds to *Antonius* by way of rhetorical amplification again indicates which way her inclinations would take her.

LITERAL TRANSLATIONS FROM GARNIER'S TEXT	MARY SIDNEY'S SHAPING
conspire against me	conspire my harm
that men, the Gods	since men, since powers divine
for her I left	for her have I foregone
incited	provoked
—	(ay me!)

disdained	contemned[VIEWED WITH CONTEMPT]
proud enemies	rageful enemy
—	(ô fool!)
punish	plague
…	…

This higher rhetorical pitch may be the language of annoy (to use Spenser's word) that marks her work here, as if anger had in part displaced the melancholy her parents' and Philip's deaths had produced. From the sketchbook experimentation of the psalms through the firming though still heavily rhymed iambic pentameter renderings of Petrarch we arrive now at French Senecanism turned into an English blank verse. It is quite a metamorphosis. Although her skills in 1590 would have allowed her easily to adopt Garnier's rhyming alexandrines as her line form, she made a conscious decision to do otherwise. It may be wondered if Mary Sidney was one of a number of poets to fall under the sway of the drumming blank verse poetics championed by playwright Christopher Marlowe at the Theatre. Marlowe's two plays of *Tamburlaine* were published in one volume this year.

In the verse of *The Ruins* he had written on Mary Sidney's mother, Mary Dudley, Spenser had referred to the Sidney children as *the sacred brood of learning and all honour*. It was indeed a mark of the Sidney children to how exacting a standard they had all been educated. In his closing Spenser advises her, *And as ye be of heavenly offspring born, / So unto heaven let your high mind aspire, / And loathe this dross of sinful world's desire*. This 'heavenly idea' would be clarified in Spenser's next comments on the countess in *Colin Clout's Come Home Again*, which will appear at the end of 1591.

In his prefatory letter to Mary Sidney, Spenser had spoken of being *bounden by many singular favours and great graces*, indicating a patronage relationship, certainly, but also a special kind of social intercourse. The nobility on the whole did not mix with the commons, although where intellectual interests overlapped social distinctions sometimes softened. Spenser closes with the words, *and so humbly kiss your hands*. In this latter there is a familiarity much greater than what one usually finds in letters of this sort.

Just weeks before James Burbage had his altercation with the Alleyn brothers, another work was entered into the Stationers' Register that may have drawn the needy actor's attention. It was a collection of miscellaneous verse by various gentlemen called *Britton's Bower of Delights*. The man primarily responsible for gathering the verses and setting them into print was Nicholas Breton. The packaging and the contents of the book reflect the patronage relationship that had developed in the year previous. Breton, another old soldier-poet to be part of Leicester's expeditionary force to the Netherlands, had seen Sir Philip Sidney shortly before his death. After the death of Leicester, Breton needed a new patron. In the summer of 1590 the Earl of Pembroke found him a position as schoolmaster. *The Bower of Delights* here in 1591 indicates Breton had spent the idle hours of the winter preparing a way to thank his benefactors.

Breton had written the leadoff piece, a very personal epitaph to Sir Philip called *Amoris Lachrimae*, shortly after Sidney's death. In the poem Breton evinces a close, even loving relationship with Sidney while he was alive and describes with some newsworthiness the events of his death and burial. What was most striking about Breton's publication here from Burbage's point of view was the emblem of 'the bear and ragged staff' with its motto, *Droit et loyal*, displayed on its title page. At this time books were sold without covers, title page out. The badge here was that of the deceased earls of Leicester and Warwick (Ambrose had also died the previous year), the very badge that James Burbage had for many years worn on his own livery coat. Despite the fact that Robert Dudley had done much to shake England out of its lingering medievalism, he appears to have been hardnosed, demanding and rather self-serving, and perhaps unscrupulous in some of his actions. When he died in 1588 the eulogies were indeed few and stingy. Breton's gesture, like Spenser's in his *Complaints*, helped to brighten the Dudley image for the sake of the earl's survivors, such as Mary Sidney and her younger brothers, as well as to preserve Sir Philip's memory.

It appears then that by the time James Burbage's needs arose in May of 1591, the Countess of Pembroke had become something of a visible patronage presence and (probably unbeknownst to Burbage unless he had read Spenser closely) a partially-realized poet. She had a protector of her own in her husband, Henry Herbert, the Earl of Pembroke, a man of position, wealth and power who had patronized players before. There was an early Pembroke's Men in the 70's. But with their marriage in 1577, he had given this up, no doubt in obeisance to his new overlord. But Robert Dudley, whom Henry Herbert and Mary Sidney had both called *father* while he yet lived, had died in 1588. Lord Robert's brother, Ambrose, the other former theatrical patron in the family, had died in 1590. Several other senior members of the extended Dudley family-faction had also died in this period. At the time of Burbage's problems, the way would have been wide open for the earl and his countess to take on such a patronage role. Though the earl's title would be attached to the name of the company, the record will overall indicate it was the countess who would take the immediate interests of the playwrights and players in hand. And that same record will indicate that overall it was the countess who lived in her Majesty's favour, not her husband.

As the players would leave for country touring at the end of June, it appears that Pembroke's Men was organized immediately rather than later in the fall. For actors there would have been Burbage's son, Richard, and any others left behind by the departure of the Admiral's Men. Some of Lord Strange's Men may have been displaced at the Rose. As well, there was her Majesty's still very bloated troupe, the Queen's Men, which one actor's will of August 1592 suggests provided some of the actors to come to Pembroke's Men. If so, there is the suggestion that the new troupe was established with her Majesty's knowledge, approval and support.

The crown and the nobility had a vested interest in the age's three main broadcasting media—pulpit, press and players—but it would be the players who gained the most economically and socially. Although the nobles generally dressed everyone well who laboured in their service, it was only with the actors that they created their sartorial equals. From the point of view of the needs of the stage, where the actors had to look like kings and queens, dukes, earls and knights, this makes perfect sense. But the actors were allowed to dress this way out in the street as well, leaving many who had in their ignorance 'capped and kneed' them, feeling resentful. Given the strictness of the dress code, this anomaly is perhaps best explained, firstly, by accepting that the governors wanted it that way and, secondly, acknowledging that the relationship between the people and the actors was, then as now, mostly adulatory.

From the Lord's Room high above and behind the action on stage, the lords and ladies would have seen the actors like somewhat larger-than-life projections of themselves to the people out front. Their own noble presence at the performance would imply approval, while their appearances provided luster and their names 'protection' to the new play as it entered the public's consciousness. But for the sharper wits in the audience, this made the actors, labouring below their noble overseers, indeed, appear like 'puppets'.

That moment when Mary Sidney and her train might occupy the Lord's Room as Pembroke's Men debuted before a London audience would come with the players' return to the city in late September or October. But while the players were still out touring the country, back in London a group of playwrights was already at work producing the first of the new troupe's plays.

The playwrights were in a class of their own. In the economic hierarchy of the playhouse, the patrons sat in their Lord's Room, the actors stood some five feet up on the stage, and at bottom, like the 'groundlings' at a playhouse performance, stood the playwrights. And though the turbulent history that lay at back of their relations should already have been sufficient warning, Mary Sidney would naively step into their production process that summer of 1591, it appears, only to help them. For her efforts she would find herself betrayed by one of the playwrights, her brother's work piratically set into print, and her own reputation sullied. The problem appears to have stemmed from the fact that she was a woman, but more specifically that she was 'a Dudley woman'.

CHAPTER 3

6 Playwrights & A Sonnet Piracy

Christopher Marlowe b. 1564

George Peele b. 1557

Thomas Kyd b. 1558

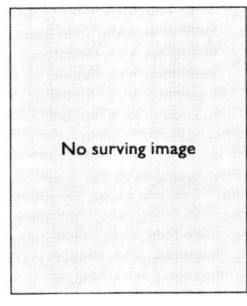
Nicholas Breton b. 1544

Robert Green b. ± 1558

Thomas Nashe b 1567

The playwrights who wrote for Pembroke's Men, summer 1591

While the companies of actors and their patrons were bound by patent and contract, the playwrights who would feed the various theatrical enterprises with new scripts, always remained aloof from that kind of commitment. As a body, they dealt with whomever they pleased, often working for an advance (with full payment coming when the finished material came in, on time). The writers of a play would have an upfront sum (which we know to have been £6 at the Rose) augmented by half the gallery take at the second performance of the play. The total pay for a new script at the Rose then was about £8, possibly more like £11 at the larger Theatre. Judging from Gosson, who had also written for the playhouse, the playwrights stood lower than the extras (who got 16p per day).

A company in residence at the Theatre would probably need a new play every month. Because of the deadlines involved, the writers were enjoined to work together as committees rather than spending a whole year working up one script alone. If one writer could frame out a story, others could, individually or in pairs, fill in the various scenes simultaneously. Given the restrictions on playing during the 47 days of Lent (Ash Wednesday to Easter Sunday), there were probably about eight playing months in a London theatrical season, and every troupe that spent the winter in town would need new plays to keep their revolving programs interesting. There must have been available pots of money from the various companies of actors as well as the inn and playhouse owners all about the city that a playwright could vie for. What was a £60 annual pot at the Rose may have been £80 at the Theatre. From two accounts we learn that there were six men writing for the Earl of Pembroke's Men over that first season, 1591–92. If one gave one's full-time attention to this company alone, and one contributed one's share to every project, the pay for the year would only have been £14 13s 4p. The extra who could find 220 days of work in the season would earn about the same. With individual principal actors earning upwards of the same amount as all that a troupe would pay for new scripts in a season, we can well understand some of the playwrights' resentment. Despite the fact that writing by committee all the while rushing to meet deadline were impositions some of the playwrights greatly resented, the majority of the era's commercial playscripts were created by this committee process. Later, when the play had been retired from the boards, whoever had bought the script could sell it for about £2 (480p) to the printers, if the script was of some especial public interest. Few, it appears, were.

While the Admiral's Men had been in residence at the Theatre, three of the principal playwrights (whose work would find its way into print) had been Christopher Marlowe, Thomas Kyd, and George Peele. Their plays (such as *Tamburlaine, The Spanish Tragedy,* or

The Battle of Alcazar), had strong roles that propelled the Admiral's star, Edward Alleyn, to the fore. Alleyn and his fellow actor and brother, John, had been great investors in scripts from these three and Burbage would have felt the sudden loss of so many perpetually popular plays going to his rival across the river. When relations between the Alleyn company and Burbage ruptured in May of 1591, the playwrights Marlowe, Kyd and Peele may have wished to follow Edward Alleyn down to the Southbank.

Even as James Burbage had to organize a new troupe, the responsibility for ensuring that there continued to be sufficient new scripts for the start of the London season in October would, under the circumstances, have fallen to him as well. It was perhaps because of the unpredictable state of affairs initially reigning at the Theatre that Burbage decided to enlist some new playwrights who had never worked directly for his playhouse before. The two writers lured to the north end were Robert Greene and Thomas Nashe. We appear to have a satirical account of Robert Greene's first encounter with James Burbage written by Greene's friend and sometime writing partner, Henry Chettle as this appeared in *Greene's Groatsworth of Wit*.

In Chettle's version of events we find our hero, now called *Roberto*, fallen out with his double-dealing courtesan, *Lamilia*. He sits on the grass singing ...*The viper's tooth is not so venomous, / The Adder's tongue not half so dangerous* ... . On the other side of the hedge sits an old actor who approaches him with the words, *Gentleman,...I have by chance heard you discourse some part of your grief, which appeareth to be more than you will discover, or I can conceipt* [WHICH MAY BE MORE SERIOUS THAN YOU REVEAL OR I CAN DISCERN]. But aware of *Roberto's* talents, the old man offers him work. For *pity it is men of learning should live in lack...men of my profession get by scholars their whole living.* *Roberto* is surprised to learn the old man is an actor for to judge by appearances, he looks like a 'great man'. (We may wonder if the old man's claim – *The twelve labours of Hercules have I terribly thundered on the Stage* – is in reference to those Leicester-inspired Hercules plays that must have become a bit of a laughing-stock after the resounding failure of Robert Dudley's Netherlands mission.) The old actor lists his many assets and impresses on the younger man what a good improvisational poet he is. Roberto is struck by his wealth though not by his poetics and demands to know how the actor means to use him. *Why sir, in making Plays, said the other, for which you shall be well paid, if you will take the pains.* The old man takes *Roberto* and leads him to the *Town's end* where he lodges him in a *house of retail*. That would be Shoreditch, beyond which was the open road to Cambridge. From several sources (including Greene himself), we learn he would fall in with one of the prostitutes of that *house of retail* and that the two would live together during the year to come.

Besides Greene, the other writer lured to the Theatre that summer of 1591 to write for the Earl of Pembroke's Men, though his stay would be explosively short, was young satirist Thomas Nashe.

The Theatre's former regular writers, Marlowe, Kyd and Peele, did not, in the event, sever their ties with the Theatre. Kyd and Marlowe, whose professional circles overlapped so as to make them immediate friends the moment the latter came to town, began working out of one room here in 1591. Together they appear to have produced plays for both the Theatre and the Rose, and possibly other troupes as well. But it is their hands along with that of George Peele that dominate the Pembroke plays that will begin to come into being this summer of 1591.

Into this group of what would already have been familiars stepped the two newcomers, Robert Greene and Thomas Nashe. Even before they became part of the Pembroke play production process, there was enough bad history between them to divide them into opposing camps. There were the hard-nosed progressives – Marlowe, Kyd, (and Peele) – who stood in opposition to the much more backward-looking middle-of-the-roaders – Greene and Nashe.

Given how acrimonious relations between the progressives and the moderates had been these past four years, we can only wonder at their being brought to work together here, even if their day-to-day relations may have been mostly arm's length. As that past turbulence is now to intrude into the present (colouring much of what the playwrights will say about Pembroke's Men, its actors and writers, and, most importantly, the first appearance of Shakespeare's hand in August of 1592), it behooves us to trace that history out.

When he abandoned his wife, child, medical studies and the patronage of the Earl of Leicester in 1586 to live 'freely' by his pen in London, Robert Greene quickly learned how hard it was to survive from the printing press even if he could produce a new romantic novella every quarter. Aside from the poor money, the lack of impact his writing was having also troubled him. Writing in the preface of *Penelope's Web* of June 1587, he used a play at the Theatre (which he only identified by its setting of Rome†) as an example of a work that had generated great public discussion when his own pamphlets thus far had hardly elicited any commentary at all. (Circumstantial evidence suggests this was in reference to a now lost play by Thomas Kyd that dramatized the life of the 3rd century Roman emperor, Heliogabalus.) But then Greene had overstepped himself and written that his readers *might as soon scoff at the rudeness of the scene, as give a plaudit to the perfection of the action.* That appeared to imply that strong acting had made 'the play of Rome' better than it really was, just the sort of jab an offended party would be sure to react to as occasion arose.

† First noted by Baldwin in *Genetics*: 3.

In the fall of that year twenty-three-year-old Christopher Marlowe, recently graduated from Cambridge, came to town with a play the likes of which the city had never experienced before. *Tamburlaine*, as exquisite as it was bold, tells the story of a poor Scythian shepherd who through acts of cunning and brutality rises to become emperor of Persia. Even across four hundred years we can still feel the crackle of its opening lines.

> From jigging veins of rhyming mother-wits,
> And such conceits as clownage keeps in pay,
> We'll lead you to the stately tent of war,
> Where you shall hear the Scythian Tamburlaine
> Threatening the world with high astounding terms,
> And scourging kingdoms with his conquering sword.
> ...

Marlowe had greatly perfected English blank verse and his play's fresh drumming style had an instant and resounding impact, especially on other writers. Marlowe immediately found a fellow traveller in Thomas Kyd, who after several years of writing comedies for the Queen's Men had turned to drama wherein he was the first to use blank verse over the course of an entire play.

Basic blank verse appears easy enough. Every line is nothing but ten syllables that go da-DUM da-DUM da-DUM da-DUM da-DUM. That no lines are rhymed makes it seemingly easier still. With little preparation but inspired by a great burst of energy, Robert Greene thought he too would write a play in that new high style. Sometime in very early 1588 Greene had *Alphonsus, King of Aragon* on the boards. Its prologue announced that t*his my hand, which used for to pen / The praise of love and Cupid's peerless power, / Will now begin to treat of bloody Mars.* Its story in a free and original manner mixes the lives of two kings of Aragon, Alphonso I and Alphonso V. That Greene was rising to Marlowe's challenge he demonstrates in much of his story, setting, language and tone. Three-quarters way through Greene has Amurack, the Turk, spur on his own troops with the call, *remember with yourselves / What foes we have; not mighty Tamburlaine, / ... but fearful boors* (LL. 1443-46). But Greene was too much the romantic, and his style appears too exaggerated to be believable. As a practiced poet, he could write iambic pentameters only too readily. What he was unaware of were the subtle, constantly-shifting techniques by which Marlowe and Kyd could sustain interest in the form over the course of five acts. Long before the end of *Alphonsus* an awful predictability sets in.

Two writers made some quick additions to that 'play of Rome' wherein new-come playwright, Robert Greene, was made the butt of a little stage ridicule. In the preface of his next novella, *Perimides the Black Smith* (S.R. March 1588), Greene tells us that he had been openly identified by the motto he had just begun affixing to the title pages of his books—*Omne tulit punctum* [PLEASURE MIXED WITH PROFIT], the motto whereby Greene, the self-promoter, hoped to entice his readers over any moral scruples they might feel about buying one of his 'love pamphlets'. Greene reveals that *two Gentlemen Poets ... had it in derision, for that I could not make my verses jet upon the stage in tragical buskins.* That would be them talking about his play. He tells us the offending matter had been in a play where *two mad men of Rome beat it out of their paper bucklers* [PAPER SHIELDS, i.e. THEIR SCRIPTS]. That would be their play.

As to who these *two Gentlemen Poets* were, he tells us this of the first. If Greene's own play failed it was because he would not *dare God out of heaven with that atheist Tamburlaine*. This hit on Marlowe is a radical departure from the *'mighty Tamburlaine'* tribute of *Alphonsus* shortly before. To apply the label of atheism to anyone was sure to make trouble with church authorities, indicating Greene's feelings against Marlowe were here running pretty high. Of the second writer involved, Greene tells us if his play failed it was because he would not *go blaspheming with the Mad Priest of the Sun*. If the parallel holds, then *The Mad Priest of the Sun* would be the title of a second play. This play does not survive but it is surmised that this is the 'play of Rome' Greene had alluded to the year before. The circumstantial evidence suggests then the blaspheming playwright is Thomas Kyd. When Thomas Nashe weighs into this argument the following year, he will first lambaste Marlowe but save his real vitriol for Kyd.

In his rage Robert Greene would denounce their verse as *impious instances of intolerable poetry*. He would not be one to *set the end of scholarism in an English blank verse*. He gives his public departure from the school of iambic pentameter writing great finality. By painting his enemies with the damning labels of atheism and blasphemy, Greene was one up again. At the end of *Alphonsus*, Greene had bravely announced his intention to write a second part. None was forthcoming.

That fall of 1588, after the Armada scare had passed, Marlowe and Kyd prepared a riposte to Greene's charges. The year before, a complete story of the legendary Faustus had first appeared at the Frankfurt Book Fair and it was this that became the basis of Marlowe's *Tragical History of Doctor Faustus*. The story of Johannes Faustus – the man who, disappointed with his studies in philosophy and religion, sells his soul to the devil in exchange for universal knowledge – is now well known. Marlowe's early production of it is a deft achievement, shimmering in its language and ideas, and truly frightening for its original audiences. And though the main story is what is interesting about the play, it is its comic subplot that provides the next paragraph in the ongoing feud with Greene.

Although *Faustus* is mostly the work of Marlowe single-handed, it is in the mixed style of the subplot that we find him working with a partner and that appears to have been Thomas Kyd. They ask what would happen if the conjuring power of a Faustus were in the hands of a clown. In their retelling of the sorcerer's apprentice tale the authors had, from all appearances, only one person in mind for it – our love-pamphleteer and would-be playwright, Robert Greene. They give their character a pointy goatee of the kind that the real-life Greene assiduously cultivated. In case anyone in the audience still entertained any doubts, the authors gave their stage character the name of *Robin*, the diminutive of Greene's first name, Robert.

Our stage Robin is presented as *poor* and *bare* and *out of service*. That would be true of the real-life Greene. He is a swearing fellow, a glutton, a womaniser and a lover of wine, much as Greene would later on his deathbed confess himself to have been. Once Robin steals one of Faustus' conjuring books he would search out some magical circles wherein *the maidens in our parish dance at my pleasure stark naked before me,* reflecting Greene's confessed weakness for the flesh. After drinking at an inn, he and his friend, Rafe, steal a silver goblet, suggesting that Greene suffered from that urge as well. When confronted by the vintner, Robin would be rid of him by conjuring up Mephistopheles himself. (It was still a felony to conjure up any spirit and here was *Robin* conjuring up his satanic majesty himself!) The *Monarch of hell* is so annoyed at being drawn forth for such a triviality that he turns *Robin* and his friend into apes! We may imagine what noises and gestures they made as they gambolled about the stage. Matters between the parties stood even again.

An opportunity for revenge came to Greene that summer when he joined a committee of writers to help the church counter a challenge to its structure. The threat had come from the extreme Protestants. Since the late 1560's, Robert Dudley, the Earl of Leicester, had become the champion of a Geneva-style reformation of the English church. This Calvinist reformation, which sought to return the church to the state it had been in before the ascendancy of Rome, wished the bishops and archbishops removed so that the congregations could rule themselves by their ministers and elders, alone or in synod. This went well beyond her Majesty's position which viewed the pillar of the church one upon which her own rule, in part, rested. But as two-thirds of the congregations were without educated preaching ministers (because of numerous abuses) despite everyone by law being obliged to pay tithes as if they did, the church's top-heavy hierarchy became the convenient sore point in the eyes of the reformers. With Dudley's death in 1588, the English Presbyterians (made up of a somewhat uneasy coalition of 'war party Protestants', Puritans, and other discontents) resorted to a series of scurrilous, highly humorous pamphlets wherein the bishops and archbishops were gleefully and unmercifully lampooned. The committee, writing under the broad group pseudonym of *Martin Marprelate,* kept their secret press continually working and constantly moving. The palace was alarmed and numerous posses were sent out. But for the next year and a half the people would be highly entertained by all *Martin* and his crew had to say.

The bishops began by publishing a pamphlet of their own whose learnedness become fodder for a stream of Martinist invective. To gain back the public opinion they had lost, the church next brought together outside writers who might undo Martin from the stage. The bishops enlisted playwright John Lyly, the Earl of Oxford's secretary, and a young satirist from Lowestoft, Thomas Nashe, who had prematurely broken off his Cambridge studies because of the death of his minister father. These two produced at least one script for the Queen's Men, who by their contract with her Majesty were obliged to play it as two separate touring companies, presumably, to spread the geographical reach of its anti-Martinist message. And, it appears, they wrote at least one script for the combined children's company that had been under Oxford's direction since the conjunction of the planets of 1583. But here in the fall of 1589 they delved too freely into matters of church and state, giving the extreme Protestants the ammunition with which to openly counterattack (producing, for example, a circulated letter by Francis Bacon and a couple of printed pamphlets by Dr. Richard Harvey). The offence given by the children's production was sufficient to cause Her Majesty to terminate the whole counteroffensive against Martin from the stage and the combined children's company was disbanded. Both the Earl of Oxford and his secretary, John Lyly, were to suffer a great loss of place at court over the matter.

The church fathers toned their assault down to producing pamphlets in Martin's style. They retained Thomas Nashe to head the committee that would come to include Robert Greene and Thomas Lodge. Under the group pseudonym, *Pasquil*, they endeavoured to match Martin and his clan blow-for-scurrilous-blow. And as each pamphlet rolled off their vetted production line, it went straight to that newly-licensed printer, Henry Chettle, for publication. (This experience, I believe, sits at the heart of Chettle's siding with Nashe and Greene in their future disputes with Pembroke's Men.)

In September 1589, in between the first and second Pasquil pamphlets, appeared Robert Greene's latest short novel, *Menaphon*. Its preface consisted of a lengthy essay-cum-letter written by Thomas Nashe and addressed *To the Gentlemen Students of Both Universities*. It is here that the battle against Marlowe and Kyd would be continued. Nashe begins by requesting the young men of Cambridge and Oxford to make Robert Greene, their *scholar-like shepherd*, welcome. Nashe acknowledges that Marlowe's new literary style had rubbed off on everyone so that now *every mechanical mate abhors the English he was born to*, attesting to its impact. The problem for the students lay in their *servile imitation of vainglorious tragedians who think they deserve poets' immortality if they can but once get Boreas by the beard and the heavenly bull by the dewlap*. Boreas was the north wind, and to get him by the beard was to direct some of his sound and fury. The *heavenly bull* was Zeus who usually reigned supreme on Olympus but had one time taken physical form as a heifer in order to carry Europa on his back to the island of Crete. These two emblems encapsulate what are to be Nashe's two central rants against Marlowe and Kyd: 1) the issue of that overly-loud blank verse and 2) the issue of importing contemporary (especially Senecan-influenced) literary materials from the continent of Europe into the island of England.

Nashe does not blame the students, only their *idiot art-masters that intrude themselves to our ears as the alchemists of eloquence, who, mounted on the stage of arrogance, think to outbrave better pens with the swelling bombast of a bragging blank verse*. Battle lines are being drawn. Anatomising the *swelling* nature of their poetry, we hear Nashe saying something to the effect that their imaginations are so full of bullying notions, their brains so flooded with a more-than-drunk bravado, and having no improvisational skill to express their virility, they void themselves of their pent-up rage in a loud, pounding blank verse; or, as Nashe more eloquently states, *Indeed it may be the ingrafted overflow of some kilcow conceit that overcloyeth their imagination with a more than drunken resolution, being not extemporal in the invention of any other means to vent their manhood, commits the digestion of their choleric incumbrances to the spacious volubility of a drumming decasyllabon.*

He comes back to Robert Greene, whom he now calls *sweet friend*. He tells him, *thy Arcadian Menaphon whose attire, though not so stately, yet comely, doth entitle thee above all other to that* [MODERATE STYLE OF SPEAKING] *which Tully in his orator termeth true eloquence.* Though not lofty, *Menaphon* was still a fine example of that musical style epitomized by Cicero (*Tully*). In the present argument, the terse, pointed style and martial rhythms of the Senecan School of writing would have represented the opposite pole, the 'immoderate style of speaking'. Nashe would see Greene square off with Marlowe in battle. He writes, *give me the man whose extemporal vein in any humour will excel our greatest art-master's deliberate thoughts, whose invention, quicker than his eye, will challenge the proudest rhetorician to the contention of like perfection with like expedition.* A challenge! Greene, the *extemporal* wit, would do battle with Marlowe, the *greatest art-master* and *proudest rhetorician*. Their weapons would be their pens. The winner would be he who could measure out perfection and speed in equal proportions. It is true that in that sort of wit-battle, Greene, the fastest pen in town, would have won handily.

But for the real revenge he has come to exact, Nashe picks Marlowe's partner, Thomas Kyd, to be his 'whipping boy'. Writers without university degrees, such as Kyd, should not try to better university men in wit combat. *Let other men, as they please, praise the mountain that in seven years brings forth a mouse,* Nashe jabs. This classical metaphor for 'all groaning, no consequence' concerns a mountain that by its heaving noises was thought to be in labour; but when a huge gap appeared in its side it was a mouse that stepped forth. The mouse here was probably Kyd's first great stage success,

The Spanish Tragedy, that had come after he had been a playwright several years. The notion is fortified by Nashe's disparaging allusion to *Elysium*, which Kyd in his play had placed within the anatomy of Hades as per late classical thinking. (For the church, Elysium was part of Heaven.) That sort of playwright had best stick to the trade of scrivener (for which Kyd had served an apprenticeship). But Kyd had wanted to be more than a secretary to the people and had pursued playwriting interests in his free time. While the university-trained poets had pursued a wide curriculum, Kyd had in his dramatic pursuits become fixated on the late Roman dramatist, Seneca, all of whose plays had been translated into English and printed in quarto between 1559 and 1567 and then in one volume in 1581. Some of them were, in part, written in blank verse. Nashe writes, *English Seneca read by candlelight yields many good sentences, as blood is a beggar and so forth. And if you entreat him fair in a frosty morning, he will afford you whole Hamlets, I should say, handfuls of tragical speeches.* Aside from the tantalizing first sighting of Ellsinore, this indeed highlights Kyd's deep reading of everything Senecan available to him. But he had taken matters a step further. With Seneca, murder, revenge, ghosts, etc. came to the audience second-hand by way of reports made by the speaking characters. Kyd's innovation was to bring all this interesting action to centre stage where his audience might take their full enjoyment of it.

But Seneca let blood line by line and page by page, at length must needs die to our stage, warns Nashe. And when the Senecan source dries up what will his *famished followers* do? Men such as Kyd would then have to *intermeddle with Italian translations,* which Nashe condemns as nothing but *home-born mediocrity.* It appears that Kyd supplemented his earnings from the stage by translating Italian pamphlets of which his translation of Tasso's *Padre di famiglia* survives. And besides that, there were Kyd's suspect French interests. Nashe writes, *otherwhile for recreation after their candle stuff, having starched their beards most curiously, to make a peripatetical path into the inner parts of the city and spend two or three hours in turning over French Dowdy where they can attract more infection in one minute than they can do eloquence all days of their life by conversing with any authors of like argument.* With daybreak, Master Kyd, in a kind of disguise, by a long, circuitous route meets up with some *French Dowdy* (a dowdy being an unattractively dressed girl or woman). *Infection* is the outcome of their *turning over*. But this is scatology played for a laugh. The issue here was turning over pages, specifically of reading imported French books in order to converse with *authors* who had similar Senecan interests. Kyd had a good knowledge of French and would have found the source story for his early version of *Hamlet* in Belleforest's *Histoires tragiques*. Kyd also procured himself a copy of the 1585 collected works of the French Senecan playwright, Robert Garnier, whose influence appears in Kyd's one surviving play from this time, *Solimon and Perseda*. (This was the same edition that Mary Sidney would work from in her translation of *Marc Antoine*.)

And then Nashe comes to the players of the Admiral's Men who were acting out those offending scenes in *Faustus* and 'the play of Rome' wherein Robert Greene had been turned into a stage mockery. Nashe warns them that though they may now wear expensive silks and ride on horseback that they not forget their recent humble origins when they *still carried their fardles* [PACKS] *on footback*. But, states Nashe, *it is no marvel, whenas the deserved reputation of one Roscius is of force to enrich a rabble of counterfeits.* Among the company of actors (the *rabble of counterfeits*) there was one highly gifted player whom Nashe dubs *Roscius*. Until his death the previous year, Roscius had been the Queen's Men's comic-actor, Richard Tarlton, England's first national star. But the Roscius Nashe has in mind is alive for he tells the actors that their fate depends on him. Here in September 1589 that could only have been twenty-one-year-old Edward Alleyn, who since his arrival on the big stage in February had become the chief attraction at the Theatre. Let the actors take care of their leader, *let them dedicate a De profundis* [PROSTRATE THEMSELVES] *every morning to the preservation of their Caesar or else this rabble would soon be back to their juggling, to mediocrity, where they could bewail in weeping blanks the wane of their monarchy.* In his novel Greene joins Nashe with a few lame shots of his own. He exposes Marlowe's Canterbury background and the fact that his father was a shoemaker, a situation that gave the cobbler's son no right to tell where another man's shoe pinched! Advantage to Greene.

(But why had Nashe stepped to the fore to defend Greene against

Marlowe and Kyd? We know Nashe held a low opinion of Greene and his romantic fluff from what he had written about Greene in his *Anatomy of Absurdity*, a wide-ranging satirical assessment of English letters Nashe had written the year before.

For one, Nashe was very much a servant of the church at this stage of his career. All the unorthodox strands running through Marlowe and Kyd's writing had no doubt marked the drumming blank verse poets in the eyes of the church.

More personally, although Nashe had his *Anatomy* ready, no printer as yet would publish it – probably due to lack of name recognition. He could not identify himself by name in the anonymous *Pasquil* pamphlets, so those works would not have immediately advanced his standing with the reading public. But a vigorous showing here in Greene's pamphlet under his own name might help establish that recognition he needed.

But the extreme thrust and parry of Nashe's language may have been motivated by more personal reasons still. Nashe and Marlowe appear to have known each other in university. Back in 1586-7 the two were among the best up-and-coming writers at Cambridge and had together written a play that would come before her Majesty twice over 1587. *The Tragical History of Dido, Queen of Carthage* took its story from Virgil's *Aeneid* and concerned Dido, the mythological founder and first queen of Carthage. Marlowe and Nashe turned the play out in lines of blank verse that indicate something of Marlowe's high aspirations but as held back by Nashe's more tempered approach. Dido, who was also known by her Phoenician name, *Elissa*, was a favourite subject to present before the Queen, a woman who like Dido was also held to be the founder of a new race of people.

But the most surprising aspect of the play lies in its opening. Here we find Marlowe and Nashe's only original contribution to the story they had found in Virgil. The play begins with the image of Jupiter dandling Ganymede upon his knee. In the words of love exchanged there is a strong homoerotic presence quite remarkable for this time. Although the matter of the authors' sexual orientation remains uncertain, later reports will claim Marlowe was gay. Nashe's proclivities remain more conjectural. In that unpublished essay of his, he had alarmingly espoused a tremendous disdain for all women generally and, like Marlowe (and Kyd), he would never take a wife. If there was some emotional bond between Marlowe and Nashe, it may have been ruptured when Marlowe suddenly left the university before the end of term in order to perform some secret but notable assignment on behalf of the government. Marlowe was then awarded his M.A. degree despite his absenteeism by order of her Majesty's Privy Council. Marlowe had next arrived in London with his play of *Tamburlaine* and established his reputation. In that same timeframe, Nashe's father had died and Nashe had had to withdraw from Cambridge without his Master's degree. Back home in Lowestoft he had in his spare hours written that satirical essay for which he had as yet no printer. Nashe may well have felt some resentment at the break in their relations as well as the totally divergent outcomes of their lives since. And Master Kyd now being Marlowe's writing partner (as he had once been) would only have sharpened Nashe's ill will towards him)

In June of the following year was entered into the Stationers' Registry an anonymous pamphlet called *Tarlton's news out of Purgatory*. Its prefatory letter, alongside the overall intent of the pamphlet, as well as the reply it would shortly elicit, all heavily suggest Marlowe and his crew were behind it. Part of the charges that Nashe under Greene's auspices had levelled against Marlowe and company concerned their use of foreign sources and their inability to translate them. Further Nashe had protested against their bringing literary infection into the country from abroad. And what he implied throughout would in one moment crystallize – Marlowe and company's writings were as *men's excrements*. In keeping with all this, the authors of *Tarlton's News* had translated into a witty, urbane and highly readable English four of the more racy stories out of that most titillating of Italian books, the *Decameron* by Boccaccio. And although its prefatorial letter bespeaks Marlowe's life point-for-point, when they came to credit *Tarlton's News*, they would only say it was from the pen of one *Robin Goodfellow*. All folklore aside, there was in the present circumstances only one Robin Goodfellow, one R.G., and that was Robert Greene. No former English translator had dared touch these Boccaccio stories, including Greene whose story for *Perimedes* had also been drawn out of the *Decameron*. The joke would then be that the Marlovians had hung this lovingly translated work of Italian bawdy around the neck of their enemy. The printer refrained from affixing his name to the title page.

But this was shortly, and with a surprising amount of good humour, to be answered by a pamphlet called *The Cobbler of Canterbury*. Its running title states it was written as an *invective* against *Tarlton's News*. The story opens on a boat full of passengers pleasantly floating down the Thames towards Canterbury on the Gravesend barge. When a gentleman pulls a little pamphlet out of his sleeve, the narrator makes bold to ask him the name of the book. *Mary, quoth he, a foolish toy, called Tarlton's News out of Purgatory.* At this news they all *fell to descanting of the book.* But it is an *ancient man that was a cobbler in Canterbury* who pronounces himself indifferent to it, *like a cup of bottle ale … 'tis not merry enough for Tarlton's vein, nor stuffed with his fine conceits: therefore it shall pass for a book and no more.* Over the course of the *Menaphon* story proper Greene had several times alluded to Marlowe's Canterbury roots and his father's profession of shoemaker. The joke here then becomes that Marlowe's humble father would hardly give his own son's work a passing grade. Thereafter the narrator recalls Chaucer's Canterbury pilgrims and suggests the passengers likewise pass their time in telling tales. Now the bawdy of Boccaccio is answered with the fabliaux out of Chaucer. In the ongoing dispute over what their models should be, the joke inherent here is that one need not go to continental sources for this kind of low-brow material, there already was enough at home! This issue of native vs. foreign sources and models rebounds in much of the work Marlowe and Greene will produce this year, indicating the issue was far more than just rhetoric.

With these differences dividing them, it is surprising to find Greene and Nashe working in close proximity to the Marlovian crew for the about-to-be-launched Pembroke's Men in the summer of 1591. Here at the point where their lives will intersect with those of the Burbage family and the patron to the new troupe, the Countess of Pembroke, it may be wondered if this gathering of writers was all due to happenstance, or if this did represent some deliberate effort to assemble what would have been the best writers then working in London. In the immediate circumstances, we would surmise that Nashe and Greene would not work side-by-side with Thomas Kyd, whom they considered to be a social inferior; but Marlowe would. Nashe and Greene could not work side-by-side with Marlowe but Peele could. Nashe and Greene could work with Peele. Greene and Peele were both romantics at heart (and great tipplers, too) and on that basis found they could work together. In the preface to Greene's *Menaphon* of 1589, after his lashing of Marlowe and Kyd, Nashe had praised a number of writers for their moderate styles. Among these he had lavished extremely warm words on the *Puritan* Peele, ranking him among the top poets alive.

This would be borne out by the way one play written for Pembroke's Men that summer appears to have been written. On the basis of what Nashe and Greene will report, supported by a history of forensic observation, it appears Marlowe and Kyd, Peele and Greene, and Nashe alone, with one or more interventions from Nicholas Breton, were the parties immediately responsible for a very large-scale re-enactment of the first stages of the English Civil War of the previous century. The play had the title, *The First Part of the Contention betwixt the two famous Houses of York and Lancaster,* when it was printed three years later. With its large cast of characters giving more or less equal time to the two sides of the conflict, the play was much more an ensemble piece not requiring a 'star' like Edward Alleyn. This would have made it an ideal vehicle for such players as James's son, now 21-year-old Richard Burbage. None of the very early Pembroke plays was hero-driven in the way material for the Admiral's Men had been. *The First Part of the Contention* may have been Pembroke's season opener in October.

Reading the script line-by-line, searching for authorial thumbprints, it appears that Marlowe (with possible help from Kyd) was the original framer, the one(s) who took the historical record as found in the 1587 edition of *Holinshed's Chronicles of England* and selectively sketched out that material into enough dramatic scenes to fill the two-hour needs of the stage. We find lines marked by Marlowe's style scattered throughout as if the scene-by-scene outline included bits of finished dialogue. The play's opening speech by the

Marquess of Suffolk, where he formally presents Margaret of France to King Henry VI of England, gives some indication of what sets that Marlovian voice apart.

> SUFFOLK. As by your high imperial Majesty's command,
> I had in charge at my depart for France,
> As procurator for your excellence,
> To marry Princess Margaret for your grace,
> So in the ancient famous City Tours,
> In presence of the Kings of France and Sicily,
> The Dukes of Orleans, Calabar, Brittany, and Alonson.
> Seven Earls, twelve Barons, and then the reverend Bishops,
> I did perform my task and was espoused,
> And now, most humbly on my bended knees,
> In sight of England and her royal Peers,
> Deliver up my title in the Queen
> Unto your gracious excellence, that are the substance
> Of that great shadow I did represent:
> The happiest gift that ever Marquess gave,
> The fairest Queen that ever King possessed.
>
> KING. Suffolk arise.
> Welcome Queen Margaret to English Henry's court,
> The greatest show of kindness yet we can bestow,
> Is this kind kiss. …

Aside from the mature, measured blank verse, the passage bristles with typical Marlovian inversions of phrase—*ancient famous, English Henry's*. But overall the play will not bear that Marlovian imprint and the tautness of the style evaporates in the royal kiss.

Here we slip into the lesser style of the writers who padded out the scenes with finished dialogue. On the basis of what we will shortly learn from Nashe as well as a number of forensic testimonies, it appears that here we find the two romantics, blustery George Peele with the aid of Robert Greene, hard at work.

> KING. … [they kiss] Oh gracious God of heaven,
> Lend me a heart replete with thankfulness,

> For in this beauteous face thou hast bestowed
> A world of pleasures to my perplexed soul.
>
> QUEEN. Th'excessive love I bear unto your grace,
> Forbids me to be lavish of my tongue,
> Lest I should speak more than beseems a woman:
> Let this suffice, my bliss is in your liking,
> And nothing can make poor Margaret miserable,
> Unless the frown of mighty England's King.

These royals sound less regal than does the marquess above. The king comes across as a simple, lusty fellow while his new queen does no better as the two-dimensional goodwife.

By contrast, the wild, prankish scenes of Jack Cade's plebeian uprising that fill out most of Act IV are written in a singular and pungent voice. This appears to be the work of comic writer, Thomas Nashe. The scenes distinguish themselves by the exuberant, plebeian prose that has something in common with the *Pasquil* pamphlets of 1589-90, as well as Nashe's other writings. Here in the play of *The Contention* the rebel Cade addresses his troupes.

> CADE. Therefore be brave, for your Captain is brave, and
> vows reformation: you shall have seven half-penny loaves
> for a penny, and the three hooped pot, shall have ten
> hoops, and it shall be felony to drink small beer, ... if I
> be king, as king I will be.
>
> ALL. God save your majesty.

The patrons, Mary Sidney and her husband, Henry Herbert, the Lord President of Wales, would eventually have to sit behind all this while it was introduced to the wider public. By their presence they would lend credibility to the work and 'protect' it as it made its way into that fractious public discussion. Though he may have been a shrewd politician, his lordship was not a literary man, leaving his wife to be the arbiter of the Pembroke cultural agenda. Mary Sidney, born and raised in a family that had thrived at court in part because of its high cultural standards, would have been a hard critic to please. Her intense, ongoing literary apprenticeship in which she had her brother's work as the gold standard before her, would have made her all the more alert to the literary issues the playwrights, by their writing, raised.

Although the exact order of events must be inferred from Nashe's actions (considered below) along with the larger context, it appears that the countess sent Nicholas Breton as her intermediary to speak with the playwrights. Possibly to encourage them, samples of more inspired writing were now to pass to them. It was an exceptional collection of poetry that none of the playwrights had ever been privy to.

There was first and foremost a cycle of sonnets the countess's brother, Sir Philip Sidney, had written to describe his doomed passion for the 'dark lady', Penelope Devereux, back in 1581. Aside from their genuine show of emotions and sweetly-tuned humour, the *Astrophel and Stella* sonnets would have provided the playwrights with many examples of how a master poet sustains interest in iambic pentameter lines over the course of an extended work. And there were also a couple of dozen equally robust sonnets, also in iambic pentameter lines, by Samuel Daniel, a poet presently in Italy who would join Mary Sidney's household the following spring. For the countess to have shared this fulsome package of what were rather 'intimate' works by the more introverted standards of the day, would suggest a conscious decision on her part that these works represented a strong model for the playwrights to emulate. Given that these playwrights of London, with their mottled history, were probably unknown to the countess, there may have been some naiveté on her part thinking she could trust them to use these works only to perfect their own craft.

The junior member of the Pembroke playwriting team, Thomas Nashe, took great umbrage at suddenly having this splendid batch of poetry thrust into his hands. Though dazzled by what he read, he was by inclination outraged to realize that Sidney's sonnets were already quite old (ten years, in fact). It was as if Nashe and the rest of the nation had been allowed to flounder a long time when these poetic gems might have offered all of them some genuine poetic guidance. At back there was a long simmering (and genuine) issue of the better courtly poets keeping their own (often superior) works in tight-knit manuscript circulation among themselves.

In order to set to right this and several other perceived injustices suffered at the hands of the Pembroke company, Nashe took a copy of the sonnets to bookseller Thomas Newman. In mid-September 1591 appeared *Sir P.S. His Astrophel and Stella. Wherein the excellence of Sweet Poesy is concluded*. Augmenting the Sidney and Daniel sonnets were a few verses from the man who had offered to become Nashe's patron until he fell into royal disfavour, Edward de Vere, the Earl of Oxford, and Thomas Campion, a student at law who was a very good lyricist

Nashe's letter, *Somewhat to read for them that list* [LIKE], was the prefatorial gateway into this heretofore hidden trove of verse. Though written in Nashe's trademark satirical manner, the letter (when laid out end-to-end) exposes fairly clearly his motive and justification for what he has done, his feelings towards Mary Sidney and the other playwrights, and his thoughts on what her ladyship's actors could expect from this great committee outpouring. Although there is as yet no sign of either Shakspere or Shakespeare, Nashe strikingly reveals the countess's wish to ingratiate herself into the playwriting process.

Nashe opens by contrasting the end of a play with the coming of this golden procession of sonnets. He sneers, *so ends the Scene* [STAGE] *of Idiots* [PLAYWRIGHTS], *and enter Astrophel in pomp*. Of those playwrights, Nashe would immediately single out Marlowe and Kyd. *Gentlemen, that have seen a thousand lines of folly drawn forth ex uno puncto impudentiae* [OUT OF ONE POINT OF IMPUDENCE], *& two famous Mountains to go to the conception of one Mouse, that have had your ears deafened with the echo of Fame's brazen towers, when only they have been touched with a leaden pen*. The last time Nashe had used this cluster of metaphors was in lashing Marlowe and Kyd in the preface to Robert Greene's *Menaphon* back in 1589. Although Marlowe and Kyd had begun adding to each other's plays from the time Marlowe came to town in 1587, the two had begun writing out of one room this year, which Nashe, in sort, corroborates. Although there is one early Marlovian Pembroke comedy, the Italianate *Taming of A Shrew* (to be considered next volume), the *Mouse* referred to here is probably the framing job done for *The First Part of the Contention.* the play which appears to underlie everything Nashe's letter refers to. That the Marlovians come first in Nashe's letter probably indicates the distant, pre-eminent position they as framers enjoyed in the creative process. If nothing else, Nashe indicates his loathing for drumming iambic verse as practiced by the school of Marlowe had not yet abated.

The next poet Nashe comes to before getting to Sir Philip's work (although it is again only to abuse him in the comparison) is Nicholas Breton. As *Britton's Bower of Delights*, with the shield of Leicester on its cover, had been published earlier in May, Nashe presents us the image of *Pan sitting in his bower of delights, & a number of Midases to admire his miserable hornpipes.* Further down Nashe will compare Sir Philip Sidney with Apollo. In mythology, Apollo on the lyre and Pan on his pipes once had a musical contest at which King Midas officiated. When tin-eared Midas chose Pan the winner, Apollo punished him by giving him the ears of an ass. One may be sure that those ass's ears would now be on Breton's admiring patrons, the Pembrokes. This opening order by its chronology would suggest that Breton as intermediary arrived after the framing-job by the *two famous Mountains* had already been completed but while the 'padders', whom we are shortly to meet, were still about their task.

But Nashe would turn away from them and speak of Sir Philip's sonnets. *Let not your surfeited sight, new come from such puppet play, think scorn to turn aside into this Theatre of pleasure, for here you shall find a paper stage strewed* [STREWN] *with pearl, an artificial heaven to overshadow the fair frame, & crystal walls to encounter your curious eyes, whiles the tragicomedy of love is performed by starlight.* It is rare that we find Nashe writing this elegantly, indicating he was, on the one hand, under the influence of the sonnets certainly but that he would indicate to those *Midases* that he, unlike Master Breton, was quite up to the task of matching Sir Philip's high romantic style.

Perhaps most striking here are the many playhouse allusions embedded in this opening passage, indicating clearly where Thomas Nashe would draw the attention of the astute reader (like the troupe's patron, the Countess of Pembroke).

| Theatre | enter | idiots |
| stage | Actor | play |

Scene	puppet	tragicomedy
heaven		argument
walls		Prologue
frame		Epilogue

But before he can describe his playhouse experience Nashe must first come to terms with the issue of the piracy and the woman he has seemingly robbed. He admits to some *presumption* even to praise Sir Philip Sidney. He knows that these jewels (Sidney's sonnets) will now *come to their hands that know not their value, and that the coxcombs of our days, like Aesop's cock, had rather have a Barley kernel wrapped up in a Ballad then they will dig for the wealth of wit in any ground they know not.* Lowbrow, ballad-loving ears would likely treat these sonnets like Aesop's cock had the jewel, which the fable tells us the bird discarded as being totally useless. But for Nashe, Sir Philip's 'poetic fame' could not be allowed to lie *imprisoned in Ladies' casks & the president books of such as cannot see without another man's spectacles.* This hit at elitism is palpable. The close proximity of 'lady' and 'president' may have escaped the notice of some but Lady Mary and her husband, the Lord President of Wales, would have personally felt the sting. It would appear that their 'Midas ears' are here joined by 'other men's glasses' suggesting that, according to Nashe at any rate, their eyesight was none of the best either. Despite the fustian, the upshot was that the Pembrokes here stood accused of hoarding something the value of which they themselves could not appreciate. Nashe betrays by this his total ignorance of the countess.

Yet at length it [SIR PHILIP'S SONNETS] *breaks forth in spite of his keepers, and useth some private pen (instead of a picklock) to procure his violent enlargement.* Nashe, the *private pen,* has now brought Sir Philip via the press to public view (*his violent enlargement*). His plea of innocence (that he was no *picklock*) is valid from a legal point of view. The laws affecting copyright were still elementary and hinged entirely on precedence of entry into the Stationers' register or actual appearance in print. The right to make copies (the *copyright*) was accorded in perpetuity to whoever did one of these first. There were no laws that prohibited one from taking someone else's writings and selling them to a bookseller or printer. That was one of the reasons the courtly poets kept their manuscripts under such tight control.

Nashe further justifies himself by stating that too long had *Astrophel (England's Sun) withheld the beams of his spirit from the common view of our dark sense*. The challenge to lift the native tongue to that smooth classical standard had been no easy matter and there had been many false starts. By the light of Sidney's sonnets Nashe now saw what *dunghill* material most of these early experiments were. *But now that cloud of sorrow is dissolved which fiery love exhaled from his dewy hair* ... . Dew was at this time thought to fall directly from heaven, Sir Philip's current abode.

Just as Spenser had addressed the countess personally in the body of *The Ruins of Time*, despite the fact that the whole poem revolved around her, so Nashe audaciously does the same here. (If his letter ever became the subject of a libel case he could, no doubt, point at this passage in his defence.) Like Spenser, Nashe begins by looking back to the root of renown from which Sidney and his sister had sprung and, again assuming that style indicated by Sir Philip's sonnets, addresses the *fair sister of Phoebus, and eloquent secretary to the Muses, most rare Countess of Pembroke*. *Phoebus* was another name for Apollo, who here stands for Sir Philip. As the *eloquent secretary* to the 'nine sisters', right off Nashe strongly hints at the countess's writerly interests, as these had presumably been communicated by Breton. Nashe writes, *thou art not to be omitted; whom Arts do adore as a second Minerva, and our poets extol as the patroness of their invention*. To say that she is *not to be omitted* is humorous in part because she is in fact the only person (aside from himself) openly named in the entire document (indicating to my mind that the letter is primarily addressed to her). By *our poets*, Nashe no doubt refers to Spenser, Fraunce and Breton, who were associated with the countess in the printed record. *Minerva*, the Roman name for the Greek goddess, Pallas Athena, was among other things, a noted patron to the arts (like the countess) and was an anagrammatic form of the countess's first name as it was usually spelled in this time, *Marie*.

Nashe claims the countess's writing outgoes that of Sappho, the beloved lyric poet of 7th century BCE whom Plato had dubbed 'the tenth Muse', this being the probable source of the *secretary to the Muses* allusion above. But Sappho's writings were lost and her 16th century reputation relied entirely on the secondhand reports of others.

Nashe is aware that the countess is driven by a larger purpose: the *Laurel Garland which thy Brother so bravely advanced on his Lance is still kept green in the Temple of Pallas*. But here in Minerva's temple Nashe would direct the countess to pursue such (feminine) recreations as religious meditation, spreading largesse and being an inspiration to (men) artists: *thou only sacrificest thy soul to contemplation, thou only entertainest empty handed Homer, & keepest the springs of Castalia from being dried up*. Castalia, a nymph pursued by Apollo, had turned herself into a spring flowing from Mount Parnassus rather than be violated by him. This had caused Apollo, by way of contrition, to bestow the power of divine inspiration upon her waters (when others, of course, drank from them). The underlying message for the countess then was: do not allow your (womanly) body to be violated by your brother, *Apollo*. Play the role convention allots you: *Learning, wisdom, beauty, and all other ornaments of Nobility whatsoever, seek to approve themselves in thy sight, and get a further seal of felicity from the smiles of thy favour*. Those *ornaments of Nobility* would be made for her, her role only being to approve (or disapprove).

And now to ensure his readers understand his intentions, he deflates all his seeming praise by admitting that (like Sappho) he only knows her at the second hand. *I fear I shall be counted a mercenary flatterer, for mixing my thoughts with such figurative admiration, but general report, that surpasseth my praise, condemneth my rhetoric of dullness for so cold a commendation*. His admiration is *figurative* because it is based only on *general report*, i.e. the report of some third party. And it is from this party that some criticism for Nashe has come. As to who that third party might be, Nashe immediately follows with another broadside against Nicholas Breton: *Indeed, to say the truth, my style is somewhat heavy-gated, and cannot dance trip and go so lively, with oh my love, ah my love, all my love's gone, as other Shepherds that have been fools in the Morris time out of mind*. The line, *oh my love, ah my love, all my love's gone,* was one of the more rhapsodic moments of Breton's *Amoris Lachrimae* as it had appeared in the *Bower of Delights* in the spring. 'Trip' and 'go lively' are dance instructions that lead us into the *Morris* allusion. The Morris was a military dance of Moorish origins that had arrived in England in the time of Edward IV. By Nashe's time it had lost its original cast of soldiers and adopted the characters of the Robin Hood tale. The *fool* in the cast had originally (*time out of mind*) been 'Mad Morion' but in the domestication had changed name and gender to become 'Maid Marian', which would make this a simultaneous hit at Breton and the countess both.

It appears that for Nashe one of the bones of contention that summer was still blank verse. He here bluntly states that he will not *sit taboring five years together nothing but to be, to be, on a paper drum*. The tabor was a small drum, used in village dances and by stage comedians as Richard Tarlton. Pounding *to be, to be* (da-DUM, da-DUM ...) on it for five years bespeaks an apprenticeship in blank verse. As all the other playwrights had come to terms with the form, the issue of Nashe's reluctance may well have arisen as they laboured to complete *The Contention*. However the other playwrights may have admonished him, Nashe's contributions to the play would resolutely all be in prose. While he was with his part of the play – the Cade rebellion – this should not have posed problems. But it appears he finished his scenes early and would enter into the work of the others padders.

Of all the writers working at the Theatre for her ladyship's new enterprise, only Nashe claims to be capable of keeping up with Marlowe. He writes, *Only I can keep pace with Gravesend barge, and care not if I have water enough to land my ship of fools with the Term (the tide I should say)*. It was on a Gravesend barge that the anti-Marlovian pamphlet, *The Cobbler of Canterbury*, had been set the year before. The *water* allusion is to 'time'. His *ship of fools* would allude to his Cade scenes, which Nashe has seemingly brought to completion before deadline. But these additions were only the better part of one act. The impression Nashe creates here is that he would have liked to contribute to the rest of the work going on but that he was shut out.

And so we come to the other padders. The summer term would soon end and what had these playwrights been doing? Of the first of these barges, whom we may take to represent Greene, Nashe writes he is like those who *to go the lighter away, will take in their freight of spangled feathers, golden Pebbles, Straw, Reeds, Bulrushes, or anything, and then they bear out their sails as proudly as if they were ballasted*

[LOADED] *with Bull beef.* Greene was known to be an exceptionally gifted copycat writer who could with ease appropriate the best in other men's styles and subject matter. It appears that in reality Nashe was still not fond of Greene's writing.

But it is for the second of these barges that Nashe has saved his particular wrath. He begins: *Others are so hardly bested for loading that they are fain to retail the cinders of Troy, and the shivers of broken truncheons, to fill up their boat that else should go empty: and if they have but a pound weight of good Merchandise, it shall be placed at the poop, or plucked in a thousand pieces to credit their carriage.* George Peele had published a poetic tribute to Sir John Norris earlier this year, a short work to which he had appended a student piece on the fall of Troy. That he had placed these *cinders of Troy* in the back of his book leads Nashe to the *poop* allusion, with its ship's and scatological meanings. Peele, even more than the other writers, liked to use his best ideas over and over. Talk of *broken truncheons* bespeaks Peele's blustery, jingoistic nature. Back in 1589's *Menaphon* Nashe had praised Peele's writing highly but now all this good feeling is gone.

Nashe reports that *such an Ass is no great statesman in the beasts' Commonwealth.* The shortcomings that Aesop paints of the ass are manifold: brainless, vain, taking credit for others' work, acting like a lapdog, and so on. Then Nashe takes three mocking hits at Peele's physical stature. If we had a picture of Peele we might be able to corroborate these. If I understand him correctly, Nashe mockingly claims Peele's ears stood up like the flaps on a Muscovite's hat [LARGE, TALL EARS], his lower lip looked like the flap of a half-open traveling bag [LOWER LIP STUCK OUT BEYOND UPPER], and his body looked as *demurely as a sixpenny brown loaf.* As a regular loaf of bread cost a penny, the *sixpenny brown loaf* would make of Peele a rather squat, roly-poly man.

According to Nashe, Peele had *some imperfections that do keep him from the common Council,* i.e. he was dictatorial and would not engage in group discussions. Yet Nashe acknowledges that he stands in high regard – *of many he is deemed a very virtuous member, and one of the honestest sort of men there are; So that our opinion (as Sextus Empiricus affirmeth) gives the name of good or ill to everything.* The philosopher Sextus had first indicated that to every argument there was an equal and opposite argument. *A whole book of this argument* [A WHOLE LIST OF HIS MANY CONS AND PROS] *would prove a worthy commonwealth matter* [A SUBJECT FIT FOR GENERAL DISCUSSION], *and far better than wits wax carnal* [MORE UPLIFTING THAN (MEN) TALKING ABOUT SEX]: *much good worship have the Author*. Nashe closes on a note of peace.

Having touched on everyone involved in the enterprise, Nashe would now come to terms with what this group playwriting process was leading to. The first problem was that *learning had lost itself in a grove of Genealogies*. If learning here represents playwriting, that *grove of Genealogies* would represent the committee producing the scripts. The cure, Nashe cheekily suggests, is not to *set an old goose over half a dozen pottle pots, (which are as it were the eggs of invention*. This humorous emblem of an *old goose* sitting on top of six half-gallon beer tankards must have hit Mary Sidney with some force for it would have all too clearly exposed her too-keen interest in the process. All that will come of this, Nashe suggests, is *such a breed of books within a little while after, as will fill all the world with the wild fowl of good wits*. There is an alchemical thread that weaves its way through this passage. (The proper emblem, as we will discover next chapter, would have been 'a phoenix from whom flocks of silver and gold birds stream', not a goose from whom come the *wild fowl of good wits*.)

Continuing in that same alchemical vein Nashe writes, *I can tell you this is a harder thing than making gold of quicksilver, and will trouble you more than the Moral of Aesop's Glow-worm hath troubled our English Apes*. Making gold out of mercury was the alchemist's dream. Just as there was no gold to be had from alchemy, according to the skeptic Nashe, so there appears to have been no tale of Aesop's glowworm, and perhaps that was the moral! Though the actors (*Apes*) might *strive to warm themselves with the flame of the Philosopher's stone, they have spent all their wealth in buying bellows to blow this false fire*. The process as outlined will not produce the desired literary gold.

Having said all he has come to say, Nashe closes abruptly, as if he would now flee the scene. *Gentlemen, I fear I have too much presumed on your idle leisure, and been too bold, to stand talking all this while in another man's door; but now I will leave you to survey the pleasures of*

Paphos, and offer your smiles on the Altars of Venus. Paphos, a city of Cyprus, was noted as a major centre for the worship of Aphrodite or Venus as the Romans called her. And this leads us to Sidney's work at hand. He signs off, *Yours in all desire to please, Tho: Nashe.*

Although this is typical Nashe, never before had he assailed one of the nobility. Given how taboo this was, it must be wondered if his fustian was not augmented by the even greater protection of some very strong patron. Whatever his relationship with the Earl of Oxford had been, the man who was best positioned to protect him in this dangerous pursuit here was John Whitgift, the Archbishop of Canterbury, whose episcopate Nashe had helped save during the *Martin Marprelate* crisis of 1589–90. Whitgift, who probably accounted Robert Dudley, the Earl of Leicester, as having been his number one enemy, could not but have enjoyed this engaging call for 'Leicester's daughter', Mary Sidney, to desist from her too bold theatrical intrusions.

The mythological Pallas may have been a kindly patron to the arts but she was also a spirited goddess of war having been born of her father Zeus's forehead, brandishing a shield and spear, which she vigorously shook. Mary Sidney appears to have gone straight to her Majesty. Her Majesty's Principal Secretary, William Cecil, ordered the Stationers' Company to impound all unsold copies of the book around 16 September. The Stationers' ledger for 18 September 1591 records the payment of 4p to porters *for carrying of Newman's books to the hall* where they were presumably destroyed. A few days later, the beadle of the company rode out to inform Master Secretary that all had been done as requested.

Despite the action against him, printer Newman by no means lost his copyright to the work. He immediately had a second bookseller, Matthew Lownes, prepare a new print-run while he himself would reprint Sir Philip's portion of the sonnets early the following year. The part that was never afterwards printed again was Thomas Nashe's *Something to read for them that list*, indicating that this was the matter where the publication had overstepped the bounds.

But things were certainly not to rest there. The damage Nashe's broadside had done would be deflected almost immediately by the man who had guided Mary Sidney's initial poetic development,

Abraham Fraunce. And he would be followed by Edmund Spenser over Christmas and Nicholas Breton the following year. Together the countess's writers would protect her reputation while divulging enough to set to right the erroneous impressions that Nashe's squibs may have produced. For Nashe this would prove to be the start of a long, tortuous struggle with the House of Pembroke, one that will animate much of the Shakespeare chronicle over the first decade.

The Patrons

Henry Herbert, the Earl of Pembroke · Mary Sidney, the Countess of Pembroke

The Players

Richard Burbage · James Burbage · William Shakspere

The Playwrights

Thomas Nashe · Robert Greene · Christopher Marlowe · George Peele · Thomas Kyd · `Nicholas Breton

The three tiers of the Pembroke company – patrons, players and playwrights.

CHAPTER 4

Defending Her Honour

The brouhaha that Thomas Nashe's preface to the pirated *Astrophel & Stella* sonnets stirred up in September 1591 would be answered over the following eight months by a number of printed pamphlets and one circulated manuscript that sought to repair the somewhat bruised reputation of the Countess of Pembroke. Although only part of Nashe and Newman's print run had escaped into the wider reading public, at court the situation would have created the sort of buzz that everyone (along the rank and file) in some (garbled) version would have been privy to. The returning university students, some of whom no doubt had copies of the original pressing with its now suppressed epistle, would have quickly learned about the matter. And back in London it would have been part of the news that greeted the gentlemen fresh returned from their country estates taking their daily stroll along the newswalks of St. Paul's and the Exchange. Although her Majesty's immediate suppression of the volume may have aroused the most initial (and possibly misconstrued) interest, exactly how Nashe had offended would in many quarters have become common knowledge.

Aside from describing the countess as an ignorant hoarder who could not be trusted as Sir Philip's literary keeper, Nashe had possibly undermined Mary Sidney most by presenting her so closely to the playwriting process – 'the goose incubating six beer tankards' emblem. The first out of the block to counter any hint of 'impiety' was Abraham Fraunce, whose *The Countess of Pembroke's Emmanuel* would appear before the year was out. Its subtitle – *Containing the Nativity, Passion, Burial, and Resurrection of Christ : together with certain Psalms of David* – summarises its contents except for the underlying, pivotal role of *Mary*. In his sparse preface Fraunce writes:

> To the right excellent and most honourable Lady,
> the Lady Mary, Countess of Pembroke.
> Mary the best Mother sends her best Babe to a Mary :
> Lord to a Lady's sight, and Christ to a Christian hearing.
>
> >   Your Honour's most
> >   affectionate.

Though Fraunce at no point overtly tips his hand by mentioning Sir Philip Sidney, the implied parallel between the tribulations of Mary, the mother of the crucified Christ, and Mary, the sister of the fallen Sir Philip Sidney, would have been lost on no one. Although *Christ* defending the countess may seem somewhat over-the-top from a modern editorial point of view, men's temper in these times was much more black and white as far as women were concerned. Making mother Mary an emblem for sister Mary imbues both with a sense of divine mission. Christian though it may be, Fraunce's work is by no means straight-laced for the cosmology is here gently overlaid with Greek mythological concepts giving us, for example, *Christ* on *Olympus*. As well, Fraunce's work is striking for the manner in which its subtext of life, death, resurrection and life again begins to lay the foundation for the Christian/Neo-Platonic defence of the countess that Nicholas Breton was preparing for publication.

From back home in Ireland, half-way through the 12 days of Christmas, Edmund Spenser made an appearance on the courtly manuscript trail whereby he would pay homage to his 19 months in England. Adopting his favourite nickname for himself of *Colin Clout*, he gave his report the name of *Colin Clout's Come Home Again*. He sent copies to his friends at the English court as a gift for New Year's Day, 1592. His poem offers a far-ranging pastoral frolic wherein everyone's identity is cloaked. But Spenser's epithets on the whole are clear either by their anagrammatic wordplay, their association and/or their consistent use over the body of his work. His work touches on much literary news, of which the following is the most pertinent to our unfolding story.

Spenser relates that his journey from Ireland to England had all been because Sir Walter Ralegh had lamented his loss of royal favour. *His song was all a lamentable lay, / Of great unkindness, and usage hard, / Of Cynthia the Lady of the sea, / Which from her presence faultless him debarred.* It was with the name *Cynthia* that Ralegh had wooed his royal mistress Elizabeth in the quite good verses he had written for her during the first days of their 'courting' in the early 80's. Tall, gallant, handsome in a rugged sort of way, intellectually intriguing and always a 'character', Ralegh rose quickly and enjoyed seven especially good years of her Majesty's favour. In the beginning there was fierce rivalry between him and Robert Dudley, who was fresh from beating off the (oh so close) French wedding negotiations. Despite their early jostling, a marriage in 1583 between Ralegh's cousin, Barbara Gammage, and Dudley's nephew, Robert Sidney (Philip and Mary's younger brother), brought peace between the families. A particularly strong relationship would develop between Sir Walter and Mary Sidney, the Countess of Pembroke, a matter Spenser may be alluding to in the passage that follows. *Then gan* [BEGAN] *a gentle bonny lass to speak, / That Marin hight* [WAS CALLED] ... .

The words Spenser has her utter are: *... right well he* [SIR WALTER] *sure did plain* [COMPLAIN; i.e. WRITE TRAGIC VERSES]*: / That could great Cynthia's sore displeasure break, / And move to take him to her grace again.* Spenser places this *Marin* close to the action of Sir Walter's new verses to the queen winning him permission to return to court. If *Marin* is Mary Sidney it may indicate that the countess was the intermediary who had brought out-of-favour Sir Walter's verses to her Majesty's attention. Spenser comes to court here as part of Sir Walter's train.

The experience of the court dazzles *Colin*'s eyes. Spenser longed to live and work in England again and goes to some pains to paint the queen in the loving hues of a man who would 'court' her in his own right. Of their meetings Spenser reports: *The shepherd of the Ocean* [RALEGH], *Unto that Goddess' grace me first enhanced, / And to my oaten quill* [i.e. RUSTIC POETRY] *inclined her ear,* who *desired it at timely hours to hear.* Spenser had brought the great neo-medieval Tudor epic that he had laboured a decade to produce, *The Faerie Queen,* with him for presentation to the Monarch. In it he sought to redefine, with a great mythic allegorical sweep, the nation's new identity as that centred upon their 'founding queen', Elizabeth, as *Gloriana*.

Spenser goes on to recall his personal experience of Sir Philip Sidney, describing him as the one *who first did lift my Muse out of the floor*. Although her Majesty had shown only grudging favour towards Sir Philip while he lived, she was sorry when he died, and the tribute would presumably have pleased her (as well as that man's sister, Mary Sidney). Further down Spenser admits that the queen's interest was in part motivated by her memories of Sir Philip – that she would listen n*ot for my skill, but for that shepherd's sake*.

From her Majesty, Spenser radiates out to a large circle of *shepherds* [i.e. POETS] who by their efforts added lustre to her Majesty's reign. For the most part they are related to the larger Ralegh-Pembroke axis. Of those we have met, we note the immediate appearance of Abraham Fraunce as *Corydon*. As Greville and Lucy did at the same time, Fraunce had in 1590 also joined the Earl of Pembroke's administration in Wales, he as a Crown Prosecutor. Here Spenser writes: *though meanly waged, / Yet ablest wit of most I know this day* – a nod at his intellectual prowess and the modest wages the Earl of Pembroke paid.

Spenser includes Samuel Daniel:

> And there is a new shepherd late up sprung,
> The which doth all afore him far surpass :
> Appearing well in that well tuned song,
> Which late he sung unto a scornful lass.

That *scornful lass* was 'Delia', the heroine of Daniel's sonnets. The sonnets Spenser had heard (or read) were probably the same ones that had appeared in the pirated edition of *Sir P.S. His Astrophel and Stella*. Given that Daniel and his master, Sir Edward Dymoke, were in France and Italy over most of 1590-91, it is doubtful that Spenser and Daniel actually met. When Nashe and Newman's pirated volume appeared in September, Daniel and Dymoke were just starting their journey back to England. But these verses written before his departure already display his musical mastery of style. Daniel had come into contact with Sir Philip's sonnets around 1588 when his brother-in-law, John Florio, began helping Fulke Greville edit Sir Philip's second *Arcadia*. Of the sonnet forms Sidney had demonstrated, Daniel had concentrated on the one wherein the sonnet's obligatory 14 lines were divided into three quatrains (three verses of 4 lines each) rounded out with a rhyming couplet. It was a form whose repetitive use over the course of a longer work, rather than tiring the reader/listener, came to be expected. The sonnets he wrote over 1588 and '89 flowed back the other way. Daniel, writing later in *Musophilus*, will say it was Fulke Greville who first brought his verses into open sight. It was undoubtedly Greville who brought Daniel's poetry to Mary Sidney's attention. And although Daniel's sonnets were at this stage already pretty, they are not philosophically deep and it is in this regard that the older Spenser (perhaps feeling challenged) now becomes quite critical.

> Yet doth his trembling Muse but lowly fly,
> As daring not too rashly mount on height,
> And doth her tender plumes as yet but try,
> In love's soft lays and looser thought's delight.
> Then rouse thy feathers quickly Daniel,
> And to what course thou please thyself advance :
> But most me seems, thy accent will excel,
> In Tragic plaints and passionate mischance.

Upon returning to England in late 1591 and finding his work piratically set into print, Daniel would over the winter months rework his sonnets, adding many new ones. The time was to be marred by an outbreak of hostility between the Dymoke household and its own overlord, the Earl of Lincoln, which Daniel escaped by suing for Mary Sidney's patronage. But to answer Spenser's specific challenge, Daniel up in Lincolnshire would also write *The Complaint of Rosamond*, wherein with a great deal of sensitivity he reworked Thomas Churchyard's tragic story of Rosamond Clifford, the mistress of King Henry II, as that had appeared in *A Mirror for Magistrates* way back in the 1550's. With this reinvented *Rosamond* Daniel succeeded in creating a piece people of the time so enjoyed that they immediately began mentioning him in the same breath as Spenser. When Daniel came to Wilton in the spring, it was ostensibly to teach the countess's children, William, Philip and Anne Herbert, but in reality it was, it appears, to write a lot of poetry, much of it initially to do with that same civil war period the playwrights were struggling with.

Next *Colin Clout* makes Sir Walter Ralegh part of this Wilton circle. *And there that shepherd of the Ocean is.* Of Ralegh's poetic skill Spenser writes: *Full sweetly tempered is that Muse of his, / That can empierce a Prince's mighty heart* – deliberately echoing what *Marin* had stated earlier in the poem. While Spenser was writing this in the fall of 1591, Sir Walter (who had stayed in England) and his older half-brother, Adrian Gilbert, chanced upon Sherborne Castle, which lay some forty miles to the west of Wilton towards Devon. Sir John Harington would record (in his later *Nugae Antiquae*) that *this castle being right in the way, he cast such an eye upon it as Ahab did upon Naboth's vineyard*. Sir Walter imagined that he could turn this church manor into a 'school' for advanced scientists and philosophers. While riding about the property, his head in the clouds, his horse tumbled down an embankment and Sir Walter's face ended up in the dirt. Was it a bad omen? His half-brother Adrian made an immediate astrological reckoning and pronounced that, on the contrary, Sir Walter should have his wish. And indeed in January of 1592, shortly after *Colin Clout's Come Home Again* arrived, Ralegh received from her Majesty a 99-year lease to Sherborne that she had wrestled out of the Church in exchange for a bishopric.

Ralegh's half-brother, Adrian Gilbert, arrests our attention for Aubrey, the antiquarian of the next century, will report that he headed the alchemy/chemistry laboratory that Mary Sidney had built for herself and her schoolhouse of children at Wilton, that he was one of many *learned gentlemen* who made Wilton appear more *like a college* than a house.

In the ongoing *Colin Clout* chronicle, Spenser next turns to the poetic spirit hovering over Wilton, Sir Philip Sidney, and the lady of the manor who mourned him.

> There also is (ah no, he is not now)
> But since I said he is, he is quite gone,
> Amyntas quite is gone and lies full low,
> Having his Amaryllis left to moan.

Here we find Spenser deliberately miming the outward features of Abraham Fraunce's hexameter style. Setting an *Amaryllis* opposite *Amyntas* had also already been suggested by Fraunce. After translating Watson's *Amyntas* in 1587, Fraunce had gone on to translate Tasso's original *Aminta* as well. He had published the two together in one volume as *The Countess of Pembroke's Ivychurch* earlier in 1591. Ivychurch was a small Pembroke manor on the River Wily, close to Salisbury, where the countess and her household apparently spent the fall after a summer at Wilton. There in the closing lines of his translation of Tasso, Fraunce had, by way of original contribution, written: *Down in a desert dale, Amaryllis found Amaranthus, / ... / Found Amaranthus fair, seeking for fair Amyntas; / And with fair new flower fair Pembrokiana presented.* Here *Amyntas* (Sir Philip) has metamorphosed into the ever-living flower, *Amaranthus*. Its appearance is discovered by *Amaryllis* (Mary Sidney) and presented to *Pembrokiana* (the countess now the embodiment of the House of Pembroke) who goes on to declare that this day will evermore be celebrated by a yearly gathering of poets and poetesses. (It may have been this gathering that first brought Spenser and the countess together.) Fraunce writes,

> And all, by all means Amaranthus flower to be praising,
> And all, by all means his Amyntas death to be mourning,
> Yea, for a just monument of tender-minded Amyntas,
> With newfound titles, new day, new dale she adorned,
> called that, Amyntas Day, for love of lover Amyntas,
> Called this, Amyntas Dale, for a name and fame to Amyntas.

In light of this we can better understand Spenser's intentions when he writes:

> Help, O ye shepherds help ye all in this,
> Help Amaryllis this her loss to mourn:
> Her loss is yours, your loss Amyntas is,
> Amyntas flower of Shepherds' pride forlorn.

After a closing rhapsodic moment wherein Spenser describes Sir Philip's pre-eminent place among them, he next turns to the ladies of her Majesty's court. Here he would, of course, again begin by offering vast compliments to the queen. But this done, Spenser turns to the ladies and here he would begin by conferring *the highest place* upon Mary Sidney whom Spenser now calls *Urania, sister unto Astrophel.* Everyone, thanks to Nashe, now knew that *Astrophel* referred to Sidney, who had but one sister. As *Urania* the countess becomes the muse of astronomy whose emblems are the starry diadem and celestial globe. In *The Tears of the Muses*, included in *Complaints* as published earlier in 1591, Spenser had written of Urania:

> Such happiness have they, that do embrace
> The precepts of my heavenly discipline;
> But shame and sorrow and accursed case
> Have they, that scorn the school of arts divine.

(Breton would soon greatly elaborate on this matter of Mary Sidney's heavenward gaze.) Back in *Colin Clout* Spenser would describe the qualities that set the countess apart:

> In whose brave mind, as in a golden coffer,
> All heavenly gifts and riches lockèd are :
> More rich than pearls of Inde [INDIA], or gold of Ophir‡
> And in her sex more wonderful and rare.

‡ Fabled source of Solomon's gold.

That certainly contrasts with the Midas' ears and the need for other men's glasses that Nashe had painted out for her. As Spenser reports, the countess was endowed with intellectual riches that set the value of her mind well above any worldly wealth. And Spenser underlines that she is unique in this, especially because she was a woman.

But the author who would most vigorously counter Nashe's challenge to the countess and himself was Nicholas Breton, whom Nashe had twice touched in his prefatorial letter to the pirated sonnets. *The Pilgrimage to Paradise, joined with the Countess of Penbrooke's love* was published in 1592 by Joseph Barnes, printer to Oxford University. It was, in fact, printed on the press that the countess's uncle and then university chancellor, Robert Dudley, had given the school back in 1585. Breton is reported to have studied at Oriel College in the mid 70's (without taking a degree). Three longtime Oxonians join him in the prefatorial material: Dr. John Case, William Gager and Henry Price, the latter two writers of university plays and close friends of the other Pembroke playwright, George Peele, another Oxonian. The spirit who was to be featured prominently in *The Pilgrimage*, Sir Philip Sidney, had in the late 60's studied at Christ Church (which was also Gager's college). The imprint would have given the pamphlet some immediate credibility.

At the head of his letter of dedication to Mary Sidney, Breton shows an all-out prostration that we do not see in the other authors she patronised, possibly indicating that the 40-something soldier-poet-schoolteacher felt himself to be vulnerable. Breton writes, *Right noble Lady, whose rare virtues, the wise no less honour, than the learned admire, and the honest serve: how shall I, the abject of fortune, unto the object of honour, presume to offer so simple a present, as the poetical discourse of a poor pilgrim's travail? I know not how, but, with falling at the feet of your favour, to crave pardon for my imperfection.* After the death of his father, Breton's mother had married the poet George Gascoigne whose attempts to curry favour at court by his pen would eat up the entire Breton family fortune during the 70's. But it did expose young Breton to the craft of literature and spectacle and as a result writing was one pastime that would carry him through the idle hours of years of soldiering. After the death of Leicester in late 1588 Breton fell on hard times until he was rescued by the Pembrokes with a teaching position in 1590. This in turn appears to have opened the way to a full-time writing career in which Breton was now to flourish.

What Breton would impress upon his readers here was that Mary Sidney was a woman worth serving with one's pen. *Who hath read of the Duchess of Urbina, may say, the Italians wrote well, but who knows the Countess of Penbrooke, I think hath cause to write better.* The Duchess of Urbina was the woman who had presided over the court that Baldassare Castiglione had brought to brilliant literary life earlier in the century in his *Book of the Courtier* (1528; 1st Eng. ed. 1561). What Nashe had hinted was Mary Sidney's desire to have the playwrights write to a higher standard here becomes the order for the English to overtake the Italians in literary excellence! That certainly places the countess's agenda on a much more elevated plane.

In a long list of comparisons, Breton distinguishes the Italian *Urbina* from the English *Pembroke*. The countess made of the writers her servants while the duchess had merely entertained hers as *followers*, a nod at the sort of patronage relationship Mary Sidney was ready to offer writers who were seriously keen to pursue their unique calling. For the English poets, the undertaking became duty as opposed to the Italians' merely remembering favours, a nod at the commanding role the countess played. For *comfort of discretion* [DISCERNING JUDGMENT] Breton calls Mary Sidney a superior *maintainer of Art*. She is a woman whose true perfections may be described; her writers will not forget her. With perhaps a glance at Nashe's hit on Peele, Breton counsels her, *think not of the ruins of Troy, but help to build up the walls of Jerusalem*. This covering over with biblical allusion what was at base a secular, though lofty undertaking – beating the Italians in literary combat – is, as we have seen, a not unusual editorial strategy.

William Gager, whose prefatory verses we shall consider just below, had already established something of a patronage relationship with the countess. Gager's Latin play, *Ulysses Redux,* had been performed in February of this year as part of a three-day festival to promote academic theatre in the face of some heavy Puritan criticism. The play was printed shortly thereafter also by Barnes on the university press. It carried a dedication to Sir Thomas Sackville, Oxford's current chancellor and himself a much admired early playwright. This was accompanied by a second dedication to Mary Sidney. Gager claims she knows him only through his writings. But he relates that the countess, in conversation with Case, had brought up his name. He hopes his poetry will be made welcome by her. As Sackville might be the *Ulysses* he animates in his play, so let the countess be Ulysses' wife, *Penelope*. Though Gager acknowledges the countess's superior intellect and judgment, he hopes she will deign to extend her hand to be kissed by this Ulysses as he makes his way onto the stage. He wrote this May 10. This dedication would indicate on which side she stood in this battle over academic play-making.

In the conclusion to his prefatory verses here in Breton's volume, Gager takes some glances at the invective Thomas Nashe had hurled in the pirated *Astrophel*. Gager speaks of the writers of *gall* who *through melancholy, or rival spite, / All poets 'sdain* [DISDAIN], *or some no Poets call.* This was recalling Nashe's aspersions on Breton's powers as a poet. *Avant* [BE GONE] *such scoffing, ... scorning spirits,* make way for the countess's authors, *... let our writers, ballad-makers, rhymers: / In her own money pay Lycambes' merits.* Lycambes was a rich and respectable citizen of Paros who with his family was viciously attacked in verses written by a young satirist named Archilosus. In Gager's allusion, Lycambes would stand for Mary Sidney while Archilosus would represent Nashe. The subtext (for those who were familiar with the story) was that Lycambes had promised Archilosus the hand of his daughter in marriage but that their relations had soured when it was discovered Archilosus had been born a bastard! *Poets fly higher, than such petty climbers, / Let this suffice, that Breton is a Poet, / She said it, we subscribe it, his books show it.* That gave Breton the countess's and the university professors' seal of approval. And so we come to Breton's work in hand.

The two parts, *The Pilgrimage to Paradise* and *The Countess of Penbrooke's Love*, are both highly allegorical pieces. The 408 verses of *The Pilgrimage* show Sir Philip Sidney and a band of five followers passing through an Arcadian landscape where they encounter the vision of a Stella-like creature. They spend time at the court of *Diana* (i.e. ELIZABETH), where all temptations are overcome because of the pilgrim's *waking wit* – that quality which for Sidney defined what it was to be consciously moral. They meet up with a hideous, seven-headed, seven-tailed creature who may represent all of Sir Philip's enemies while he lived. The monster seeks to thwart his passage but on the other side of the path appears an angelic creature who informs the pilgrim that t*he labour, that thy love hath tane* [taken] *in hand ... / Have got thee grace in mercy's glorious eyes / To find the path that leads to paradise.* The angelic creature disappears, leaving the pilgrim to battle the beast. After slaying it with his wisdom, the pilgrim travels over the sea and arrives in paradise, in allegorical fashion mirroring Sir Philip's defeat of his enemies at court with his wit and then sailing to the Netherlands where he would meet his death.

With the hero's passing we come to the 144 verses of *The Countess of Penbrooke's Love*. The 3:1 ratio in the verse count in favour of

Sir Philip indicates the basis upon which her place in the public's consciousness would be founded. Although the name Pembroke was often written in this time of phonetic spelling as *Penbrooke*, one cannot help but wonder if Breton, in light of the subject he will now present, is not intentionally punning.

At the opening of the piece Breton takes us to the scene of *a plot of earthly paradise, / Upon a hill* where *the Muses made a Maze*. At the centre of the maze t*here sits a grace, that hath the world at gaze, / which Phoenix is but name unto a nature*. There are two potent Neo-Platonic images here. The *maze*, or labyrinth, represents the world of confusion through which the pilgrim must pass in order to come to the centre from where the world may be seen for what it is. It is the start of the alchemist's so-called 'Great Work'. And representing the final stage of that work we find the *Phoenix*, the alchemical symbol for the *lapis philosophicus*, or 'philosopher's stone', that material whose presence by its essential power was instrumental in turning base materials into silver and gold.

At the very top of the alchemist's multi-tiered labour appears the phoenix out of whom silver and gold birds emerge.

after Libavius. *Alchymia*. Frankfurt, 1606.

Breton's work was to treat this matter of the *Phoenix* with some urgency. And the manner with which he uses it resonates with certain things Nashe had said the September before. In hindsight it may be surmised that this had been Breton's defence of the countess before the playwrights the summer before. We remember Nashe's long pseudo-alchemical metaphor in which he had cast Mary Sidney not as a phoenix, but as *an old goose*. And rather than flocks of silver and gold birds streaming from her, Nashe had predicted nothing but *the wild fowl of good wits*. And as to who the real phoenix was, Nashe had in his preface emphatically written: *Dear Astrophel* [SIR PHILIP], *that in the ashes of thy Love livest again like the Phoenix* – indicating the same three images Breton uses – *phoenix, love* and *ashes*. But Nashe had continued: *Oh might thy body (as thy name), live again likewise here amongst us: but the earth, the mother of mortality, hath snatched thee too soon into her chilled cold arms, and will not let thee by any means be drawn from her deadly embrace, and thy divine Soul, carried on an Angel's wings to heaven, is installed, in Hermes' place, sole prolocutor* [SPOKESPERSON] *to the Gods. Therefore mayest thou never return from the Elysian fields like Orpheus; therefore must we ever mourn for our Orpheus*. If there was a *phoenix*, according to Nashe, Sir Philip was it by the works he had left. Further, Nashe insists Sir Philip was irrevocably dead and if he did any speaking now it was in heaven (not on earth). This would not have been as callous as it sounds if Nashe had only been responding to claims Breton had already set forth.

But now Breton and his Oxford crew would set Nashe straight again. In his letter of commendation at the head of the volume, the noted Oxford Aristotelian, Dr. John Case, would assure the book's readership that the countess was the phoenix here. He writes that Mary Sidney is *that rare Phoenix … the sweetest Phoenix*, whose *colours … are in your* [i.e. BRETON'S] *book*. Addressing the notion of *love* as that is found in Breton's title – *The Countess of Penbrooke's Love* – Case writes that this is *not the Love of Martha, but the Love of Mary who loved much, who loveth Christ. This Love made Mary Magdalene's tears, and maketh the best Mary living* [MARY SIDNEY] *to ascend to Jerusalem and there to seek her lover in the Temple*. (This reflects much the same strategy Fraunce had first used in *Emmanuel*.) Case continues: *But finding him not among the Doctors she taketh the wings of an Eagle, & in her sacred thoughts flieth above the Sun, never ceasing to seek, till she have found her Lover*. After Philip's death Mary Sidney had indeed found him back through her literary 'labours of love'. This was presumably the 'royal wedding' out of which this 'phoenix' here appears. *Lo here is Love, and here is labour, but the labour is light, where the Love is great. For the heart there only liveth, where it loveth. Marvel not therefore if this lovely Lady become a pilgrim upon earth, and pass the sea, and wilderness of this world, till she enjoyeth her Love.* So Mary Sidney (like her brother before her) was also now a *pilgrim*, a seeker, a poet. The *Love and pilgrimage of that peerless Lady*, Case writes with some intimacy, *is as a crystal of truths well known unto me.* Aside from his work at the university, the doctor had since 1589 also been one of the canons of Salisbury Cathedral, whose spires were just visible from the hilltop at Wilton.

In *The Countess of Penbrooke's Love* Breton would describe how Philip's death had motivated Mary to do what she was now doing. He has the countess plaintively ask her brother: *But, what should I? shall I ? or can I give? / To thee: for all, that thou hast given me?* The challenge was formidable and the countess had to work hard to overcome her shortcomings so that her *humble heart may in repentance prove, / The dearest passage of thy love's direction.* She would be the conduit of his wishes – his literary oracle. Her goal in this was only to *live to thee, in thee, and but with thee, / My dearest life, and only truest love: / where heaven and earth do all the comfort see, / That faithful passions in the soul may prove.*

And the place where they would meet was in her breast. *Come lamb, come love, come lie betwixt my breasts / where zealous love, and true repentance rests.* The notion of the heavenly spirit of her brother finding a place in her earthly bosom resonates with how the countess chose to represent herself pictorially throughout her life.

What appears as immodesty takes on much clearer

after

Jean de Courbes

meaning when the self-representation is considered within Breton's context here. For it is this place (... *where heaven and earth do all the comfort see*) that Sir Philip will find his resting place. Further down Breton will in two places refer to this very special place as a *phoenix nest*.

At the beginning of *The Countess of Penbrooke's Love*, just after Sir Philip's passing, many artists and artisans try to fill the vacuum her brother's death has left in Mary Sidney's life. *The world came in, with presents many a one,* writes Breton, *But, yet, alas, her love could like of none*. Pleasing her demanding humour becomes the arduous pursuit of jewelers, clothiers, musicians, soldiers, farmers, lawyers, courtiers, scholars, sailors, shepherds and finally poets. She could judge the pains that they had taken and rewarded them accordingly. Of these, the poets perhaps fared least well. Breton writes:

> The poets came, and brought in their inventions,
> But well she knew their fancies were but feigned:
> The muses brought the truth of their intentions
> Which in their kinds were kindly entertained:
> But yet the best, with all her worthiness,
> Touched not the humour of her happiness.

She could see the poets' work for what it was. The muses (to whom the countess was secretary) brought correction to their shortcomings, from which the poets had all greatly benefited. But even then the best that they brought forth failed to meet the countess's high expectations. Left to herself (except for the *unseen* Breton), she moans, *this world is but a weed, / who lives on earth that in the heavens hath been?*

This interplay of sister and brother is everywhere present in Breton's work. When Breton speaks of the *phoenix* at the end, it is to describe its now *two in one* nature, as if brother had found an earthly home within sister. As the *phoenix* (he the heavenly, she the earthly part), they are the *lapis* whose touch turns that which is base into silver and gold. The goal stated at the beginning of Breton's book was that the countess wished to overtake the Italians in the art of fine writing, so Breton closes by presenting her as the force that will bring this about.

And indeed over the course of that first season some *lapis* did begin to rub off on those plays the Earl of Pembroke's Men were performing. A new hand began the task of turning the base material into silver and gold just in the way the countess wanted. This newcomer to the script production process had a sharp eye for detail and possessed generally wider knowledge and experience than did the other playwrights. The new hand would take the liberty to rewrite some of the text, most notably the royal and female parts. We can see what the new hand brings to the table by placing *The Contention betwixt the two famous Houses of York and Lancaster* beside the rewritten version. As before, the play opens with the Marques of Suffolk having just returned from France with King Henry's new bride, Margaret of Valois, now Queen Margaret of England. The Shakespearean changes are marked in bold.

ORIGINAL VERSION	REWRITTEN VERSION
SUFFOLK:	SUFFOLK:
As by your high imperial Majesty's command,	As by your high imperial majesty
I had in charge at my depart for France,	I had in charge at my depart for France,
As procurator for your excellence,	As procurator **to** your excellence,
To marry Princess Margaret for your grace,	To marry Princess Margaret for your grace;
So in the ancient famous City Tours,	So, in the **famous ancient** city Tours,
In presence of the Kings of France and Sicily,	In presence of the Kings of France and **Sicil**,
The Dukes of Orleans, Calabar, Brittany, and Alonson.	The Dukes of Orleans, Calaber, B**retagne** and Al**ençon**,
Seven Earls, twelve Barons, and then the reverend Bishops,	Seven earls, twelve barons and **twenty** reverend bishops,
I did perform my task and was espoused,	I **have** perform**ed** my task and was espoused,
And now, most humbly on my bended knees,	And humbly now **up**on my bended knee,
In sight of England and her royal Peers,	In sight of England and her **lordly** peers,
Deliver up my title in the Queen,	Deliver up my title in the Queen
Unto your gracious excellence, that are the substance	To your **most** gracious **hands**, that are the substance
Of that great shadow I did represent:	Of that great shadow I did represent;

The happiest gift that ever Marquess gave, The fairest Queen that ever King possessed **KING HENRY:** Suffolk arise. Welcome Queen Margaret to English Henry's Court.	The happiest gift that ever marquess gave, The fairest queen that ever king **received**. **KING HENRY:** Suffolk arise. Welcome, Queen Margaret:

The new poet is very attentive to courtly nuances and pays attention to ceremonial detail: *royal* is downgraded to the more correct *lordly*, *knees* changed to the ceremonially more correct *knee*. It is small stuff to most ears but significant enough to galvanize the new hand. An editorial decision has been made to give all French place names their French form, betraying some knowledge and sympathy for that language and culture. Those peculiar Marlovian inversions—*ancient famous*, *English Henry's*—are either righted or eliminated, the new hand being somewhat contemptuous of that sort of artificiality. The new author would also immediately dispel the notion that a woman should be something *possessed*. But on the whole the intrusions are minimal indicating that the new hand generally liked what the Marlovians had written.

It is when we come to those 'fluffed-up barges' of Robert Greene and George Peele that the intrusions begin to intensify.

ORIGINAL VERSION	REWRITTEN VERSION
... **KING HENRY:** ... The greatest show of kindness yet we can bestow, Is this kind kiss: [they kiss] Oh gracious God of heaven, Lend me a heart replete with thankfulness, For in this beauteous face thou hast bestowed A world of pleasures to my perplexed soul.	... **KING HENRY:** ... **I can express no kind*er* sign** of love **Than** this kind kiss. [they kiss]O **Lord, that lends me life,** Lend me a heart replete with thankfulness, For thou hast **given me** in this beauteous face A world of **earthly blessings** to my soul, **If sympathy of love unite our thoughts.**

The imperious *we* is corrected to *I* – the king is addressing the queen now, not the nation. The first king's rather lusty response to the kiss is transformed into an elegant expression of emotion in the second text. The nigh oath-like exclamation, *Oh gracious God of heaven,* is turned into the more psalm-like, *O Lord, that lends me life,* an alteration that now adds resonant force to *Lend* in the next line. What in the first is the offer of a *world of pleasures* now becomes a much more tempered *world of earthly blessings*. And there is immediate indication that the new poet has given the nature of true love some thought, as indicated by the pithy addition of *If sympathy of love unite our thoughts,* a line that demonstrates with some vigour the new poet's romantic outlook. It is when we come to the first female presence in the play that the intrusions suddenly turn from grey to black, as if the new hand had a special expertise here none of the other poets possessed.

ORIGINAL VERSION	REWRITTEN VERSION
THE QUEEN: Th'excessive love I bear unto your grace, Forbids me to be lavish of my tongue, Lest I should speak more than beseems a woman: Let this suffice, my bliss is in your liking, And nothing can make poor Margaret miserable, Unless the frown of mighty England's King.	THE QUEEN: **Great King of England, and my gracious lord,** **The mutual conference that my mind hath had** **By day, by night, waking and in my dreams,** **In courtly company, or at my beads,** **With you mine alderliefest sovereign,** **Makes me the bolder to salute my King** **With ruder terms, such as my wit affords** **And overjoy of heart doth minister.**
KING HENRY: Her looks did wound, but now her speech doth pierce, Lovely Queen Margaret sit down by my side: And uncle Gloucester, and you Lordly Peers, With one voice welcome my beloved Queen.	KING HENRY: Her **sight did ravish**, but her **grace in** speech, **Her words y-clad with wisdom's majesty,** **Makes me from wondering fall to weeping joys,** **Such is the fullness of my heart's content.** Lords, with one **cheerful** voice welcome my **love**.
ALL: Long live Queen Margaret, England's happiness	ALL: Long live Queen Margaret, England's happiness.

The new poet would dispense with that two-dimensional modesty and endeavour to fill out the person of the queen fully while still acquiescing to expectations of female humility. She addresses her new husband first in grand terms (*Great King of England*) and then in co-equal terms (*my gracious lord*). She immediately responds to the king's proviso (*if sympathy of love unite our thoughts*) by describing the non-stop thought she has given to their meeting here. Her Spenserian call of *alderliefest* is answered by the king's *y-clad* in his next speech, indicating the new poet was not adverse to a little neo-medieval sheen where appropriate. The king's response to the queen's speech with its five finely crafted lines now reaches an emotional crescendo to which the group salute – *Long live Queen Margaret, England's happiness* – becomes a true overflowing.

And as for what the new hand would do with Thomas Nashe's parts of the play, we may consider the following sample as being in many ways typical of what happens throughout Act 4.

ORIGINAL VERSION	REWRITTEN VERSION
CADE. Therefore be brave, for your Captain is brave, and vows reformation: you shall have seven half-penny loaves for a penny, and the three hooped pot, shall have ten hoops, and it shall be felony to drink small beer, and if I be king, as king I will be.	CADE. Be brave **then**; for your captain is brave, and vows reformation. **There** shall **be in England** seven halfpenny loaves **sold** for a penny; the three-hooped pot shall have ten hoops; and **I will make** it felony to drink small beer. All **the realm** shall be in common, and in Cheapside shall my palfrey go to grass. And **when** I am king, as king I will be –
ALL. God save your majesty.	ALL. God save your majesty!
CADE. I thank you good people, you shall all eat and drink of my score, and go all in my livery, and we'll have no writing, but the score & the Tally, and there shall be no laws but such as comes from my mouth.	CADE. I thank you good people. **There shall be no money,** all shall eat and drink **on** my score, and **I will apparel them** all in **one** Livery, **that they may agree like Brothers, and worship me their Lord.**
DICK. We shall have sore laws then, for he was thrust into the mouth the other day.	BUTCHER. **The first thing we do, let's kill all the Lawyers.**

On the issue of blank verse versus prose (one of Nashe's great issues in his letter of September 1591), the new hand is magnanimous. It serves the purposes of the new poet to let the commoners continue speaking in prose so that they distinguish themselves from their versifying betters. The humour is mostly left intact, too, though there are continuous additions, much of it in the same acerbic, punning style. (The new hand appears to have a terrible weakness for punning.) And though most of the additions here work well enough, the new hand would now and then overdo it so that the dialogue loses its proletarian realism and takes on the new hand's hard-to-suppress high-mindedness. (A full presentation of the twin texts of this play is at **www.tiger-heart.com**.)

Although it is doubtful that these additions to the play would necessarily have made *The Contention* more successful commercially (it is now longer by a third with some of it rather more recherché), the additions do give the script a quality whereby the play could with some comfort come before the court, if that should ever be the case.

This was the scenario into which William Shakspere of Stratford would step, delivered from his legal problems back home and into the hands of this Pembroke company of players in London. Later legends from the acting fraternity report that when he arrived in the city, Shakspere was first given the task of looking after the parking and security of patrons' horses, a task at which he appears to have excelled. Given his far-ranging experience dealing in coin, commodities and people, we can see how this responsibility would have been rather straightforward for him. Most of the horse traffic came from Westminster and the Inns of Court during the season, suggesting that William Shakspere came to London between October 1591 and June 1592. This is corroborated to a degree by the fact that Nashe made no allusion to him in his Pembroke snapshot of September 1591, while Robert Greene, writing shortly in August 1592, will paint him in large.

But after a stint of guarding the horses, Shakspere moved up onto the stage and became an actor. Given his size and roguishly handsome features (according to the later Chandos portrait, anyway), he would at the least have cut an above-average visual presence. If he did have speaking parts right away, he would have had to temper his Warwickshire accent for these London audiences. In the fledgling Pembroke troupe, the actors would have come from the ranks of other professional companies—tough ground for a 27- or 28-year-old rookie. But tradition would maintain that he never played any role bigger than the ghost in *Hamlet*, making him throughout his years in London no more than an extra as far as acting was concerned.

Was it he who within months had worked his way up from parking attendant to actor and then playwright, giving these Pembroke scripts that quality Mary Sidney was calling for? Although Master William no doubt had smarts of all sorts, setting aside the issue of literary talent, it remains that there is little in Shakspere's background to suggest that he would have changed this and other Pembroke scripts in the highly particular ways that the new hand does.

Perhaps the person who best knew what the countess wanted and how to get it was the countess herself. She had continued to develop her skills as a poet, having begun from a broad base that had narrowed into a keen blank verse interest. She had the right sort of resources in place to assist her. She had the time and inclination. But she was a woman and a noble woman at that. Gender lines at court may have been somewhat blurred because there was a woman on the throne but in the general population they remained sharp. Nashe had demonstrated the countess's naiveté even to engage with the playwrights at arm's length. If Mary Sidney had wished personally to intercede in the scripts her players were performing, she would have had to cloak her actions.

Her ladyship's predicament was probably known to her husband, as well as to Abraham Fraunce and Fulke Greville. Perhaps their fellow member on the Welsh Council, Sir Thomas Lucy, recounted his story of the poacher, William Shakspere, and the case he intended to bring against him. Sir Thomas may have even recounted, as the townspeople of Stratford did to visitors in the next century, that this William had composed a facetious little verse about the old knight that Lucy intended to bring forward in court as well. It may have been in such a moment there crystallized in Fulke Greville's mind the respective good William Shakspere and Mary Sidney could do each other, a matter in which he could with ease and discretion personally play that role of *Master* he would at the end of his life claim to have played.

William Shakspere did have particular attributes to recommend him for that sort of assignment. He was of a known Warwickshire family. He had the ability to read and write augmented by long experience of worldly affairs. And if he could improvise a merry country verse, for which we have the two samples from the end of his life as proof, that would have been all to the better. Such a man could go to London, learn the business of the playhouse, go onto the stage in some small roles and, if the need arose, humbly acknowledge himself to be the poet, William Shakespeare. Most people would believe that if told. The exception of course would be the discerning, skeptical few and, in what may have been the first real test of his credibility, that summer William Shakspere would come face-to-face with the most discerning of them all, Robert Greene.

CHAPTER 5

Nashe With A Paddle & Greene's Month Of Dying

The spring of 1592 was marred by a much greater than usual outbreak of plague that grew worse as the days warmed. London was the port of entry and its huddled masses were hard hit. Those with license to travel immediately evacuated to the countryside while those without were ordered to remain in the city and carry on as best they could. The plague was like a malignant spirit wending its way up and down the streets, mowing down this house of people, passing that. It had happened many times before but this time it would be more intense and much longer lasting.

At first the playhouses remained open despite the deaths surging out of control with the warming weather. Then in the third week of June there was a riot among some apprentices who had gathered near the now enlarged Rose, not for the day's play it appears, but to engage in some fisticuffs with rival apprentices. The matter came to the immediate attention of the Privy Council who the same day ordered all the playhouses closed for the time being; they were within the week ordered to remain closed until such time as the infestation abated. That way the players' season was curtailed but by a few days. (It was good to have powerful friends.)

It was now time for summer touring. The players loaded their gaily-bedecked wagons with their scripts, musical instruments and chests of costumes and props, and began the slow trot out of town along the nation's outlaw highways for an indefinite bout of country touring. All mounted on horses or riding in the wagon, they would have made a most splendid and welcome sight, especially when all dressed in their matching livery coats bearing the arms of the noble houses they served.

While Lord Strange's Men went into Kent and the Queen's Men headed for Southampton, town records tell us, the Pembroke company headed north. What survives of the first leg of their inaugural tour is an account book entry from the period June-August 1592 for the town of King's Lynn, seventy miles north of London. Here the troupe was paid 20 shillings (a single pound) for a civic-sponsored performance. For a summer troupe of 12-15 players this was already an average of about 16-20p per person. The actors were generally allowed to collect what they could from the audience at the end of performances as well, pushing their wages even higher. The cost of living was about half in the country what it was in London.

Of the six original playwrights who had laboured for Pembroke's Men over the course of the season, 1591-92, only Thomas Nashe had seen fit to storm off and tell tales out of school. Upon terminating his relations with the company in September 1591, he left with modest wages, a very rich packet of sonnets, and, it appears, some insights into how the chronicle histories of England (which he berated elsewhere for their dryness) could be turned into exciting historical drama. While Marlowe, Peele and Greene had continued with the middle years of the civil war in a play called *The True Tragedy of Richard, Duke of York,* Nashe stepped back in Holinshed's chronicle to the happier early part of King Henry VI's reign, when England had won battles against France and had even burned that upstart witch, Joan of Arc. For Nashe, this latter matter no doubt would have been a salutary lesson to all uppity women who would endeavour to do men's work! The play, called *Harey VI* by Henslowe in his business daybook, first appeared on the boards of the Rose playhouse at the beginning of March 1592. *Harey* was performed 14 times until that bit of rioting closed all the playhouses in mid-June. We know that Nashe considered Edward Alleyn to be the best lead in London and so the move to the Rose would have been natural for him.

It appears to have taken Nashe some five months to write the play of *Harey*. In *Pierce Penniless,* the pamphlet he was working on, he would claim that some 10,000 spectators had seen the play during its spring run. That was an average of some 715 per performance – quite good, and probably typical. The Rose probably held no more than about 1,500 people even after Henslowe's expansion the previous

Christmas. In his preface to the pirated sonnets, Nashe had claimed that only he could keep up with *Gravesend barge* [i.e. MARLOWE] and with this play of *Harey* he would have made good on his boast. (On his own Marlowe had never written more than one play a year.) Henslowe paid £6 upfront and half of the galleries at the second performance. Although the practice was to charge double prices only at the premieres, we note that with *Harey* double prices were still in effect second time around. Good on Nashe! This perhaps gave Nashe some £8-9 in total for his 5 months of labour.

It would now take him another five months to complete his next project, the appropriately-titled pamphlet *Pierce Penniless*. Pamphlets generally paid far less than plays, only £2-3, though Nashe may have bargained for more. Though he always affixed the title, gentleman, to his name on the covers of his printed pamphlets, it is clear that Nashe would come to the end of another fiscal year in which his earnings would remain quite some distance below the £20 per year and counting that denoted a 'gentlemanly standing'.

On his way to completing that pamphlet of *Pierce Penniless his Supplication to the Devil,* Nashe had, with the onset of plague conditions in London, gone to the Archbishop of Canterbury's country residence of Croydon. It may be surmised that church hospitality was always there to help keep Nashe alive during the lean times. It was at Croydon, under Archbishop Whitgift's gaze, that Nashe finished his satirical reply to what the Pembroke writers had said over the previous half year regarding his letter of September 1591. At the end of July 1592, his pamphlet ready, Nashe travelled to London. The Archbishop had personally provided the censor's authorization for its printing, indicating that from the start it had met with his and the bishops' approval. It is the traditional ploughman's name, Piers, that has been distorted into Pierce, giving us the image of a poor, simple rustic but simultaneously the all-seeing, thrusting-after-truth crusader Nashe would now play.

No matter how we read the work, *Pierce Penniless* remains one of the most vital and one of the most unusual pamphlets printed in that era. There are within it a number of component parts that the author has deliberately shuffled in the presentation. It is the printer,

John Busby, who would first alert us to the fact in a note placed after the title page. There Busby states that the *dedication, epistle and proem* [PREFACE] *have been inserted conceitedly in the matter.* Indeed, to stretch the pages of the book out is to see that the order of its component parts is back to front. It begins with a kind of epilogue, continues with its main body, and then concludes with an introduction, a letter to the reader and a kind of dedication. It is as if after having read the book as presented, Nashe would lure us into reconsidering everything in the backward glance. Indeed, what appears to be stirring on first reading takes on a much more hideous intent when the book is reconsidered in this back to front fashion.

The dedication would then start at: *But from general fame, let me digress to my private experience, and with a tongue unworthy to name a name of such worthiness, affectionately emblazon to the eyes that wonder, the matchless image of Honour, and magnificent rewarder of virtue, Jove's Eagle-born Gannymede, thrice noble Amyntas.* It appears that Abraham Fraunce's (and lately Spenser's) Amyntas epithet for Sir Philip Sidney has now reached critical mass. The private experience would refer to Nashe's study of those writings by Sidney he had in his possession. Nashe again paints Sir Philip as the true exemplar of 'the compleat man': *In whose high spirit, such a Deity of wisdom appeareth, that if Homer were to write his Odyssey new (where, under the person of Ulysses, he describeth a singular man of perfection, in whom all ornaments both of peace and war are assembled in the height of their excellence), he need no other instance to augment his conceipt, than the rare carriage of his* [i.e. SIDNEY'S] *honourable mind.*

The other poets would have continued with words of praise for Sidney's sister, Mary, as even Nashe had audaciously done the September before. But here he would attack her chief defender, Nicholas Breton. *Many writers and good wits are given to commend their patrons and Benefactors, some for prowess, some for policy, others for the glory of their Ancestry and exceeding bounty and liberality: but if my unable pen should ever enterprise such a continuate* [CHRONICLING] *task of praise, I would embowel a number of those wind puffed bladders, and disfurnish their bald pates of the periwigs Poets have lent them, that so I might restore glory to his right inheritance, and these stolen Titles to their true owners.* The last time Nashe had addressed his own shortcomings as a writer was in his September letter where he had immediately followed with a spoof of Breton. And here he threatens that if he should ever sing Sidney's praises, he would use the occasion to have a go at those who sang his praises now. Here we may be sure that *those wind puffed bladders,* those *bald pates* dressed in the wigs of better poets, is all meant for Breton and his Oxford crew.

Nashe claims he would be Sir Philip's defender *if it would so fall out (as time may work all things),* [that] *the aspiring nettles, with their shady tops, shall no longer overdreep* [DROOP OVER] *the best herbs, or keep them from the smiling aspect of the Sun, that live & thrive by his comfortable beams.* One senses in the undercurrent that *the best herbs* refer to Nashe himself while poets closer to Sidney's legacy, like the countess and Breton, would form *the aspiring nettles* that stifle the deserving (though denied) underlings from the Sun (i.e. SIDNEY'S LITERARY LEGACY). Nashe gives every indication here and elsewhere that he imagines there being much more to Sidney's legacy than he was privy to, as if much still lay locked away in 'Lady Mary's casket'. But he was misinformed for the reality (in terms of the wash of history, at any rate) was that both Sir Philip's major pieces were now in print and all the rest, aside from the original Arcadia, were a lot of occasional bits and bobs. Nashe naively makes a call for greater egalitarianism — *none but Desert* [THE DESERVING] *should sit in Fame's grace.* As he himself was the 'deserving', so the *Fame* at whose feet he would sit was Sidney. Nashe concludes, *none but Hector be remembered in the chronicles of Prowess, none but thou, most courteous Amyntas, be the second mystical argument of the knight of the Red-cross.* Hector, the commander of the Trojan forces in their war with Greece, was admired for his compassion and adherence to the code of nobility, like Sidney. In the actions *of the knight of the Red Cross,* the hero of the opening book of Spenser's *Faerie Queene* (1590), there is a moral mirror for Sidney's exemplary life.

And now, strangely, Nashe would tear a strip out of that latter poet, Spenser, for not having already performed that *continuate task of praise.* Treading very carefully, he writes: *And here (heavenly Spenser) I am most highly to accuse thee of forgetfulness, that in that catalogue of our English Heroes, which ensueth the conclusion of thy famous Faerie Queen, thou wouldst let so special a pillar of Nobility pass*

TIGER'S HEART IN WOMAN'S HIDE

unsaluted. The very thought of his far derived descent, & extraordinary parts, wherein he astonieth [ASTONISHES] *the world, and draws all hearts to his love* [POETRY], *would have inspired thy forewearied Muse with new fury to proceed to the next triumphs of thy stately Goddess* [i.e. THE FAIRY QUEEN]. On the concluding pages of the general print run of *The Faerie Queene* there had appeared a string of dedicatory sonnets to certain nobles of her Majesty's court, none of which had mentioned Sir Philip Sidney. Feeling he has the poet cornered, Nashe milks the matter over the course of a page, even penning a glib sonnet to sustain the merriment.

> Perusing yesternight, with idle eyes,
>   The Fairy Singers' stately tuned verse,
> And viewing after Chapmen's wonted guise††,
>   What strange contents the title did rehearse;
> I straight leapt over to the latter end,
>   Where like the quaint Comedians of our time,
> That when their Play is done do fall to rhyme,
>   I found short lines, to sundry Nobles penned;
> Whom he [SPENSER] as special Mirrors singled forth,
>   To be the Patrons of his Poetry:
> I read them all, and reverenced their worth,
>   Yet wondered he left out thy memory.
>   But therefore guessed I he suppressed thy name,
>   Because few words might not comprise thy fame.

†† Itinerant peddlers' usual manner

(Actors at the end of plays fell to dancing, not rhyming; elsewhere in *Pierce*, Nashe refers to the jigs of the newsmongers, who turned their news not into dances but rhymed ballads.) With regards to Spenser, however, Nashe was again out of the loop. In the volume of *The Faerie Queene* he was reading from, what had appeared as blank pages had in a select number of copies (possibly printed for a more restricted courtly circle) contained further verses of dedication, among which was the following.

> To the right honourable and most virtuous Lady,
>   The Countess of Penbroke.

Remembrance of that most Heroic spirit,
> The heavens' pride, the glory of our days,
> Which now triumpheth through immortal merit
> Of his brave virtues, crowned with lasting bays,

Of heavenly bliss and everlasting praise;
> Who first my Muse did lift out of the floor,
> To sing his sweet delights in lowly lays;
> Bids me most noble Lady to adore

His goodly image living evermore,
> In the divine resemblance of your face;
> Which with your virtues ye embellish more,
> And native beauty deck with heavenly grace:

For his, and for your own especial sake,
> Vouchsafe from him this token in good worth to take.

There were quite a few other patrons who, for whatever reason, did not have their dedications included in the general edition of 1590. This was written at a time when Spenser had probably only recently visited Mary Sidney, possibly for the first time. He recalls the memory of Philip, with whom Spenser had had direct traffic in the late 70's when he was secretary to Sidney's uncle, Robert Dudley. Already we find here the image he would later repeat in *Colin Clout's* (*Who ... floor*). We note Spenser's observation that the countess looked a lot like her brother, a matter to which portrait remains attest. And as well there is the suggestion of that Uranian cluster that Colin Clout would later echo. Overall, it appears that Spenser had been guilty of no omission, as Nashe would have his equally misinformed readers here in *Pierce* believe.

After his own sonnet, Nashe continues: *Bear with me gentle Poet, though I conceive not aright of thy purpose, or be too inquisitive into the intent of thy oblivion* [NOBLE RESERVE; i.e. SILENCE ON SIDNEY]: *for, how ever my conjecture may miss the cushion, yet shall my speech savour of friendship, though it be not allied to judgment.* Nashe includes the matter, he claims, for the sake of their countrymen that live *out of the Echo of the Court,* so that they might know of Sir Philip's *invaluable virtues, and show myself thankful (in some part) for benefits received.* As Sidney had died well before Nashe appeared in print those benefits could only have come indirectly through studying those parts of Sidney's literary legacy he had before him. It is a strange affair, Nashe goading the man then acknowledged to be the supreme living poet among them. But in the further backward glance it becomes obvious that this chipping at Spenser's credibility is done as part of a larger offensive.

Continuing in the backward glance we next come to the letter to the reader. Nashe begins: *Gentle Reader, tandem aliquando* [FINALLY] *I am at leisure to talk to thee.* Nashe rants against the low quality of literature filling the stalls along Paul's churchyard, the inane rhyming of the ballad-making newsmongers of Westminster Hall. And there was his own pressing need for support—*for a good Patron will pay for all. Aye, where is he?* He admits his readers will question his motivations for writing a supplication to the Devil for patronage.

Although he could have had a supportive patron in the countess, had he wanted, in what follows we discern some of the reasons why he could under no circumstances serve her. Nashe calls for the whip of an Aretino (the earlier Italian satirist remembered as the 'Scourge of Princes') to use *against our English Peacocks, that painting themselves with church spoils, like mighty men's sepulchres, have nothing but Atheism, schism, hypocrisy, & vainglory ....* Just as we may be sure Nashe would be that whip, the Peacocks would be those nobles who had thrived from church properties given them by King Henry VIII at the time England's monasteries were dissolved. No one had enjoyed King Henry's generosity in that regard more than the House of Pembroke who became by it one of the richest houses in England. (And therein lay not only Nashe's resentment but that of his supporters in the church, as well.) Nashe continues unflatteringly: *Oh how my soul abhors these buckram giants, that having an outward face of honour set upon them by flatterers and parasites, have their inward thoughts stuffed with straw and feathers.* This appears to present us with an accusation of unorthodox thinking levelled against Henry Herbert, the present Earl of Pembroke. *Far be it, bright stars of*

Nobility, and glistering attendants on the true Diana [i.e. THE QUEEN], Nashe assuages, *that this my speech should be any way injurious to your glorious magnificence: for in you live those sparks of Augustus' liberality, that never sent any away empty.* This was more to recall 'hospitality' as it had been practiced up to the generation before but which now in this new period of intensive capital accumulation had suddenly all but disappeared (to which Nashe's letter elsewhere abundantly attests).

Having passed the dedication and letter to the reader (such as they are), we now come in our backward journey to what would be the introduction. It is here we discover why Nashe could not possibly go to the countess for the patronage he so desperately needed. This introduction is presented as a conversation between *Pierce* (alias Nashe) and the *knight of the post*, the figure who will carry his letter to the Devil in hell. Pierce would know certain things from him, such as what hell is and what devils are. The post replies with some general remarks but in short order begins to draw an extraordinary picture of a *right earthly Devil*. It comes in answer to Pierce's question of what the Devil is that he receives the following reply.

Some claim, the knight of the post states, *that the Devil is but a pestilent humour in a man, of pleasure, profit, or policy, that violently carries him away to vanity, villainy, or monstrous hypocrisy.* The outrageous behaviour such a temperament breeds—*dishonourable prodigality; intemperate venery* [OVEREATING MEAT]*; self-love; murder; treason; theft; cozenage; cutthroat covetousness; Macchiavillism; Puritanism; under-hand cloaking of bad actions with Commonwealth pretences; Italianate conveyances* [MURDER BY POISONING]*; to use men … and then cast them off; to seek the destruction of those that know his secrets; to destroy those he had employed in any murder or stratagem*—at first reading appears to be no more than the nasty underbelly of their times, did they not, as a particular catalogue of misdeeds, bear such resemblance to the alleged misdeeds of Robert Dudley, the Earl of Leicester (especially as these had been reported in a rash of pamphlets that had appeared after the breakdown of the French wedding negotiations in the early 80's). Now this would all be circumstantial did the knight of the post not immediately follow with the conceited tale of a *Bear* whose point-by-point story laid beside Robert Dudley's life would indicate Nashe very much had Dudley's emblem of 'the bear and ragged staff' in mind while composing it. And in it Nashe would pack quite a little bombshell that would not only explain many of his actions throughout but do serious harm to the reputations of Dudley's survivors here in 1592.

It is called the *tale of a Battledore*. A *battledore*, also called a hornbook, was one of those paddle-like boards upon which children then learned to read and practice their writing. As well the word was used for any large laundry paddle or shuttlecock racket. All meanings bear on Nashe's intentions – read what comes out of the wash and poing! it's back in your court.

The story begins: *The Bear on a time, being chief Burgomaster* [CHIEF CIVIC OFFICIAL] *of all the Beasts under the Lion, gan think with himself how he might surfeit in pleasure, or best husband his Authority to enlarge his delight and contentment.* From the beginning of the reign in 1558 until the end of his life Robert Dudley had remained her Majesty's prime emotional interest, placing him (*under the lion*) in the number 2 position. Talk of *husband* glances at Leicester's long pursuit of marriage with the queen. Under that special royal favour, Dudley had enjoyed great power.

Having devoured all kinds of viands, the Bear now longs for horseflesh, and discovers a Camel grazing in a meadow. Noting his size and well-shod hoofs, the Bear decides to catch him by guile. When the Camel bows to him, the Bear plans to grab him by the neck and strangle him. To his surprise, rather than bowing, the Camel *lifted up one of his hindmost heels, and stroke* [STRUCK] *him such a blow on the forehead that he overthrew him.* Among Leicester's whispered misdeeds the one with which talk of horseflesh would resonate most particularly was with 'the Master of the Horse' affair of 1560.

Upon her succession to the throne in 1558 the Queen had immediately made Robert Dudley her Master of the Horse, the second most important post in the royal household after that of the Lord Chamberlain. There appears to have been a desire for marriage on both their parts. Unfortunately Dudley was already married. But in 1560 his wife of ten years, Amy Robsart, died after a fall down a pair of steps caused her neck to break. As the Privy Council came to terms with the real possibility that the Queen could now marry and produce an heir, even Dudley's enemies were ready to acquiesce to the inevitable. News of the death (along with the talk of the marriage) travelled to all the capitals of Europe. In Paris the news aroused a great deal of indignation, which the English ambassador, Sir Nicholas Throckmorton, recorded at firsthand. Among the intelligence sent back to Lord Treasurer William Cecil (a man opposed to the match), was the flippant remark by Elizabeth's chief rival, nineteen-year-old Mary Queen of Scots (then momentarily on the throne of France), that Dudley would have had squashed at any cost: *"The Queen of England is going to marry the Master of her Horses, who has killed his wife to make room for her"*. The Lord Treasurer told her Majesty to immediate and devastating effect. All the happy enthusiasm the Royal Maid had entertained for the wedding was suddenly, dramatically to evaporate. She had wanted to make Dudley the Earl of Leicester first, but when the patent she had ordered was presented for her signing the queen took a knife and cut the paper into pieces. It would be several years before that project was revived. Throckmorton had indeed *stroke him such a blow on the forehead that he overthrew him*.

Angry beyond endurance, the *Bear* consults with the *Ape* to determine how he might be revenged. The *Ape* may stand for Dudley's Italian physician, one Dr. Julio. He advises the Bear to dig a hole *right in the way where this big boned Gentleman should pass*. The story later put out by the anti-Leicester propagandists was that Julio concocted a poison that was placed in Throckmorton's salad when he came to a banquet at Leicester House, which by delayed reaction would kill him. There were rumours that Dudley had quietly eliminated others who had opposed him through poison although nothing has ever been proved.

Continuing on his way, the Bear passes a grove where a herd of Deer *were a-ranging; whom, when he had steadfastly surveyed from the fattest to the leanest, he singled out one of the fairest of the company, with whom he hoped to close up his stomach ... .* Many women were overcome by Dudley's magnetism. The *fairest* of the women in his life had been Lettice Knollys, the rather beautiful, vivacious 28-year-old wife of the Earl of Essex. But this *deer* was under the protection of a *forester*. *Therefore,* [BEAR] *determined slyly and privily to poison the* stream where this jolly Forester wonted to drink; and as he determined, so he did. The rumour was that Dudley had also poisoned the Earl of Essex in order that he might marry his widow. (This was after the failure at Kenilworth for Dudley to secure her Majesty's hand in marriage.) The Bear knows his life would be in peril if caught, *though not with the Lion, whose eyes he could blind as he list.* It was true that nothing appeared to undermine for long her Majesty's emotional dependence on her 'dear Robin' Dudley.

The Bear devours other animals as Dudley was alleged to have murdered other people. *Yet newfangled lust, that in time is weary of welfare, at last brought him out of love with this greedy, bestial humour; and now he affected a milder variety in his diet.* The Bear *bethought him what a pleasant thing it was to eat nothing but honey, especially given the great store of it there was in that Country.* He seeks to persuade the Husbandmen *that they might buy honey cheaper than being at such charges in keeping of Bees, for what should such idle Drones do with such stately Hives.* The *Bees* here would stand for the Bishops, talk of *honey* a cloak for money, those *stately Hives* a glance at the issue of how the church was to be structured – with or without those *idle Drones*. Within the context of Dudley's life we reach the early 80's and the start of the looming Presbyterian crisis.

As he aged, Dudley had more and more come to champion a Geneva-style settlement for the church in England. The Geneva reformers had radicalized the movement by calling for a return to the structure of the Christian church that had existed before the ascendancy of Rome. The hierarchy of bishops and archbishops, besides costing a great deal, created a lot of intermediaries in the individual's relationship with God and came by some to be seen as a corrupting Roman innovation (that, among other things, impeded parish improvements). But as much as her Majesty was moved by Genevan reformist thinking, she would resist this innovation to the end.

To persuade the people, the Bear engages the Fox, *and promised to have his Patent sealed, to be the King's Poulterer forever, if he could bring it to pass.* 'King' Robert Dudley had in 1585 brought Thomas Cartwright, a Puritan divine with a trenchant pen then living in the Netherlands, back to England and established him as the Master of Leicester's Hospital in the town of Warwick (just up the road from Stratford). Unusually Dudley issued Cartwright (the *poulterer*) a deed for life (*forever*) to the hospital. This angered none more than Archbishop Whitgift. Cartwright and Whitgift had been vehement enemies since the 60's. Whitgift, back then Vice Chancellor of Cambridge, had deprived Cartwright of the position of Lady Margaret Professor of Divinity to which Cartwright had been fairly elected in 1569. But now Cartwright was to help implement a shadow Presbyterianism throughout those territories under Dudley's control.

The Bear drops out of the story just as Robert Dudley died in 1588. But the Fox remains. *With that he grew in league with an old Chameleon, that could put on all shapes, and imitate any colour.* The *Chameleon* would in all likelihood represent clergyman John Penry, the fiery young Welsh preacher purported to have been the chief pen behind the *Martin Marprelate* pamphlets, although others were involved. Despite the great efforts made to nab them, like a true *chameleon*, the Martinists eluded detection for a stretch of some 18 months. The Fox, according to Nashe, dresses him *sometime like an Ape to make sport, and then like a Crocodile to weep, sometime like a Serpent to sting, and by and by like a Spaniel to fawn* – reflecting the jagged rhetorical mood swings the Martin pamphlets had evinced.

Nashe continues with his allegory. *In this disguise, these two deceivers* [CARTWRIGHT AND PENRY] *went up and down, and did much harm under the habit of Simplicity, making the poor silly Swains believe they were cunning Physicians.* The Fox and Chameleon do an excellent job selling their plan (*the novel folly*) to the people (*the headlong vulgar*) – indeed, the Martin pamphlets were a resounding success. But a Fly discovers them *and heard all their talk and buzzed in Linceus' ears the whole purport of their malice.* Linceus, the eagle-eyed Argonaut who accompanied Jason on the quest for the Golden Fleece, probably stands for the Archbishop on the ship of state, the Fly the informant who first reported Martin's identity. Quickly *they are apprehended and imprisoned, and all their whole council detected.* The uprooting of the movement led to Cartwright's arrest and trial by the church's Court of High Commission in 1590. He was kept in custody until late 1592 and then exiled to the Channel Islands where he would remain until 1598. Penry and his printer Waldegrave escaped north to Scotland in 1590 but Penry returned to England in 1592, was apprehended and hanged the following year.

How likest thou my tale, friend Persie? asks the knight of the post, have *I not described a right earthly Devil unto thee, in the discourse of this bloody-minded Bear? Or canst thou not attract the true image of hypocrisy, under the description of the Fox and the Chameleon?* And to put this crew in good company, the tale is rounded out with a ten-page translation of *De Illorum Daemonum* by Georgius Pictorius (published in 1563) wherein a host of conventional hellbound devils is described.

The ramifications of this are profound. Stripping away the allegorical veneer it becomes clear that Nashe (under the protection of his church masters) would here openly lay responsibility for the Martin Marprelate fiasco, a matter that was one of the government's most serious challenges over 1588-90, on what Robert Dudley, the Earl of Leicester, had set into motion while yet alive. Given that Dudley was dead, this bold public assertion could only have damaged that man's survivors, not in the eyes of the public, where Martin had been popular, but with those for whom Martin had been such a problem, such as the queen. Further, given that Nashe's poverty and need for patronage are the recurring themes of his pamphlet, it appears the message Nashe would impart was that for him to go to this Dudley line for patronage was akin to striking a deal with this *right earthly Devil*. No, if Nashe had to make a supplication to any malignant spirit, he would rather go straight to the Devil himself!

And so it is that we now come to the main body of his book, his far-ranging letter to Satan. In line with its underlying concern for Nashe's empty purse, the letter makes a fervent plea for the Devil to rope in the influence of the seven deadly sins so that Nashe's and all poor people's condition might be improved. His anatomy of sin, very much in line with his medieval thinking, is well illustrated with satirical hits on many of his contemporaries, including Breton and the countess.

In the first week of August 1592, Nashe momentarily came to town to arrange for *Pierce*'s printing with publisher John Busby. The book was entered into the Stationers' register on 8 August and would be in the stalls in about a month. His fellow playwright-pamphleteer, Robert Greene, was still in London and before Nashe returned to the Archbishop's manor in the country, he and Greene gathered for what would be a very merry carouse. It was later reported by several parties that there was a great deal of Rhenish wine and pickled herring at their party of which Robert Greene took a surfeit.

Despite Nashe's penury, it had been a year of highs for Greene. Aside from his constant playwriting, he had since his arrival in Shoreditch written a series of pamphlets that detailed the workings of London's criminal class. That woman he had met in that *house of retail* in Shoreditch was the sister to a noted thief who went by the name of 'Cutting Ball'. These two appear to have been excellent raconteurs, nimbly able to lay bare the organization and special insider's language that animated the whole of their underworld activity. Greene, the budding reporter, wrote it all down and in November of the previous year had appeared the first of what became known as his *conny-catcher* pamphlets, the most successful of his extended works. By his incredibly prodigious output, Master Greene earned upwards of £30 this year though it would all be dissipated by his lifestyle.

The day after the banquet with Nashe, Greene awoke to find a swelling about his waist that grew worse day by day. In *Greene's Groatsworth of Wit* the reason is tersely given: *his immeasurable drinking had made him the perfect Image of the dropsy.* Dropsy is that condition where fluids accumulate under the skin because of liver or kidney failure. In Greene's day the condition was not yet understood even if the relationship between it and alcohol abuse was. The heavy drinking of the previous day had therefore been the last straw. The medical help he found, though expensive, proved ineffective.

As Greene had never managed to save, his small earthly accumulation dwindled rather quickly and the next we hear he is homeless and living in the street. This sudden hard reality – to be seriously ill, out of money, and living in the street – must have been very distressing. In the street he might have died. But ironically a cobbler's wife by the name of Mrs. Isam took pity on him and moved him into her home in the Dowgate area in the centre of the city. She washed his shirt, which was very decrepit at his arrival. According to

Nashe she was a very big woman *who had an arm like an Amazon.* Although the affliction was no doubt unsettling, it appears not to have altogether incapacitated Greene. We get some sense of his activity from his selling the fifth instalment of his conny-catcher pamphlets here in mid-August to Henry Chettle's mate, printer John Danter, well before it was ready. No doubt Greene negotiated an advance. The book that Danter entered into the Stationers' Register on 21 August was to be called *The Repentance of a Conny-catcher,* and was to include the lives of two notable cozeners who came to sorry ends, Ned Browne and a man named Morton. It appears the story of Browne was left as collateral for later after Greene's death Danter would publish this as *The Black Book's Messenger.*

And at about the same time, Greene had a meeting with his theatrical employers, the Earl of Pembroke's Men. The episode is recounted in a cogent letter Greene would write to his fellow playwrights, Marlowe, Nashe and Peele, which would appear in the posthumous *Greene's Groatsworth of Wit.* It is with this desperate, vengeful letter that we receive the next snapshot of the Pembroke enterprise, but now as it was with the addition of William Shakspere the actor plus Shakespeare's hand.

Greene's letter begins, *To those gentlemen, his quondam* [FORMER] *acquaintance, that spend their wits in making plays, R.G. wisheth a better exercise, and wisdom to prevent his extremities.* Those *gentlemen,* according to the letter, are Christopher Marlowe, Thomas Nashe and George Peele plus two other playwrights not otherwise identified. Greene begins by asking them to take heed so that what has happened to him does not happen to them.

He addresses the first of three playwrights. *Wonder not (for with thee will I first begin), thou famous gracer of tragedians, that Greene, who hath said with thee, like the fool in his heart, "There is no God," should now give glory unto his greatness . . . .* The scholarship is generally agreed that *famous gracer of tragedians* is meant for Christopher Marlowe, each of whose plays had continued as blockbusters season after season. Marlowe's new drumming poetics in 1587 had become the theatrical standard by 1592. Some of *Groatsworth*'s first readers would remember the charge of atheism Greene had hurled at Marlowe in the introduction to *Perimedes* back in 1588. And where the charge had there been expressed as a glancing blow, here the matter is pounded home with some vengeance over the course of a long, rambling paragraph. It is possible that Greene had drawn succour from Marlowe's unorthodox views, which held that religion was but a superstition meant to hold simple people in awe. The last year had been a particularly libertine time in what had already been a morally-challenged life for Greene and he may well have felt himself influenced by Marlowe's 'every man for himself' bravado (though Marlowe shared neither of Greene's weaknesses for drink and courtesans). But the realization that he was dying had no doubt suddenly and furiously brought to the fore Greene's always-present fear of damnation (a theme that runs like a thread through his work): *penetrating is his power, his hand lies heavy upon me, he hath spoken unto me with a voice of thunder, and I have felt he is a God that can punish enemies.*

Greene turns to the second of the playwrights, Thomas Nashe, whom he addresses in much warmer tones. *With thee* [MARLOWE] *I join young Juvenal, that biting satirist.* The first to second century Roman poet, Juvenal, who claimed to have been driven to write satire by the indignation he felt for life around him, is a fit epithet for the now 25-year-old Nashe. Greene claims that he *lastly with me together writ a Comedy.* This work, if it is a play, remains unidentified. In what survives of their writing, there is their common assault on the Harvey brothers of Cambridge (as found in the about-to-be-printed Pierce's letter to the Devil and Greene's *Quip for an Upstart Courtier* as was published back in June). Greene tells Nashe, *Sweet boy, might I advise thee, be advised, and get not many enemies by bitter words: inveigh against vain men, for thou canst do it, no man better, no man so well: thou hast a liberty to reprove all, and name none; for one being spoken to, all are offended; none being blamed no man is injured.* Greene would here counsel Nashe to stop his habit of identifying too openly those he would lampoon. Nashe's relationship with the Pembrokes appears to emerge next. Cryptically Greene writes: *Stop shallow water still running, it will rage, or tread on a worm and it will turn: then blame not scholars vexed with sharp lines, if they reprove thy too much liberty of reproof.* To 'stop running water' was to 'pen' it. The phrase *shallow water still running* suggests a 'brook'. That would make Penbrook. Pen a brook, i.e. build up a head of water, and *it will rage if released*, like the Pembrokes had done when Sir Philip Sidney's sonnets had piratically appeared under Nashe's auspices. The *worm* allusion may suggest that Greene agrees with Nashe that the Pembrokes suffered from lack of eyesight. The *scholars vexed with sharp lines* would bring into focus Breton, Peele and the countess in the case of the preface to the pirated sonnets and the countess, Breton and his Oxford crew, Spenser, and others in the soon-to-appear *Pierce Penniless*. Greene overall would recommend Nashe curb his freedom.

Greene now comes to the third of his addressees, George Peele. *And thou no less deserving than the other two, in some things rarer, in nothing inferior; driven (as myself) to extreme shifts* [EMPLOYMENT], *a little have I to say to thee: and were it not an idolatrous oath, I would swear by sweet St. George, thou art unworthy better hap* [LUCK], *sith* [SINCE] *thou dependest on so mean a stay* [POSITION]. Namesakes aside, George Peele's whole surging inclination towards nationalism makes St. George, England's patron saint, a coherent allusion for him. Peele's dependency on the playhouse to help make ends meet mirrors Greene's own.

The letter continues with the recent experience Greene has had with the actors that causes him to write now. *Base-minded men all three of you, if by my misery you be not warned: for unto none of you (like me) sought those burrs to cleave: those Puppets (I mean) that spake* [SPOKE] *from our mouths, those Antics garnished in our colours.* The reference to *those burrs* would suggest the old actor James Burbage, his son Richard, and the rest of the Burbage family. Talk of *Puppets* and *antics* leads us to the troupe as a whole. Greene goes on to tell them of the specific interaction he recently had with them.

He writes, *Is it not strange that I, to whom they all have been beholding* [BEHOLDEN], *is it not like that you, to whom they all have been beholding, shall (were ye in that case as I am now) be both at once of them forsaken?* We clarify Greene's meaning by stripping the sentence down to its simpler 'I' form: 'Is it not strange that I, to whom they all have been beholden, shall (in that case as I am now) be at once of them forsaken?' This speaks of the association between Greene and the actors, that they had needed his services, but that now in his illness (*that case as I am now*) they have deserted him. Because of the reference to his illness, we can date this meeting to the month of August 1592. The words, *at once*, particularly evoke a dismissive attitude on their part towards him.

Where the encounter took place Greene does not specify but it may well be that he caught Pembroke's Men in rehearsal at the closed Theatre. The journey from the Isams' home in Dowgate to the Shoreditch playhouse would have been just over a mile. With the playhouses closed because of plague the actors would have needed no new material just now while Greene was probably more desperate than he had ever been – a most unfortunate synergy! From his own admission of sharp dealing with other troupes, we may wonder if he already had outstanding debts with the Pembroke company. From their point of view it may not have appeared feasible extending credit to a dying man. Undermining Greene's bargaining position further, the actors now apparently had one within their own ranks who had given those scripts Greene and his partners had written some new polish, bringing them up to a much finer courtly quality.

In his encounter with the actor, Greene appears not to have taken appearances at face value and it is this matter that his letter would now address. The loaded piece of intelligence was written in such a way as to slip by the censor and then to be read properly only by the addressees of his letter, the playwrights. Singling out the actor, Greene writes, *Yes trust them* [THE ACTORS] *not, for* [among them] *there is an upstart crow, beautified with our feathers ... .* In general Elizabethan usage, the word *upstart* was derisively used for those who had newly risen to wealth and position (as opposed to the old and established). That already creates the impression of empty airs. In one passage of *A Quip for an Upstart Courtier* that he had published in June, Greene had described commoners who pass themselves off as gentlemen as *upstart changelings*, adding the nuance of 'counterfeit' to its meaning. As to referring to the actor as a *crow*, in *The Defence of Conny-catching* from earlier this year we find Greene telling the story of a man who falsely claims to have travelled the continent of Europe. He writes there: *Thus decking himself like the Daw with the fair feathers of other birds, and discoursing what he heard other men report, he grew...plausible among young gentlemen.* The daw, a member of the crow family, is likewise decked out in the feathers of others. The *upstart crow* bespeaks a newcomer who is not what he appears. The glance at *our feathers* would have alerted the playwrights that this concerned their work in particular.

As to what this 'bogus bird' among the actors had done Greene writes: ... *that with his* **Tiger's heart wrapped in a Player's hide,** *supposes he is as well able to bombast out a blank verse as the best of you.* The actor only *supposes*, or imagines, he is capable. 'Bombast' was the cotton wool used to stuff or pad clothes. To pad the *blank verse* was to add new material to the play scripts – the drill of which the other playwrights knew only too well. The next statement we expect to hear is one telling us how the new hand stacked up compared with the old, practiced hands. But there is not a single word of criticism or praise relating to the new material to be found in the whole of Greene's letter. The news Greene would impart was of a wholly different nature.

There are two phrases that are deliberately set off from the rest by the use of a bolder typeface. In the first of these we learn that this actor had a *Tiger's heart wrapped in a Player's hide*. Most first readers presumably would have taken this to mean the man was an actor of some fury. Some may on reconsideration have wondered why 'tiger'–men generally were lions, women tigers. But Marlowe, Peele and possibly Nashe would have been able to read right to the heart of the allusion. After its time, Greene's deeper intentions would lie buried for almost two centuries until it was noticed by one Thomas Tyrwhitt in the 18th century that this was actually a slightly reworked line out of Pembroke's second civil war play, *The True Tragedy of Richard Duke of York*. But there the line stood as: *O tiger's heart wrapped in a woman's hide*. When we consider the line from the point of view of its original context, Greene's intentions to the writers become even clearer. In the scene the captive Duke of York is ranting against his captor, Queen Margaret, for killing his son and now giving him a cloth stained with his boy's blood. Towards the end of his Marlovian outburst, he states

> Thou art as opposite to every good,
> As the Antipodes [poles] are unto us,
> Or as the south to the Septentrion‡.

‡Northern constellation of the Great Bear

> O tiger's heart wrapped in a woman's hide!
> How couldst thou drain the life-blood of the child,
> To bid the father wipe his eyes withal,
> And yet be seen to bear a woman's face?

What the playwrights would have realized immediately was that in the matter of who was padding out the scripts, Greene would have them seek out a woman behind the actor.

In the equation of which they were all a part, there really was only one woman who was in a position to do this but Greene will not touch this. He would now identify the actor who had made the claim of authorship: ... *and being an absolute **Johannes fac totum**, is in his own conceit the only Shake-scene in a country* [COUNTY]. With this Greene appears to finger William Shakspere, fresh out of the country of Warwick where, until the troubles with Sir Thomas Lucy, he had lived. *Johannes fac totum* is the second phrase to appear in that bolder typeface. The Latinate term, *fac totum,* designated any man who dealt with the world at large as the business agent for another. Perhaps the most compelling read of this phrase we can give is when we remember that for a decade John Shakspere had remained in hiding for debt during which William had acted as his 'outside agent'. William's father was listed in the church registry as Johannes. This would indeed have made of his son a *Johannes fac totum ... in a country.* This would have been a devastating revelation of what had been the Stratford man's 'university'. The moniker, *Shake-scene,* brings William's identity to the fore even as it mocks his involvement with the stage.

That Pembroke's Men were momentarily back in London in this time frame is corroborated by an independent piece of evidence. On 19 August 1592 an actor of Shoreditch named Simon Jewel, apparently in the first throes of plague infection, wrote up his final will and testament. That places his event in the same timeframe in which Greene had his encounter with the players. From the itemized inventory in Jewel's will we learn of his shares in the apparel, horses and wagon of his troupe. There is also his livery coat and his *playing things* with a chest to transport them in. He speaks of the wagon being *new bought*, which would fit a company that had just been out on its first tour like Pembroke's Men. The name, Simon, was not then common but is one that has been found embedded in the first quarto edition of *The Taming of a Shrew*, a play in the Pembroke repertoire. There is a very careful reckoning of moneys owed to him and by him and a distribution of his few earthly goods among his friends. The meagreness of his possessions alongside the small role in *Shrew* leave the impression of a young man just starting his career.

And then, coming as a sudden realization of other money yet to come, Jewel speaks and the lawyer writes: *Item my share of such money as shall be given by my Lady Pembroke or by her means I will* [WISH] *shall be distributed and paid towards my burial and other charges.* It is but a tiny glimpse but that phrase – *by my Lady Pembroke* – implies a personal familiarity on Jewel's part. It is noteworthy that he expects the countess to make the payment personally, an unusual disclosure of her closeness to the actors of the company. It further indicates (as does all else) that it was Mary Sidney and not her husband who took the day-to-day interests of the troupe in hand.

Prior to the realization of the countess's money to come, Jewel had assigned his horse to cover the cost of his funeral. Now a fair horse could be bought for a pound, although the actor may have had better. After the realization of the money to come, Jewel assigns it to cover his burial costs. Plus he surmises there may be enough left over to cover his other charges. The exact size of the payment coming to Jewel is unknown, but if his was but a share then we are looking at a payment of some £15-18 to the company, at the least. When noble country manors entertained travelling troupes of players in the summertime the payment to them was generally on the order of £1-3. Given the money here, it appears something of a different order was afoot.

The matter appears not far to seek. Her Majesty was on procession in the West Country this summer and was due to arrive at the Pembrokes' north Wiltshire manor of Ramsbury about 25 August, less than a week away. This was just such an occasion that the countess had known would come, one reason she would have encouraged the playwrights (and presumably her players) to come up to the highest standard possible. Given that Pembroke's Men would win the honour of playing half the dates at court this coming

Christmas, her Majesty's visit here would have given the countess an excellent opportunity to present her troupe before the queen. If so, then a rewritten *Richard, Duke of York* (as Greene alleges) would make impeccable sense. Simon Jewel would not make the sixty-mile journey from London to Ramsbury. He died within a couple of days for his will was proved 23 August. The parish register indicates he had lived in Holywell Street, and was hence a neighbour of the Burbages. Jewel's condition would have made the players all the more sensitive to physical afflictions, a matter that may have aggravated Greene's bargaining position.

Greene continues his letter by telling the other playwrights: *O that I might intreat your rare wits to be employed in more profitable courses: & let those Apes imitate your past excellence, and never more acquaint them with your admired inventions. I know the best husband of you all will never prove* [TURN OUT TO BE] *an Usurer, and the kindest of them all will never prove a kind nurse: yet whiles you may, seek you better Masters.* It is clear that Greene would not have the playwrights stop writing, only that they stop writing for the Pembroke company. He finishes, *it is a pity men of such rare wits should be subject to the pleasure of such rude grooms* [BOORISH SERVANTS]. Calling the troupe grooms reflects their servile status in relation to their noble masters.

Greene now writes he could include two more writers who had written *against* [FOR] *these buckram gentlemen.* That the troupe had a total complement of six playwrights is corroborated by Nashe's emblem of them as 6 *pottle pots*. As to who these two others were, Greene does not say, though we have considered Thomas Kyd and Nicholas Breton. Buckram was fine linen stiffened with paste that by figurative extension came to mean ostentatious, stiff and stuck-up. But *let their own works serve to witness against their own wickedness, if they persevere to maintain any more such peasants.* As to other writers who might come in the future, Greene writes, *I leave them to the mercy of these painted monsters, who, I doubt not, will drive the best-minded to despise them.*

Having blown off this steam, he calms himself by offering some meditations for moral living. *Delight not (as I have done) in irreligious oaths; Despise drunkenness...; Fly lust....* But no sooner started than Greene is back to his real theme. He writes, *and when they soothe you* with terms of *Mastership*, *remember Robert Greene, whom they have so often flattered, perishes now for want of comfort*. When he was working for the company, they had called him *master*, but now that he is sick and dying, they give him nothing. He compares the playwrights' lives to *so many lighted tapers* [CANDLES] *that with wind-puffed wrath may be extinguished*. He beseeches the playwrights: *Trust not then… to such weak stays* [EMPLOYMENT]. In closing he writes *…a whole book cannot contain their wrongs which I am forced to knit up in some few lines of words*. He signs off with *Desirous that you should live, though himself be dying, Robert Greene*.

Greene felt very hard done by. Just the list of names he calls the players—*apes, antics, puppets, rude grooms, buckram gentlemen, peasants, painted monsters, weak stays*—indicates the depth of his anger (and loss of dignity). But despite the supposed lack of room to list all their wrongs, his diatribe against them in the end boils down to just one complaint: *remember Robert Greene, whom they have so often flattered, perishes now for want of comfort*. He had asked for money and they, for whatever reasons, had denied him.

Without any support, with none of his friends venturing into the city to visit him, and with only the limited hospitality of the Isams, Greene was reduced to miserably crying out for a cup of wine from his hostess. The swelling continued up his body, his neck and, in the end, his face. On 3 September he died. According to Gabriel Harvey, one of the first reporters on the scene, Mrs Isam took his death very hard and for his burial made him a garland that she laid on his head. The following day she and her husband took the corpse down to the new churchyard near Bethlehem Hospital, some ways south of the city, and had Greene's remains more economically interred there. The cost of his burial sheet was 4 shillings, the burial itself 6 shillings 4 pence. It indicates that even the humblest of funerals already cost the sizeable sum of 10s 4p (just over half a pound).

Though Greene would counsel the other playwrights to abandon the troupe, the forensic evidence would indicate that the remaining playwrights, Marlowe, Kyd and Peele continued working for Pembroke's Men. It is their voices that will continue to be heard in the stream of plays now to emerge—the conclusion to the civil war saga, *Richard III*, along with *The Comedy of Errors* (the two plays that may have been Pembroke's offerings at court that coming Christmas), and *Titus Andronicus* in the new year.

The printed record would eventually indicate that Robert Greene was right about his first claim – someone had indeed padded out their original play. As with the *Contention*, there are two versions of *The True Tragedy of Richard Duke of York*, which laid out side by side once again indicate what that new hand would bring to the board.

There are many editorial intrusions, the most surprising of which (for this observer) is the barrage of punctuation the new poet adds – commas, semi-colons, colons and periods – enough to add some 7 minutes to the running time. But this new hand understands the more paused delivery of nobles and especially royals and the added punctuation, when observed as described in the Prologue, allows these characters to sound more convincingly regal.

The sprinkling of textual intrusions on the whole indicates a higher level of satisfaction on the part of Shakespeare with regards to the work of the original committee, although the poet makes enough outright additions to add another forty minutes to the play's overall length. The intrusions begin to blacken the moment the first female steps unto the stage. The male writers, though all very good, could not, it appears, write a full-blooded female character to Shakespeare's satisfaction. The additions are marked in bold while stage directions and character names have been left untouched.

ORIGINAL VERSION	REWRITTEN VERSION
THE TRUE TRAGEDY OF RICHARD DUKE OF YORK	THE THIRD PART OF HENRY THE SIXTH WITH THE DEATH OF THE DUKE OF YORK
ll.196-229 ... Norfolk. And I'll to Norfolk with my followers.*Exit.* Montague. And I to the sea from whence I came. *Exit*	Act 1, scene 1, ll.208-273 ... Norfolk. And I to Norfolk with my followers. Montague. And I unto the Sea, from whence I came. Henry. **And I with grief and sorrow to the Court.**

Enter the *Queen* and the *Prince*.	*Enter the Queen.*
Exeter. My Lord here comes the Queen, I'll steal away	Exeter. Here comes the Queen, **Whose Looks bewray her anger:** I'll steal away.
King. And so will I.	Henry. **Exeter** so will I.
Queen. Nay stay, or else I follow thee.	Queen. Nay, **go not from me, I will** follow thee.
King. Be patient gentle Queen, and then I'll stay.	Henry. Be patient gentle Queen, and I will stay.
Queen. What patience can there? ah timorous man, Thou hast undone thyself, thy son, and me, And given our rights unto the house of York. Art thou a king and wilt be forced to yield? Had I been there, the soldiers should have tossed Me on their lances points, before I would have Granted to their wills. The Duke is made Protector of the land: Stern Falconbridge Commands the narrow seas. And thinkest thou then To sleep secure? I here divorce me Henry From thy bed, until that Act of Parliament Be recalled, wherein thou yieldest to the house of York The Northern Lords that have forsworn thy colours, Will follow mine if once they see them spread, And spread they shall unto thy deep disgrace. Come son, let's away and leave him here alone.	Queen. Who can be paient in such extremes? Ah **wretched man, would I had died a Maid? And never seen thee, never borne thee Son, Seeing thou hast proved so unnatural a Father. Hath he deserved to loose his Birthright thus? Hadst thou but loved him half so well as I, Or felt that pain which I did for him once, Or nourished him, as I did with my blood; Thou wouldst have left thy dearest heart-blood there, Rather than have made that savage Duke thine Heir, And disinherited thine only Son.**
	Prince. **Father, you cannot disinherit me: If you be King, why should not I succeed?**

Henry. **Pardon me Margeret, pardon me sweet Son,**
The Earl of Warwick and the Duke enforced me.

Queen. **Enforced thee?** Art thou King, and wilt be forced?
I shame to hear thee speak: ah timorous **Wretch,**
Thou hast undone thyself, thy Son, and me,
And given unto the House of York **such head,**
As thou shalt reign but by their sufferance.
To entail him and his Heirs unto the Crown,
What is it, but to make thy Sepulchre,
And creep into it far before thy time?
Warwick is Chancellor, and the Lord of Callice,
Stern Falconbridge commands the Narrow Seas,
The Duke is made Protector of the **Realm,**
And yet shalt thou be safe? Such safety finds
The trembling Lamb, environed with Wolves.
Had I been there, which am a silly Woman,
The soldiers should have tossed me on their **Pikes,**
Before I would have granted to **that Act.**
But thou preferst thy Life, before thine Honour. And seeing thou dost, I here divorce **myself,**
Both from thy **Table** Henry, and thy Bed,
Until that Act of Parliament be **repealed,**
Whereby my **Son is disinherited.**
The Northern Lords, that have foresworn thy Colours,
Will follow mine, if once they see them spread:
And spread they shall be, to thy foul disgrace,
And utter ruin of the House of York.
Thus do I leave thee: Come Son, let's away,
Our Army is ready; come, we'll after them.

King. Stay gentle Margaret, and hear me speak.	Henry. Stay gentle Margaret, and hear me speak.
Queen. Thou hast spoke too much already, therefore be still.	Queen. Thou hast spoke too much already: **get thee gone.**
King. Gentle son Edward, wilt thou stay with me?	Henry. Gentle Son Edward, thou wilt stay with me?
Queen. Aye, to be murdered by his enemies. *Exit.*	Queen. Aye, to be murthered by his Enemies.
Prince. When I return with victory from the field. I'll see your Grace, till then I'll follow her. *Exit.*	Prince. When I return with victory to the field, I'll see your Grace: till then, I'll follow her.
	Queen. Come Son away, we may not linger thus.
King. Poor Queen, her love to me and to the prince her son, Makes her in fury thus forget herself. Revenged may she be on that accursed Duke. Come cousin of Exeter, stay thou here, For Clifford and those Northern Lords be gone I fear towards Wakefield, to disturb the Duke.	Henry. Poor Queen. **How love to me,** and to her Son, **Hath** made **her break out into terms of Rage**. Revenged may she be on that **hateful** Duke, **Whose haughty spirit, winged with desire, Will cost my Crown, and like an empty Eagle, Tire on the flesh of me, and of my Son, The loss of those three Lords.** I'll write unto them, and entreat them fair; Come Cousin, **you shall be the Messenger.**
	Exeter. **And I, I hope, shall reconcile them all.** *Exit*

Given that her Majesty was about to arrive at the countess's home of Ramsbury for a processional visit this August of 1592, a longer, more discerning *Richard Duke of York* would make perfect sense. The countess understood what it meant to have all things ready for the queen. The wash of history we have considered thus far would indicate that of all the people involved with Pembroke's Men, it was, as Greene suggests, a woman, in particular their patron Mary Sidney, who was far and away the best positioned to be that final copy editor with the discretionary power to change anything not yet meeting royal expectations. What Breton had hinted with his alchemical-allegorical depiction of the countess as the lapis appears to have been spilling out now into the working scripts. Indeed the changes made to the play of *Richard* did imbue it with glimmers of silver and gold not present in the original.

CHAPTER 6

Is It Mary?

In his exchange with the players, Greene had learned that someone had rewritten at least one of the Pembroke scripts. Greene's *Tiger's heart* allusion brings into the same timeframe – August of 1592 – the three texts that contain a form of the line. There is first of all the play, *The True Tragedy of Richard Duke of York* (as this was printed in 1595 but assumed to have been first written and acted over the 1591-92 season). Next would come the rewritten version by the new, Shakespearean hand (as this would appear as *The Third part of King Henry the Sixth* in the First Folio of 1623). And last would come Greene's letter, which by its knowledge of the overwriting has to follow the other two.

Aside from Greene's probing the city's criminal underclass (in that series of conny-catcher pamphlets he had produced this past year), there was also his acute stylistic sensitivity (as evidenced by his twelve years of often writing in other men's styles), his outright knowledge of the play in question, his participation in the Pembroke company almost from the beginning, not to forget his contempt for the players generally. This would all have made of him one of the Stratford man's very sharpest of tests, if indeed William Shakspere was only posing as the author of the changes. If Greene had thought Shakspere was the author then Greene should have reacted to the writing, but this he does not do. What he would only impart to his fellow playwrights was his take on the authorship question: look for a woman behind this man. We could dismiss Greene as a sick and intemperate witness and be done with it if what he lets slip were not so convincingly corroborated by all we have already seen. A further test awaits us now.

We have reconstructed all that is known of William Shakspere's life up to the time of this first Shakespearean unfolding and have suggested there is a gap. The education and experience of life we have found for him would not, on their own, have prepared him to do what the new hand specifically does. This is not for a moment to propose that a man coming from Shakspere's background could not be a poet, even a great poet, only that he would not be a poet in the specific ways that Shakespeare is. History indicates that the man from Stratford was a poet for which we have the two funerary verses from the end of his life (considered in the opening pages of this volume) as well as the report of a third verse in connection with his problems with Sir Thomas Lucy. The two surviving poems do, by their generally earthier tone and outlook, find a great deal of resonance with what we have found of the Stratford man's life so far. But they indicate that even at the end of his life, Shakspere himself had not yet attained that subtlety of thought or meticulous musicality that are the hallmarks of everything the poet, Shakespeare, will write.

But the patron of the troupe, Mary Sidney, the Countess of Pembroke, had the interest, the motivation, the skill as well as the means specifically to do what Shakespeare would now do. And with her Majesty's impending arrival at her north Wiltshire manor of Ramsbury here in August of 1592, Mary Sidney would have had an immediate and genuine motive for applying what she had learned these past five years to the text of *Richard Duke of York* in order to bring the play up to royal expectations.

Now any person proposed as a solution to the Shakespeare authorship question must inevitably appear before 'the tribunal of good sense' where it must be demonstrated that the candidate's life corroborates exactly everything that will spike in Shakespeare's now well-defined authorial profile. Although William Shakspere's case, when considered in this way, is far from persuasive, anyone who would take the mantle from him will have to be satisfactory in every regard. Although many alternates have been proposed (Francis Bacon, Edward de Vere, Christopher Marlowe, etc.), not one of these lives can do that to the satisfaction of the scholarship. But the Countess of Pembroke's pre-Shakespearean life does provide, I believe, that clear and exact corroboration that would suggest hers is a candidature worthy of further, ongoing research.

Mary Sidney was born on 27 October 1561 at Tickenhill Palace (the former home of Prince Arthur and later of Princess Mary, the Catholic Tudor). Tickenhill sat on a hillside overlooking the town of Bewdley in Shropshire, England. (As happenstance would have it, Bewdley was only thirty miles northwest of Stratford.) Mary Sidney was thus born 2½ years before William Shakspere. At the other end she would outlive him by some 5½ years. (Master Shakspere and the countess would be buried beside different arms of the Avon River!)

In their respective experiences of life, however, it was Mary Sidney who got what we might term the 'Shakespearean upbringing'. The year before her birth Queen Elizabeth had named her father, Sir Henry Sidney, to the post of Lord President of Wales. Mary's father was hence the governor of Wales as well as the four adjoining English counties known as the Welsh marches. Brilliant and hard-working though he may have been in his service to the queen, young Mary's place at court (as did his) came through her mother, Mary Dudley. She was the daughter of John Dudley, the Earl of Warwick and the Duke of Northumberland, whom Queen Mary had executed for his too-eager role in placing Lady Jane Grey on the throne. And she was the sister of Robert Dudley, the Earl of Leicester, who now occupied that space next to the throne that her father had in the court of King Edward VI.

Mary Sidney's parents were married the year before King Edward's death and both had played roles in the abortive nine-day reign of Queen Jane I. Both had had to plead for their lives once Catholic Mary Tudor came to the throne. Mary Sidney's mother's brothers, Robert and Ambrose Dudley, were put in the Tower where the Princess Elizabeth briefly joined them. Robert Dudley and the princess may have fallen in love here, though some say they were already enamoured. Throughout Queen Mary's reign this emotional bond between Princess Elizabeth and the dashing, young duke's son blossomed. With Queen Mary's death in 1558, Elizabeth came to the throne and immediately made Lord Robert her Master of the Horse, his brother Ambrose, the Master of the Armoury, and then two years later their sister's husband, Sir Henry Sidney, the Lord President of the Welsh Council. In the high politics of usurpation and beheadings, danger, love and ultimate success, the family stories already contain sufficient to fire a Shakespearean imagination.

The principality but especially the marches were full of old castles and, as her father's administration was obliged to hold court in the various towns of the jurisdiction, Mary Sidney would over the course of her childhood reside in many of them. Aside from his many official duties, her father was also an active member of that new group called the *antiquarians* who thought they could yet make a more complete reconstruction of their own English history if they could but gather together all the surviving documents. He was very active on the antiquarians' manuscript trail. Wherever he was posted, Sir Henry gathered the scattered records of his jurisdictions and, for the first time, placed them in purpose-built chambers. He owned copies of *Grafton's* and *Froisard's* chronicle histories of England. Later, after her Majesty had made him Lord Deputy of Ireland as well, Sir Henry had his Clerk of the Irish Council, Edmund Molineux, write all the parts of *Holinshed's Chronicles* touching on the history and conditions of Ireland. There was a concomitant interest in geography and cartography, which finds testimony in Sir Henry's support of John Gough's survey of Ireland and Christopher Saxton's mapping of Wales.

The Sidney parents took great care to give all their children a broad, exacting humanist education whose curriculum extended well beyond what the more humble village grammar school could then offer. Mary Sidney was lucky not only to be a part of the Tudor flowering in education for noble daughters, which had started in earnest earlier in the century, but, more significantly, to be the offspring of already highly literate parents (this at a time when literacy was still making first, tentative inroads in most families). In the birth-order, she followed in the footsteps of her studious older brother, Philip. The parents (along with the queen they served) had excelled in all the subjects such a schoolhouse then offered: religion, French, Latin, Italian, a little Greek and Hebrew, classical literature and history, geography, arithmetic and geometry, astronomy, needlework and music. As the Sidney parents were in direct service to the queen, their task would have been (as with so many parents of the time) to prepare their children eventually to take on those roles they were playing. To prepare her, Mary Sidney was educated according to the same royal curriculum. As her Majesty and her own parents had been rather gifted students, the bar the older generation set would already have stood high. Though the Sidney parents exercised lots of 'tough love', their children Philip and then Mary appear to have been naturally ready to exceed expectations.

In the teaching of religion, we note that the Sidney family account book shows a copy of Foxe's very Protestant *Book of Martyrs* purchased for each child. Shakespeare would later know this book intimately. Over the course of Mary's childhood, her uncle, Robert Dudley, patronised the printing of the Genevan edition of the Bible in England. This was a highly politicised version whose sidebar interpretations were full of Protestant radicalism. This is the edition we will find Mary Sidney working from in her later psalm metrification exercises. Though there are references to other English editions of the Bible in the poet's works, the allusions on the whole indicate that the Geneva Bible was part of Shakespeare's desk reference.

There was in the Sidney schoolhouse a heavy emphasis upon learning languages, and none more so than French. Mary's father, Sir Henry Sidney, had been trained at Prince Edward's castle school where he had excelled at French, later leading at least one English embassy to France for Queen Elizabeth. The Sidneys accounted themselves as having originally come to England out of France back in the reign of Henry II. The parents engaged native French speakers to teach the children. When Mary's brother, Philip, was presented at the French court in August 1572, he impressed his hosts with the native quality of his French. King Charles IX made Sidney a baron of the French realm and gave him the arms of 'the Swan', because the French equivalent, *cygnet* (pronounced seen-yay), was the closest the heralds could come to the Englishman's Frenchified name, *de Sideney* (pronounced de-see-de-nay). In London the Sidneys supported the French Huguenot church. During her later literary apprenticeship we find Mary Sidney demonstrating a translator's knowledge of the language. French will be the one contemporary foreign language with which Shakespeare, as we have already somewhat seen, will exhibit the greatest familiarity.

While all the children were thoroughly grounded in Latin, as may be expected, the language curriculum was further expanded to include Italian. Mary Sidney's mother, Mary Dudley, had been tutored privately in a home that would early celebrate the best Italy had to offer. She was one of the few ladies at court who could, like the queen herself, actually speak contemporary Italian. The Sidney parents again brought in native speakers to teach the children, including Lodowick Bryskett (the son of Italian Protestant refugees) and, again according to the family account books, one *Mistress Maria the Italian.* It appears Mary Sidney again exerted much early effort for her later apprenticeship works also show her making highly competent translations from Italian into English. John Aubrey would in the next century report having seen the great library at Wilton built by the countess in her time. His eyes were particularly mesmerized by the substantial collection of Italian books–*all their poets,* he excitedly noted. Aside from exhibiting an apparent ability to read contemporary Italian novels in the original, Shakespeare will later make Italy the overall favourite place of the dramatic imagination.

In the matter of music, the family account books record that young Mary was instructed in the lute and virginal, receiving a new lute for her 10th birthday. Given that her Majesty took her own considerable musical skills very seriously, we can imagine the standard the girl had to work towards. Later Shakespeare will demonstrate a musician's quipping familiarity with musical terms, instruments and concepts.

Although Mary Sidney's uncle Robert came within a hair's breath of marrying the queen on a couple of occasions, her Majesty, who was fearful of losing her primacy, had always found reason to jerk back. But Queen Elizabeth's emotional need to have Lord Robert nearby would never entirely leave her, he in the end being her one true love. It must be said of him that though he was always ready to serve his queen reasonably faithfully, his ardent desire to marry only lasted so long as the queen remained within her childbearing years (until approximately 1578). But these would be the years of Mary Sidney's childhood and first coming to court. The special, never-to-be-consummated dynamic between Dudley and the Queen created the circumstances in which the trappings of romance could play some visible, ongoing role.

Although young Mary's family patronised a broad range of books in these early years, in the beginning when the queen and Dudley's passions were most ardent, they were instrumental in opening the native print culture to the more aggressive kind of romance literature found in Ovid and some more recent authors out of Italy and France. This would suddenly open the envelope of what was considered 'acceptable reading' at the time.

Up to 1564 Arthur Golding had been tutor to his nephew, Edward de Vere, the 17th Earl of Oxford, an irascible and at times violent boy whose service Golding appears glad to have left. In December of 1564 Golding's momentous translation of Ovid's *Metamorphosis* appeared as a New Year's gift to his new patron, Robert Dudley. Although these stories of change and transformation were pagan in origin, Ovid's work (or so Golding argued) presented *outwardly most pleasant tales and delectable histories, and fraught inwardly with most pithy instructions and wholesome examples.* Golding found *favour and gentleness* at Dudley's hands and over the next three years brought *Metamorphosis* to eleven books. No classical volume (both in its original Latin and its Englished version here) would so fill Shakespeare's poetic imagination.

In 1566 William Painter, the Clerk of her Majesty's Armoury, published a collection of mostly very short tales called *The Palace of Pleasure*, which he dedicated to Mary Sidney's other uncle, Ambrose Earl of Warwick. As Master of the Armoury, Ambrose Dudley would already have been Painter's master. Its title page carried the Dudley device of 'the bear and ragged staff', indicating that his collection of tales had found acceptance well before printing. In his dedication to Dudley, Painter rhetorically asks: *To whom may be given a Theatre of the world, and stage of human misery, more worthily than to him that hath with comely gestures, wise demeanour, and orderly behaviour, been an actor in the same?* As these tales were in large measure directed at a female readership, Painter likewise compliments Warwick's new wife, Anne Russell, *whose courteous and countess-like behaviour glistereth* [GLISTENS] *in court amongst the troupe of most honourable dames.* Of significance, we find among its 66 short tales the stories of Lucrece, Coriolanus, Timon of Athens, and Gileta of Narbonne, all of which will later be spun out by Shakespeare into original poetry and plays. Books of this sort would have provided a young reader like Mary Sidney with a wide, Shakespearean sweep of Mediterranean characters, place-names and plot devices. That this led her in later life, if her library is to be believed, to procure copies of the original Italian sources would all be in line with Shakespearean expectations.

Similarly, Geoffrey Fenton, a well-travelled 28 year-old agent for Sir Henry Sidney residing in Paris, had published in 1567 a number of liberal translations of the romance stories of Bandello as *Certain Tragical Discourses.* He dedicated the book to Mary Sidney's mother, Lady Mary Dudley, whom he compliments on her *sincere and devout order of living, held up as a looking glass to behold.* Out of one of its stories would come the subplot of Shakespeare's *Othello.*

The writers obviously had the young and old, the males and females in mind. Painter writes that these tales of *unlawful love, and the foul practices of the same* which *being thoroughly read and well considered, both old and young may learn to avoid the ruin, overthrow, inconvenience and displeasure, that lascivious desire and wanton will doth bring to their suitors and pursuers.* At the conclusion of his tale of the adulterous Pandora, Fenton writes: *Let also the young ladies and little girls learn to direct the course of their youth by the contrary of this example.* But despite their defensive moral underpinnings, the appearance of these stories, with their relatively open depictions of all sorts of abominable behaviour, while refreshing to some, alarmed others. Roger Ascham in *The Schoolmaster* (printed within months of both the *Discourses* and *Palace*) appears to have Painter and Fenton in mind when he rails against those *fond books, of late translated out of Italian into English, sold in every shop in London, commended by honest titles the sooner to corrupt honest manners, dedicated over boldly to virtuous and honourable personages, the easlier to beguile simple and innocent wits.* For Ascham these stories were enticements to ill living and a subversion of true religion. *What toys, the daily reading of such a book, may work in the will of a young gentleman, or a young maid, that liveth wealthily and idly, wise men can judge, and honest men do pity.*

The litterateurs, like Fenton, argued that reading must be broader than just the *noble acts of good men*, that only by exposure to wrongdoing would young men and women come to know *the utmost that vice promises to her followers.* Happily Mary Sidney's family liked these tales and all three writers—Golding, Painter and Fenton— were to thrive under their respective lords, although there would be 'more serious' books of a religious nature from two to follow in due order. (The Dudley-Sidneys may have been extreme Protestants but they were definitely not Puritans.) It goes some way to indicating that from the very start Mary Sidney was born into just that sort of book culture that sits so comfortably at the romantic heart of Shakespeare.

How that culture of romance affected the life of young Mary Sidney may be further adduced from a surviving artefact to come from that time that her uncle Robert was preparing for the queen's Kenilworth visit of 1575.

Philip Sidney Robert Dudley The Queen Katherine Dudley Henry Hastings

Mary Dudley Mary Sidney Anne Russell Ambrose Dudley

Untitled. Anonymous. Undated.

There is a painting remaining at Mary Sidney's childhood summer home of Penshurst Manor in Kent that shows the whole family together with the queen. On the basis of their relative ages and other circumstances, the painting appears to date back to 1572.

On the basis of the painting's style, it may have been the work of an unidentified painter who left similar canvasses of the French court surrounding the Duc d'Alençon (later King Henri III). We know that Mary Sidney's brother, Philip, started his tour of Europe in France and was in Paris the summer of 1572. Everywhere he went during his three-year European journey, young Sidney commissioned articles or enlisted men to go to England to help his uncle reshape Kenilworth Castle into the grand staging ground for what would be the most grandiloquent wedding proposal ever mounted by an Englishman. Given the £60,000 that was spent, this canvas before us here would have been no more than a bauble. If it was decided to hang it somewhere where her Majesty might see it, and she did stop long enough to take it in, the painting's underlying message would have been rather transparent to her.

At the centre of the circle there is a couple engaged in a lively, passionate dance. Her Majesty did love to dance. Elizabeth would have recognized herself in the radiantly beautiful woman who reaches above everyone else in the room. Below her stands her ever-dashing 40-year-old paramour, Robert Dudley, here ready 'to love and to hold'–her Majesty's ready support and steady anchor. And to this wooing dance Lord Robert has brought the members of his family. (In these times one married an extended family much more than a single individual.)

Just below the couple's gaze (to the right) is Lord Robert's sister, the radiant 27-year-old Katherine Dudley. Katherine and the queen were as close as sisters. When the man standing beside her, her 36-year-old husband, Henry Hastings, the Earl of Huntingdon, died in 1595, Katherine would move into the bedchamber next to Elizabeth's for the rest of the reign. (Childless Aunt Katherine adored the Sidney children.)

On a level with Katherine Dudley, on the other side of the canvas, her Majesty would have recognized Lord Robert's nephew (and Mary Sidney's older brother), 18-year-old Philip Sidney. If he appears unnaturally radiant in that darkened background, it is because his childless uncles, Robert and Ambrose, had both named him their heir. If it looks as if he is about to make a grand entrance, it is that once Philip returned from Europe in 1575, he would be formally presented to the queen (along with his sister, Mary, and his friend, Fulke Greville) and would then need employment from her Majesty. Well-educated, extremely well-read, impeccably groomed and mannered, highly talented if a tad high-strung, Philip had early amazed the members of his extended family who saw in him a perfection they themselves could not attain. Philip's features here emblematise the bright promise his life still holds.

Returning to the lower right, we find in the seated couple, the Sidney children's other uncle, 44-year-old Ambrose, the Earl of Warwick, and his wife the countess, Anne Russell (age unknown). She, too, was one of Elizabeth's favourite ladies-in-waiting. If Ambrose's ham and thigh appear pronounced, it is probably because her Majesty was known to have enjoyed his physical good looks. She liked to quip that on the basis of physique alone she would have chosen Ambrose over Robert!

Opposite, on the other side of the dance floor, we find Lord Robert's other sister and the Sidney children's mother, 41-year-old Mary Dudley. Despite her prominent place and size in the overall composition, her face is the only one not shown. Back in 1562 her Majesty had caught smallpox and Mary Dudley had unstintingly nursed the queen through the ordeal. As a result she caught the pox herself and was left so badly scarred that she ever after hid her face from public view with masks and veils. The emblem of the angel in the bench she sits on would have reminded her Majesty of sacrifices made.

And the bright, attentive little girl sitting in front of her would be her daughter, 11-year-old Mary Sidney. Although the girl is but a small presence in this greater constellation, her place, sitting as she does on the inner ring, is far from insignificant. She joins with the other women in blithely regarding the happy couple at the centre. (In sharp contrast, other than Robert Dudley, all the men in the room avert their gaze.) This sisterhood of powerful, educated and cultured women formed Mary Sidney's immediate role models, the women she was learning to emulate. Her physical place in the canvas then would indicate that she was already an accepted member of that circle. Shortly after Kenilworth we find Nicholas Breton's stepfather, George Gascoigne, writing this of Mary as part of the

Woodstock processional visit of 1575: *Though young in years, yet old in wit, a gest* [BEARING] *due to your face, / If you hold on as you begin, who is 't you'll not deface?* Her Majesty was known to appreciate strong intellects and would have found young Mary agreeable on this basis alone. The relationship between the monarch and the countess was founded then on years of first-person interactions. This would have made Mary an effective negotiator in the competition for playing dates at court when she becomes patron to the players in 1591.

Had Queen Elizabeth married Lord Robert, Mary Sidney and the rest of the people assembled here would have become England's new 'royal family'. This gives us some appreciation for just how much was at stake. Although the painting is no doubt a contrivance, an emblematic moment, it does nevertheless indicate that as far as her family and its courtly aspirations were concerned, Mary Sidney was to be pushed forward.

Looking back over those years before Mary Sidney joined her Majesty's train one is struck by the nature of the backdrop against which her early life unfolded. As the Lord President's daughter, Mary had spent the law terms from October to June primarily at Ludlow Castle but also in travelling along the law circuits to those castles and fortified manors (from Bewdley to the isle of Anglesey) where the English-Welsh court sat on a seasonal basis. As they travelled from town to town they would form a large procession made up of heralds, the sergeant-porter, the servants, squires, chaplains and clerks, the clerk of the council, the law sergeants, the judges, knights and peers, treasurers and secretaries, and then her father on his white steed. After him came the wagons and litters containing the ladies and children. Footmen, henchmen and guards surrounded all. The Elizabethan way of governing called for a show of pomp and power that would make an unassailable impression upon the people. The girl before us would grow up on the inside of this looking out. It is this same courtly point of view that will later inform all that Shakespeare will write.

Mary Sidney's early connection with Wales would be maintained throughout her life. Besides her later Welsh husband, Henry Herbert, and the many properties she would come to hold there through her marriage to him, his appointment to the Welsh Presidency after the death of her father would occasionally draw Mary Sidney back to Ludlow. Aside from an easy familiarity with the Welsh and their idiosyncrasies, Shakespeare will later also exhibit an animated Anglo-Celtic sympathy for the lives of the 'fairy folk', who will occupy many important stage roles to come.

Because of the success of his administration in Wales, Mary's father was simultaneously appointed Lord Deputy of Ireland in 1565 and the family would spend the next five years at Dublin Castle and about the Irish Pale. The experience of Ireland was to be much more militaristic, with Mary Sidney often witnessing the departure of her father at the head of large bodies of troops to endure sometimes difficult winter campaigns. Curiously, though there are statements about the hardships of winter campaigning, Shakespeare speaks from the point of view of the females left behind. Shakespeare would later express some sense of Irish matters and also exhibit an appreciable knowledge of military matters. Wilton would later also have a pronounced military side. Aubrey describes the armoury there in the next century as *a very long room ... very full where there were sufficient muskets, pikes, lances, and armour to dress sixteen thousand men, horse and foot.*

As the Lord President's and the Lord Deputy's daughter, Mary Sidney was close to one of the ablest statesmen in Elizabeth's realm, Sir Henry giving her throughout her childhood glimpses into the workings of a well-ordered, stage-sized court, at peace and at war, with all its attendant personages observing all that courtly protocol. Shakespeare would later come to the task of writing with a considered understanding of that kind of life, a keen awareness of what it meant to govern justly and an appreciation for just how heavy that can make a crown.

Young Mary Sidney's experience of these two jurisdictions reverberates with another of the more pronounced spikes in Shakespeare's later authorial profile. It has been noticed, especially by members of the legal professions, that Shakespeare had somewhere been able to pick up an appreciable knowledge of law. There is in the poet an easy command of legal language, an ability to depict courtroom drama, and a philosophical appreciation of how the law works as if the poet had had some meaningful, formative experience of it. In Mary Sidney's case, both Ludlow and Dublin had as their primary mandate to prosecute English law and there were gaols and courtrooms within the walls of both castles. These courtrooms were but several steps from the front door of her family's apartments and would have potentially offered her a daily diet of living courtroom drama. The English judges had their apartments within the castle walls. During the day they were joined by noisy swarms of lawyers, witnesses and family drawn to the various proceedings. The great hall brought the whole administration together for the midday meal. There were also gallows, which at Ludlow stood just below the Sidneys' apartments. Sir Henry Sidney was a keen apologist for the rule of law. The chronicler Hooker relates the arrival of the Sidney family at Dublin on 13 January 1566. *When he* [SIR HENRY] *received the Sword* [OF STATE], *he made an eloquent Speech, setting forth what a precious Thing good Government is, and how all Realms, Commonwealths, Cities, and Countries do flourish and prosper, where it is maintained.* Mary's father understood the importance of precedence in the prosecution of law and at both castles gathered the battered court records together and, as with the administrative records, built archives for them, as much to improve their accessibility as to prevent their further deterioration. In both jurisdictions he had had (again for the first time) all new legislation printed and distributed, indicating there may have been printing shops at both castles. It gives some sense of his forward-looking mind, an inspiration to the children he was so carefully nurturing.

On top of whatever experiences of the law her childhood among judges (and lawyers) may have given her, Mary Sidney's legal education would be augmented in a highly particular way by her marriage to Henry Herbert in 1577. Her portion in the marriage was jointure for life in a large portfolio of properties covering parts of Dorset, Wiltshire, Devon, Glamorgan and Monmouth. As mentioned, together these produced the extraordinary annual income of £1,000 for the countess's personal use. As landlady to hundreds of families, Mary Sidney would have had before her examples of the entire range of legal agreements that governed landlord-tenant relations in the Elizabethan age. And it is this particular slice of the law over which Shakespeare will later exhibit the greatest mastery!

Her brother Philip also had an interest in the law, in which study he recruited his squire, the law student Abraham Fraunce, to be his tutor. After Philip's death, Fraunce's *Lawyer's Logic,* recognized by the scholarship as one of the key texts to shape Shakespeare's formal legal logic, was composed and first taught at Wilton.

Though their responsibilities kept the Sidneys at their posts in Wales and Ireland, there were breaks in the year during which by sea and land they would travel to wherever the court happened to be. Right from the beginning of the reign, the Sidney family made every effort to spend Christmas at court, where Mary's father familiarly became *Harry* to her Majesty. They were privileged to be part of her Majesty's 'Christmas family'. Usually several plays, often by the troupes patronized by Mary Sidney's Dudley uncles were part of the twelve-day Christmas festivities. Mary Sidney would have come to the responsibilities of theatrical patronage in 1591 with an historical appreciation for what Christmas at court entailed. She would be part of that family right to the end of the reign in 1603.

In 1564 Sir Henry Sidney had been inducted into the Knights of the Garter, England's highest order of knighthood, and the annual Garter celebrations at Windsor became another part of the family's itinerary. Later Shakespeare will write a 'Garter comedy' called *The Merry Wives of Windsor* where the poet presents an outrageous satire of one of the other Garter families who stood in opposition to the Sidneys for some important posts at court. (As they will so often do in Shakespeare's imagined world, it is the women who in the end prevail!)

Wherever the Sidneys were over the course of Mary's childhood, the three-month summer recess was generally spent at their manor of Penshurst in Kent. It lay only thirty miles south of London. Kent was said to offer the most pleasant summers in England. Young King Edward VI had bequeathed the four thousand acre estate onto Mary's grandfather, Sir William Sidney, who had been Edward's nursery guardian and later household steward. As the prince's mother, Jane Seymour, had died twelve days after his birth, it was Mary's Sidney grandparents, father and aunts who became the prince's surrogate family. But of these it was Mary's father who became inseparably close to Edward. The two appear to have been temperamentally well suited. The young king would die in Sir Henry's arms.

The device that Grandfather Sidney created for the family's coat-of-arms, readily evident at Penshurst and other places where the Sidneys left their mark, was the pheon. This broad, barbed bolt, when affixed to a shaft, made for a deadly instrument of war. Sir William undoubtedly had seen many of these over the course of his early military career. But by turning the spearpoint earthwards it had made a form of the first letter of his name, W. In the presentation of her own identity, Mary Sidney would all her life closely identify with this emblem, that despite everything else, she was first and foremost a Sidney. Within it we already find a **W**, a William, a W.S. and the better part of a spear!

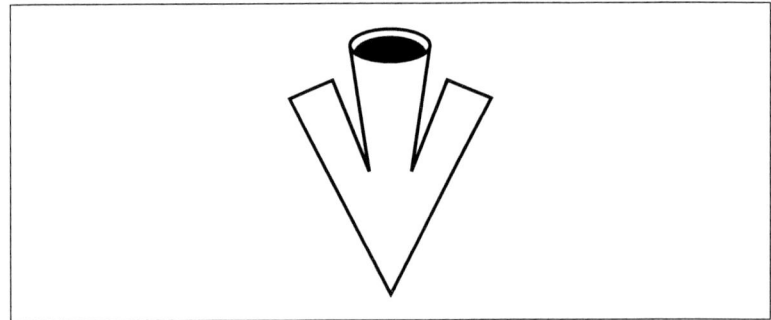

The Sidney pheon

After the death in early 1575 of Mary's younger sister, Ambrosia Sidney, her Majesty wrote to offer condolences and to say that Mary could come to court to continue her education under her care. Over the period 1575-77 while Mary Sidney was one of her Majesty's Maids of Honour, she had the experience of living in close quarters with the queen for an uninterrupted duration. The maids stood high in the pecking order and enjoyed daily contact with the queen. They spent parts of the day in the Privy Chamber where her Majesty received petitioners and ambassadors in their presence. It would have given Mary Sidney a direct view of the workings of government at the highest level. The queen regularly took the maids for brisk walks. Happily Elizabeth was a highly literate woman and there were libraries and time set aside for daily reading in all the palaces she inhabited. Much of the day the maids continued their education. After supper finished at 6, evenings were given over to chapel, ensemble music making, dancing, and embroidery. Some evenings there was a play. The maids enjoyed free room and board plus £40 a year.

Although Mary Sidney already had a long experience of theatre as that was practiced in her father's court as well as before her Majesty, as a maid she would have had uninterrupted access to all the tableau-, masque- and play-making to come before the queen, at court and on progress, over the course of seven seasons. While Mary Sidney lived at Westminster, up in Shoreditch her uncle's troupe, Leicester's Men, were building the Theatre, the first public playhouse. One of the last plays she saw as a maid was *The History of Error* (1577), which on the basis of its title alone has often been thought a possible precursor for Shakespeare's *The Comedy of Errors*.

Elizabeth could be harsh with those of her maids who wished to marry but Mary Sidney's proposed marriage to the very much older Earl of Pembroke in 1577 appears to have ruffled no feathers with her. The countess's seasonal visitations to court continued much as they had before. In 1580, at the age of 18, Mary Sidney entered a five-year period in which she bore four children. Despite her many maternity absences, the bond between sovereign and subject appears to have remained strong. We note that in 1583 the queen gave Philip Sidney a lock of her hair to give to his sister, a special mark of favour. Although no reason immediately appears in the record, the countess would bear no further children after 1584. She was then still only 23 years old.

After the deaths of her parents and brother Philip in 1586, Mary Sidney remained at home for almost two years. Although she already carried within her a rich array of experiences pertinent to the poet's craft, that muse of hers may have been allowed to slumber had it not been so ruefully, painfully and extraordinarily aroused by the death of her brother and then the arrival of her brother's all-knowing squire. These appear as the events that precipitated the radical redirection in the young countess's life. By her brother's example and Master Fraunce's guidance, Mary Sidney learned all the basics pertinent to the poet's craft. It was a happy synergy – as her children were at their lessons, the countess could delve into her own further development.

The Armada scare of summer 1588 brought members of the extended Sidney family together at Wilton. The Spanish disaster appears to have invigorated the countess. (As Sir Philip had been felled by a Spanish bullet, anti-Spanish feeling would remain high at Wilton for decades to come.) While her husband, the Earl of Pembroke, and his mounted knights rode north to plunder Spanish shipwrecks, she and the rest of her household prepared a grand processional entry into Westminster for the Queen's Accession Day celebrations in November. The Spanish ambassador reported back to Madrid: *On Thursday the wife of the earl of Pembroke made a superb entrance into this city. She has been for more than a year on her estates in the country. Before her went 40 gentlemen on horseback, two by two, all very finely dressed with gold chains. Then came a coach in which was the Countess and a lady, then another coach with more ladies, and after that a litter containing the children, and four ladies on horseback. After them came 40 or 50 servants in her livery with blue cassocks.* This event appears to signal that Mary Sidney was ready to step into the breech left by her Uncle Robert's death two months earlier. But those blue cassocks would suggest she went to court as a Sidney, not a Dudley or a Herbert.

Over the course of the next year the countess delved into those translations of Petrarch's Italian and Garnier's French, the edges of which we have considered. The manner in which her broad metrical experiments funnel into a singular interest in drumming iambic meter would indicate that she, too, fell under the sway of Marlowe's poetic revolution well before she became patron to the players.

As Mary Sidney was made unhappy with Fulke Greville's edition of *Arcadia*, presenting the story in its unfinished state, she and the other scholars of Wilton had since 1590 begun to create what would turn out to be a 250-page ending for Philip's novel. They did it by reworking material out of the first version of *Arcadia* Philip had written for his sister ten years before. The countess edited the finished Books I-III as well, deliberately deleting, for example, the less moral actions of the princes. She betrays in this the same bias towards royal rectitude that Shakespeare will in rewriting the Pembroke playscripts. And, significantly, it indicates that not even her brother's work was above being 'corrected' by her – as if all really were now under her gaze. As this Arcadian project went forward, the piracy of September 1591 appears to have forced Mary

Sidney into a reconsideration of Philip's sonnets as well. The version printer Newman republished early in 1592 came with hundreds of editorial changes, all of them of a nature that would suggest her intercession. Editing and rewriting Philip's *Arcadia* and sonnets would have drawn Mary Sidney into a very deep, word-by-word, line-by-line reconsideration of all her brother had written. If Mary is Shakespeare then this would explain why Philip's Arcadian spirit so indelibly permeates all of Shakespeare's early original comedies like *The Comedy of Errors, Love's Labours Lost, The Two Gentlemen of Verona*, and will then rebound regularly throughout the entire Shakespeare corpus.

And then in May of 1592 the countess began to write under the influence of a new poet in her household, Samuel Daniel, whose full contribution to the Shakespeare saga will be one of the subjects of my next volume. The three most important contemporary English influences on Shakespeare's style here at the beginning will later be judged to have been the poets Sidney, Daniel and Spenser. If Mary is Shakespeare then we can see how and why this is so.

Given her family's long commitment to theatre at court alongside her own long personal experience of it, it seems logical that when the countess became patron to the players in 1591 she would want to bring them before her Majesty as her family had done in the decades before. By the time that first opportunity arose in August of 1592, Mary Sidney would have had a strong sense of what it took to please her Majesty from the stage. This experience would have been invaluable to someone overlooking the scripts of her players in anticipation of such a royal visit. It is no stretch imagining the countess, with her cultured background, obvious motivation, heightened literary sensibilities and quickly-evolving editing skills, being tempted to give those scripts of her players a final tweak. Although the limitations placed on what women could do during the Tudor century were generally more liberal than they would become in Jacobean times, they were still far more constrained than they would be in later modern society. In the matter of writing, while Mary Sidney was doing 'pious' psalm metrifications (as quilt pieces) she was unassailable. Her exact, though rhetorically amplified, translations of works by continental male authors may have raised some eyebrows but, being well done and the subjects being serious, they appear to have garnered only admiration. The labours she was bestowing upon finishing the *Arcadia* moved her unto fuzzy territory although the circumstances – doing what she could to mend her brother's broken legacy with the help of a number of upright, scholarly men living in her household – should have deflected any criticism. But for her to begin refining the works of (not always reputable) men like Greene, Marlowe, Kyd, Nashe and Peele – works first destined for the common stage – would potentially have left many feeling very uneasy. Even after Nashe had only hinted at her too great interest in the playwriting process (the *old goose* incubating six *pottle pots*), the defence mounted by Fraunce and Breton was to deflect any *impiety* by presenting Lady Mary as a parallel to Mary, the mother of Jesus, or Mary Magdalene, Jesus' companion. But Breton had taken matters a step further, giving Mary Sidney by a strange alchemy the power to make that literary gold that had formerly been her brother's domain.

There were other examples of nobles helping along the stage material destined first and foremost for royal performance. In his heyday in the 80's, when he was royal overseer of the children's companies, the Earl of Oxford had padded (quite successfully, it is reported) the scripts of the comedies written by John Lyly and others that the children performed at court and in the public halls. But they had undone themselves during the Martin Marprelate crisis and the 1590 suppression of the children's companies opened the court calendar for the adult troupes. That first Christmas at court after Martin, the Queen's Men predominated. At Christmas 1591 it was the newly amalgamated Strange-Admiral company which took the majority of the playing dates. But with the Queen's Men starting to falter, perhaps there was a chance for the newcomers, the Earl of Pembroke's Men, that Christmas of 1592.

The Pembrokes' north Wiltshire manor of Ramsbury lay in the path of the queen's progress that summer of 1592. The court appears to have arrived around 25 August and left around the 29th. Little immediate record of the visit remains. However, in the matter of court appearances, we surmise that Pembroke's Men were successful for they would receive half the playing dates at court that coming Christmas.

There remains one small piece of comedy that appears to have been performed before her Majesty during the visit. Happily it survived in Francis Davison's 1602 Pembrokian miscellany, *A Poetical Rhapsody*. There we find *A Dialogue Between Two Shepherds, Thenot and Piers, in Praise of Astrea*. Its subtitle reads: *Made by the excellent Lady, the Lady Mary, Countess of Pembroke, at the Queen's Majesty's Being at Her House at   , Anno* [IN THE YEAR] 15 . Although Davison would suppress some of the crucial details, the visit to Ramsbury would, in fact, turn out to be the only processional visit to a Pembroke home during that part of Elizabeth's reign that Mary Sidney was the countess. The visit of August 1592 then becomes the most likely occasion of its performance. Its contents would strongly suggest this is so.

The dialogue consists of ten short exchanges between two shepherds, *Thenot* and *Piers*. While *Thenot* would find words with which to offer just praise to *Astrea* (the mythological goddess of Justice who here stands for Elizabeth), his clever opponent in the match, young *Piers*, with schoolboy glee would contradict him at every turn. Her Majesty may have recalled *Thenot* from Spenser's *Shepherd's Calendar* where the old shepherd had told the tale of 'the oak and the briar' to instruct a young, dismissive herder's boy named *Cuddy*. The tale *Thenot* there tells is of an impetuous young bramble who requests the lord of the field to cut down a royal oak withered with age. Once done the bramble suddenly finds itself cruelly exposed to the elements. This little fable bears down heavily on Mary Sidney's intentions here before the queen in her ongoing skirmish with Thomas Nashe. For now rather than *Cuddy* accompanying *Thenot* (as in Spenser's original), it is *Piers* who is the rude, clever boy. Although Nashe's *Pierce Penniless*, with its attack on the memory of Robert Dudley, would not be released for another week, word was probably already circulating. However the name is written – Pierce or Piers – the sound remains the same. The last three exchanges of the dialogue presented before the queen are as follows:

...

Thenot. As heavenly light that guides the day, 43
 Right so doth shine each lovely Ray,
 That from Astrea flieth.

Piers. Nay, darkness oft that light enclouds,
 Astrea's beams no darkness shrouds
 How loudly Thenot lieth [LIES]!

Thenot. Astrea rightly term I may,
 A manly Palm, a Maiden Bay,
 Her verdure [GREENERY] never dying.

Piers. Palm oft is crooked, Bay is low,
 She still upright, still high doth grow,
 Good Thenot leave thy lying.

Thenot. Then Piers, of friendship tell me why,
 My meaning true, my words should lie,
 And strive in vain to raise her.

Piers. Words from conceit [FANCIFUL EXPRESSION] do
 only rise,
 Above conceit her honour flies;
 But silence, nought [NOTHING] can
 praise her. 60

If the allegory holds, then *Thenot* would stand for the countess who by her actions would only seek to praise her Majesty with just words. *Piers* would stand for Nashe who would negate the countess's actions with nothing but funny, clever, contradictory words. But the countess would give Nashe a purge here before the queen by leading him to his own natural conclusion—that only silence could then truly praise their sovereign. Might that persuade the queen!

Her Majesty, as *Astrea* goddess of justice, would now have to sit in judgment. Should the young, cocky, intriguing and always funny Thomas Nashe, whose wit had served her Majesty's needs so well during the Marprelate mayhem, be allowed further free reign or should he be, as the countess here suggests, brought to heel? (As my next volume will demonstrate, Nashe would keep his freedom and continue his little war on the House of Pembroke throughout the fall and winter with no action being taken against him until later in 1593.)

With *Thenot and Pierce* the countess indicates that in that satirical vein she could engage as well as the next quipping poet, even if her place at court (having the monarch's direct ear) would eliminate her need to 'shout'. That *Thenot* shows us Mary Sidney writing in an original comic vein is something we have not met with elsewhere in her apprenticeship works. That she could exercise this vein with such seeming familiarity before the queen betrays a well-established relationship between them even if *Piers and Thenot* indicates (significantly) that the countess had to petition the monarch just like everyone else. It further acknowledges the high level of protection that Nashe stood under.

Beside *Thenot and Piers*, there is another early piece that is entirely from Mary Sidney's own mind and hand. It is the dedicatory poem that she prefixed to her first version of the completed book of psalms. Called *To the Angel Spirit of the most excellent Sir Philip Sidney*, it remains a beautiful, heartfelt elegy that describes the special place her brother held in all her actions. Although it is but a small sample, it gives us again a sense of which way her voice would go if it were free to express its own mind – just as Shakespeare would be free with *Richard Duke of York*.

Although the verses of *Angel Spirit* are 7 lines long, they depart from rhyme royal by their *abbabba* rhyme scheme. But in their lines they again offer a good sampling of Mary Sidney's handling of iambic pentameter. As Shakespeare's additions to *Richard Duke of York* are also in iambic pentameter, the two provide us with something of a level surface on which to compare them and to ask if the hand that wrote the one could also have written the other.

MARY SIDNEY. TO THE ANGEL OF THE MOST EXCELLENT SIR PHILIP SIDNEY (75 LINES)	SHAKESPEARE'S WHOLE-LINE CONTRIBUTIONS TO RICHARD DUKE OF YORK (FIRST 75 EXAMPLES)
To thee pure Spirit, to thee alone addressed Is this joint work, by double interest thine, Thine by his own, and what is done of mine Inspired by thee, thy secret power impressed. My Muse with thine itself dared to combine As mortal staff with that which is divine: Let thy fair beams give lustre to the rest. That Israel's King may deign his own transformed In substance no, but superficial tire [ATTIRE]: And English guised in some sort may aspire To better grace thee what the vulgar formed: His sacred tones age after age admire Nations grow great in pride and pure desire So to excel in holy rites performed. O had that soul which honour brought to rest Too soon not left and reft [BEREAVED] the world of all. What man could show which we perfection call, This precious piece had sorted with the best. But ah! wide-festered wounds that never shall Nor must be closed, unto fresh-bleeding fall, Ah memory, what needs this new arrest? Yet blessed grief that sweetness can impart Since thou art blessed. Wrongly do I complain, Whatever weights my heavy thoughts sustain Dear feels my soul for thee. I know my part Nor be my weakness to thy rites a stain – Rights to aright, life-blood would not refrain: Assist me then, that life what thine did part.	Cheered up the drooping Army, and himself, Richard hath best deserved of all my sons: The Queen this day here holds her Parliament, But little thinks we shall be of her counsel, By words or blows here let us win our right. And kneel for grace and mercy at my feet, For he that interrupts him, shall not live. Why whisper you, my Lords, and answer not? My Conscience tells me he is lawful King. I am content: Richard Plantagenet Enjoy the Kingdom after my decease. Farewell faint-hearted and degenerate King. In whose cold blood no spark of Honour bides. Turn this way Henry, and regard them not. And neither by Treason nor Hostility, To seek to put me down, and reign thyself. And I with grief and sorrow to the Court. And never seen thee, never borne thee Son, Seeing thou hast proved so unnatural a Father. Hath he deserved to loose his Birthright thus? Hadst thou but loved him half so well as I,

Time may bring forth what time hath yet
suppressed
In whom thy loss hath laid to utter waste
The wrack of time untimely all defaced,
Remaining as the tomb of life deceased:
Where, in my heart the highest room thou hast;
There, truly there, thy earthly being is placed
Triumph of death: in life how more than blessed

Behold, O that thou were now to behold,
This finished long perfection's part begun
The rest but pieced as left by thee undone,
Pardon, blessed soul, presumption overbold:
If love and zeal hath to this error run
'Tis zealous love, love that hath never done,
Nor can enough, though justly here controlled.

But since it hath no other scope to go,
Nor other purpose but to honour thee,
That thine may shine where all the graces be;
And that my thoughts (like smallest streams that flow,
Pay to their sea their tributary fee)
Do strive, yet have no means to quit nor free,
That mighty debt of infinites I owe

To thy great worth which time to times enrol
Wonder of men, sole born, soul of thy kind
Complete in all, but heavenly was thy mind,
For wisdom, goodness, sweetness, fairest soul:
Too good to wish, too fair for earth, refined
For Heaven, where all true glory rests confined;
And where but there no life without control.

O when from this account, this cast-up sum,
This reckoning made the audit of my woe,

Or felt that pain which I did for him once,
Or nourished him, as I did with my blood;
Thou wouldst have left thy dearest heart-blood there,
Rather than have made that savage Duke thine Heir,
And disinherited thine only Son.

Father, you cannot disinherit me:
If you be King, why should not I succeed?
Pardon me Margaret, pardon me sweet Son,
The Earl of Warwick and the Duke enforced me.

As thou shalt reign but by their sufferance.
To entail him and his Heirs unto the Crown,
What is it, but to make thy Sepulchre,
And creep into it far before thy time?
Warwick is Chancellor, and the Lord of Callice,

And yet shalt thou be safe? Such safety finds
The trembling Lamb, environed with Wolves.

But thou preferst thy Life, before thine Honour.

And utter ruin of the House of York.

Our Army is ready; come, we'll after them.

Come Son away, we may not linger thus.

Whose haughty spirit, winged with desire,
Will cost my Crown, and like an empty Eagle,
Tire on the flesh of me, and of my Son,
The loss of those three Lords torments my heart:
I'll write unto them, and entreat them fair

What is your quarrel? how began it first?

Sometime of rase [SCRAPING] my swelling passions know,	
How work my thoughts, my sense, is stricken dumb	Your right depends not on his life or death.
That would the more than words could ever show;	
Which all fall short. Who knew thee best do know	Now you are heir, therefore enjoy it now:
There lives no wit that may thy prayer become.	By giving the house of Lancaster leave to breathe,
	It will outrun you, father, in the end.
And rest fair monuments of thy fair fame,	
Though not complete. Nor can we reach, in thought,	No; God forbid your grace should be forsworn.
What on that goodly piece, time would have wrought.	
Had divers so spared that life (but life) to frame	I shall be, if I claim by open war.
The rest: alas such loss the world hath nought	
Can equal it, nor O more grievance brought,	I'll prove the contrary, if you'll hear me speak.
Yet what remains must ever crown thy name.	
	Thou canst not, son; it is impossible.
Receive these hymns, these obsequies receive,	
(If any mark of thy secret spirit thou bear)	That hath authority over him that swears:
Made only thine, and no name else must wear. I	
can no more dear soul, I take my leave,	Then, seeing 'twas he that made you to depose,
My sorrow strives to mount the highest sphere.	
	Your oath, my lord, is vain and frivolous.
	Therefore, to arms! And, father, do but think
	How sweet a thing it is to wear a crown;
	Within whose circuit is Elysium
	And all that poets feign of bliss and joy.
	Why do we finger thus? I cannot rest
	Until the white rose that I wear be dyed
	Even in the lukewarm blood of Henry's heart.
	And whet on Warwick to this enterprise
	And tell him privily of our intent.
	In them I trust; for they are soldiers,
	Witty, courteous, liberal, full of spirit.
	While you are thus employ'd, what resteth more,
	But that I seek occasion how to rise,
	And yet the king not privy to my drift,
	Nor any of the house of Lancaster?

	And therefore fortify your hold, my lord.
	Ay, with my sword. What! think'st thou that we fear them?

These two samples indicate rather more congruence than divergence. Given Mary Sidney's known and Shakespeare's surmised learnedness, there is surprisingly the same unique tendency towards one-syllable words, epitomized by the regular occurrence of ten-word iambic pentameter lines. These occur at about the same rate in both samples.

MARY SIDNEY	SHAKESPEARE
Thine by his own, and what is done of mine	By words or blows here let us win our right.
Too soon not left and reft the world of all	Hadst thou but loved him half so well as I,
Dear feels my soul for thee. I know my part.	Or felt that pain which I did for him once,
But since it hath no other scope to go,	Tire on the flesh of me, and of my Son,
Do strive, yet have no means to quit nor free,	How sweet a thing it is to wear a crown;
Which all fall short. Who knew thee best do know	Ay, with my sword. What! think'st thou that we fear them? [11 WORDS]
I can no more dear soul, I take my leave,	

Mary Sidney's *Angel Spirit* packs an average of 8.17 words per line. Shakespeare's rate would be relatively consistent over the course and average out at about 8.10. It indicates that the countess's pre-Shakespearean thumbprint lines up exactly with Shakespeare's in this regard.

Although the practice gently declined over the years, Shakespeare would be the greatest creator of hyphenated words of that age. True to that curve we find Mary Sidney's rate of compounding here in *Angel Spirit* exactly in line with Shakespearean expectations. The two texts above yield the examples of *wide-festered, fresh-bleeding* and *life-*

blood for Mary and *faint-hearted* and *heart-blood* for Shakespeare. Of further idiosyncratic note, both samples contain multiple examples of lines stopped mid-sentence, a sign of advanced poetic development.

MARY SIDNEY	SHAKESPEARE
Since thou art blessed. Wrongly do I complain,	I am content: Richard Plantagenet
Whatever weights my heavy thoughts sustain	Enjoy the Kingdom after my decease.
Dear feels my soul for thee. I know my part	And yet shalt thou be safe? Such safety finds
Nor be my weakness to thy rites a stain	The trembling Lamb, envi-roned with Wolves

One measure of the sophistication of the stage poet's craft was the ability to break beyond the bounds of the single iambic pentameter line unit in the depiction of thought or action. The trap to avoid was letting the line unit become the unit of thought. But both samples here overall strongly indicate that the problem with Mary Sidney as with Shakespeare goes completely the other way. In both samples there is a constant struggle to rope in the tumble of ideas that would quickly overtop the bounds of a line.

Would a woman capable of writing as well as this have needed to turn over that final grooming of her players' playscripts to that newcomer among her players, William Shakspere, when she herself demonstrably already possessed all the necessary skills, expertise, resources and sense of style to do what Shakespeare now does and will continue to do? The wash of history up to August of 1592, the month in which Robert Greene looked into the nature of the actor Shakspere's claim to authorship, would strongly indicate that Mary Sidney, the Countess of Pembroke, the patron of the company, was the *woman* Greene had in mind. As we shall discover over the next several volumes, this is how everyone afterwards would take things.

At heart, the countess had an enormous motive force behind her. Survivors who take up the causes of the fallen are often very driven people. *Angel Spirit,* like Breton's *Countess of Penbrooke's Love,* tells that Philip's *secret power* had *impressed* itself upon her, her *Muse* combining with his as *mortal staff with that which is divine.*

This marriage of heaven and earth permitted part of him to live on through her. Though he might be a *tomb* and *monument*, he now had life in *the highest room* of her heart – that 'phoenix nest'. Though hers was *presumption* (she only being a woman), she was driven by *zealous love, love that hath never done, / Nor can enough, though justly here controlled*. The *love* she feels has turned to endless labour and, just as Breton also describes it, that labour consisted of writing. Although Mary Sidney would early on here still cloak this action with the acknowledgment that she, as a woman, did work under restrictions (i.e. was *controlled*), when she later rewrote the poem she would strike this line out and replace it with something closer to her heart: *Nor can enough in world of words unfold*.

Once set free in that 'heavenly realm', not soon brought down! Though the literary remains suggest that her ladyship's writing career would abruptly end in 1593, another set of remains indicates Shakespeare's long writing career was just getting underway.

The test for Mary Sidney now becomes whether she by her presence can bring about a better understanding of the thirty-some years of archival matter related to Shakespeare to lie before us. In the present state of Shakespeare biographical studies, many documents alluding to the poet have had to be silently passed over because their intentions could no longer be deciphered. With Mary Sidney as a central part of the unfolding chronicle, we shall now have occasion to bring them all back for renewed consideration.

EPILOGUE

The Chronicle Before Us

The prehistory and the first year of the chronicle proper now lie behind us. It is the first crescent of the orb turning into a new day. Thirty-one more years lie before us awaiting our reconsideration. In this first year we have been able to establish Mary Sidney's proximity, motive, and means to do what Shakespeare will now continue to do. As she has never been made integral to any biography of Shakespeare while her place in those Shakespearean remains is indelible, a re-examination of events is, I believe, called for. I invite all readers who may be piqued by the question to engage with me in sifting through these Elizabethan as well as later Jacobean remains to find back all the facts that yet remain embedded in the bedrock. From this will emerge a much more reasonable *and* detailed presentation of the order of events.

In volume 2 of my own ongoing chronicle reconstruction I will continue with Thomas Nashe and consider what he had to say in the wake of Greene's death on the subject of Pembroke and Shakespeare. We shall meet Greene's literary executor, Henry Chettle, and determine his role in setting Greene's letter to the playwrights into print plus consider his apology later in the year for damages the letter had done. We shall find Marlowe addressing the countess in print this fall and consider his evolving role in the Pembroke play production process. We shall follow Pembroke's Men through their Welsh tour of fall 1592 leading up to their performances at court over Christmas 1592-93, and determine which of their plays would make the most sense within these two politically distinct performance spaces. We will consider what the remaining Pembroke playwrights – Marlowe, Peele and Kyd – did to continue the flow of such Shakespearean scripts as *The Comedy of Errors, Richard III* and *Titus Andronicus*. We will find the countess's *Antonius* in print and contextualise the book within the contemporary politics of England's relations with France. We shall meet the Cambridge academic-turned-reporter, Gabriel Harvey, and hear what he had to say on the authorship of the first Shakespeare work in print, *Venus and Adonis* (1593), and determine if he is right in his claim that this was the countess's lesson to Nashe on what the young satirist's failings were. We will consider the new poet at Wilton, Samuel Daniel, and determine just how sharp a Shakespearean focus his work there will have. We shall consider what Mary Sidney added to the rewritten *Arcadia* (when it is printed in the spring) and set that beside Shakespeare's early Arcadian passages. And as the political clouds darken over, we shall determine what the Shakespearean plays, *Titus Andronicus* and *Love's Labours Lost,* have to say in the context of the upheavals that will overtake the countess, her players, playwrights and dear Sir Walter Ralegh in the summer of 1593. But coming to her defence, we will meet with an exquisite collection of poetry written by a particular coterie of nobles and gentlemen whom we may dub 'the knights of the phoenix nest'. We shall set some further remarks by Harvey beside what is known of the sudden termination of Pembroke's Men and compare his claim of the countess's 'victory' with what is known of the establishment of the new company of actors, the Lord Chamberlain's Men. We shall consider what it would have meant for Shakespeare to enjoy the immediate protection of the palace. This will bring us to the beginning of 1594.

Placing Mary Sidney in the central position of the chronicle allows a more thorough and convincing sort of the record than has been possible up to now. Francis Bacon, whose case originally arose because of his and Shakespeare's purportedly similar legal backgrounds, is nowhere near the scene here and, as my next volume will indicate, was, in fact, allied to the rival camp of the young Earl of Essex. Today's frontrunner in the authorship debate, Edward de Vere, the Earl of Oxford, as my presentation here has already suggested, is some ten years out of sync with the Shakespeare chronology, his heyday already having come and gone by 1591. Perhaps the most compelling of the alternate Shakespeares proposed to date is Christopher Marlowe because of his proximity to the first unfolding of Shakespearean material. But as my presentation has indicated, he cannot possibly be Shakespeare for the simple reason that we have now found the two writing side-by-side.

I acknowledge that I am not the first person to have noticed the affinities between the Countess of Pembroke and the poet, Shakespeare, and I hope that all those with any insights into any part of the solution will come forth with whatever findings they have. A complete and impartial re-examination of the whole of what the Elizabethan and Jacobean archives contain on Shakespeare, from the prehistory to how it is all laid to rest in the end, is ultimately what is called for. Although I would not be presumptuous, I do realize that bringing a task of this magnitude to completion may, like the *Oxford English Dictionary* project, require the efforts of large numbers of readers and scholars willing to make the re-appraisal that produces a new consensus. My website **www.tiger-heart.com** offers information for all those who may be interested in joining this search.

Legend teaches that the phoenix lies in its ashen, dormant state half a millennium before being again aroused. The 500th anniversary of the first appearance of Shakespeare's hand on the stage gives us until the year 2092 to set to right any outstanding issues.

BIBLIOGRAPHY

AUTHOR'S ACKNOWLEDGMENTS.

Although her book does not appear in my bibliography, I caught my first glimpse of Mary Sidney and her multi-faceted role in Joy Hancox's *The Byrom Collection* (London: Jonathan Cape, 1992).

I must acknowledge three scholars without whose particular labours I would have been 'in the wilderness' a long time. There is first, Professor E. K. Chambers (1856-1954) whose monumental gathering of everything related to Shakespeare that was known up to 1930 proved half the battle already done. Similarly I acknowledge the extensive work that Professor Margaret Hannay has done to gather and present all that is known about the life and works of Mary Sidney, the Countess of Pembroke. Third, I recognize Charles Nicholl for his study of Thomas Nashe, the work that opened my eyes to the age's satirical underpinnings in terms of presenting 'the news'. I admit immediately that none of these scholars, nor any of the others whose works appear below, came to that reconstruction I have begun to present here and may, for whatever reason, wish not to be associated with a work such as mine. Nevertheless, I thank them.

F.F

SECONDARY SOURCES

Adams, Joseph Quincy. *Chief Pre-Shakespearean Dramas.* Cambridge, Mass.: The Riverside Press; Houghton Mifflin Co., 1924.

Adlard, George. *Amy Robsart and the Earl of Leicester ... and a History of Kenilworth Castle.* London: John Russell Smith, 1870.

Albright, Evelyn May. *Dramatic Publication in England 1580-1640.* New York: D.C. Heath and Company, 1927.

Arnold, Janet. *Lost from her Majesty's Back.* Wisbech: Costume Society, 1980.

BIBLIOGRAPHY

Aubrey, John. *Aubrey's Brief Lives*. Oliver Lawson Dick, ed. Ann Arbour, MI: University of Michigan Press, [1957].

Aubrey, John. *The Natural History of Wiltshire*. John Britten, ed. Newton-Abbot: David and Charles, 1969.

Axton, Marie. 'Robert Dudley and the Inner Temple Revels'. Cambridge, *Historical Journal*, 13 March 1970.

Baldwin, Thomas Whitfield. *On the literary genetics of Shakespeare's plays, 1592-1594*. Urbana: University of Illinois Press, 1959.

Bellany, Alastair. *The Politics of court scandal in early modern England: news culture and the Overbury affair, 1603-1660*. Cambridge: Cambridge University Press, 2002.

Berleth, Richard. *The Twilight lords: Elizabeth I and the plunder of Ireland*. Lanham, MD: Roberts, Rinehart, 2002.

Brennan, Michael. *Literary Patronage in the English Renaissance: the Pembroke family*. London: Routledge, 1988.

Brennan, Michael. "William Ponsonby: Elizabethan Stationer." in *Analytical & Enumerative Bibliography*, 7 (1983): 91-100.

Brigden, Susan. *New worlds, lost worlds: the rule of the Tudors 1485-1603*. Harmondsworth: Penguin Books, 2000.

Briggs, Julia. *This Stage-play World: Texts and Contexts, 1580-1625*. 2nd ed. Oxford: OUP, 1997.

Bruce, Alastair. *Keepers of the kingdom: the ancient offices of Britain*. London: Weidenfeld & Nicolson, 1999.

Butler, Lionel and Chris Given-Wilson. *Medieval Monasteries of Great Britain*. London: Michael Joseph, 1979.

Cambridge History of English and American Literature (1907-21), vol. 3 Renascence and Reformation. XVII. The Marprelate Controversy. http://www.bartleby.com/213/1701.html

Campbell, Lord John. *Shakespeare's Legal Acquirements Considered*. London: J. Murray, 1859.

Chambers, E.K. *William Shakespeare: a Study of Facts and Problems.* Oxford: Oxford University Press, 1930.

Chambers, E.K. *The Elizabethan Stage.* Oxford: Clarendon Press, 1923.

Cheney, Patrick. *Marlowe's Counterfeit Profession: Ovid, Spenser, Counter-Nationhood.* Toronto: University of Toronto Press, 1997.

Clark, Eleanor Grace. *Ralegh and Marlowe, a study in Elizabethan fustian.* New York: Russell and Russell, 1965.

Clegg, Cyndia Susan. *Press censorship in Elizabethan England.* Cambridge: Cambridge University Press, 1997.

Collins, Arthur. *Letters and Memorials of State, in the reigns of Queen Mary, Queen Elizabeth, King James, King Charles the first, part of the reign of King Charles the second, and Oliver's usurpation.* London: printed for T. Osborne, 1746.

Conley, C.H. *The First English Translators of the Classics.* New Haven, CN: Yale University Press, 1927.

Cook, Ann Jennalie. *The Privileged Playgoers of Shakespeare's London, 1576-1642.* Princeton: Princeton University Press, 1981.

Cross, Claire. *The Puritan Earl: The Life of Henry Hastings Third Earl of Huntingdon 1536-1595.* London: Macmillan, 1966.

Crupi, Charles W. *Robert Greene.* Boston: Twayne, 1986.

Dawley, Powel Mills. *John Whitgift and the English Reformation.* New York: Charles Scribner's Sons, 1954.

Duncan-Jones, Katherine. 'Sidney in Samothea: a Forgotten National Myth'. in *Review of English Studies.* n.s. v26 no98 May 1974: 174-177.

Duncan-Jones, Katherine. *Sir Philip Sidney: courtier poet.* New Haven: Yale University Press, 1991.

Duncan-Jones, Katherine. *Ungentle Shakespeare: scenes from his life.* London: The Arden Shakespeare, 2001.

Dunlop, Ian. *Palaces and Progresses of Elizabeth I*. London: Cape, [1962].

Eccles, Mark. 'Samuel Daniel in France and Italy'. *Studies in Philology*. xxxiv, 1937: 148-67.

Edmond, Mary. "Pembroke's Men." *Review of English Studies*. n.s. v.25 no 98 May 1974: 129-136.

Elliott, John R., Jr. *Playing God: Medieval mysteries on the modern stage*. Toronto: University of Toronto Press, 1989

Elton, G.R. *England under the Tudors*. London: Methuen, 1974.

Empson, William, *Faustus and the Censor: The English Faust-book and Marlowe's 'Doctor Faustus'*. Oxford: Blackwell, 1987.

Encyclopædia Britannica (1777-84). www.search.eb.com/shakespeare/classic/C00021.html

Fox, Alistair. *The English Renaissance: identity & representation in Elizabethan England*. Oxford: Blackwell Publishers, 1997.

Freeman, Arthur. *Thomas Kyd: Facts and Problems*. Oxford: Clarendon Press, 1967.

Gardiner, Father H.C. "Mysteries End; an investigation of the last days of the medieval religious stage." *Yale Studies in England*. v.103, 1967.

Garnier, Robert. *Two tragedies: Hippolyte and Marc Antoine*. Christine M. Hill and Mary G. Morrison, eds. London: Athlone Press, 1975.

Gibson, Wendy. "Sidney's Two Riddles." *Notes and Queries 24* (1977): 520-21.

Greville, Fulke, Baron Brooke. *Life of Sir Philip Sidney*. 1st pub. 1652. Introd. by Nowell Smith. [Oxford]: Clarendon Press, 1907.

Gurr, Andrew with John Orrell. *Rebuilding Shakespeare's Globe*. London: Weidenfeld and Nicolson, 1989.

Gurr, Andrew. *The Shakespearean Playing Companies.* Clarendon: Oxford, 1996.

Gurr, Andrew. *The Shakespearean Stage, 1574-1642.* Cambridge: Cambridge University Press, 1980.

Hamilton, A.C. *Sir Philip Sidney: a study of his life and works.* Cambridge: Cambridge University Press, 1977.

Hannay, Margaret P. "'How I these studies prize': the Countess of Pembroke and Elizabethan Science" in *Women, Science and Medicine 1500-1700: Mothers and Sisters of the Royal Society,* Lynette Hunter and Sarah Hutton, eds. Phoenix Mill, UK: Sutton Publishing, 1997.

Hannay, Margaret P. *Philip's Phoenix: Mary Sidney, Countess of Pembroke.* New York and Oxford: Oxford University Press, 1990.

Hannay, Margaret P. "Mary Sidney Herbert, Countess of Pembroke." http://www.siena.edu/hannay/MarySidney.htm

Harbage, Alfred. *Annals of English drama 975-1700.* rev. by S. Schoenbaum. London: Methuen, [1964].

Herbert, Sidney, 16th Earl of Pembroke. *Wilton House* [VISITORS GUIDE]. n.p.=n.d.

Hogue, Arthur R. *Origins of the common law.* Indianapolis, IN: Liberty Fund, 1986.

Honan, Park. *Shakespeare, a life.* Oxford: Oxford University Press, 1999.

Horne, David H. *Life and Minor Works of George Peele.* New Haven: Yale, 1952.

The House of Commons, 1558-1603. P.W. Hasler, ed. London: H.M.S.O., 1981.

Howell, R. *Sir Philip Sidney, the Shepherd Knight.* London: Hutchison, 1968.

Huffman, Clifford Chalmers. *Elizabethan Impressions: John Wolfe and His Press.* New York: AMS Press, 1988.

Hull, Suzanna. *Chaste, Silent and Obedient: English Books for Women, 1475-1640.* San Marino, CA: Huntingdon Library, 1982.

Illustrations of British History, Biography and Manners [1838]. Edmund Lodge, ed. Westmead, England: Gregg, 1969.

An Introductory Sketch to the Martin Marprelate Controversy 1588-90. Edward Arber, ed. New York: Burt Franklin, 1895.

Jenkins, Elizabeth. *Elizabeth and Leicester.* London: Phoenix Press, 1961.

John Dee's Library Catalogue. Julian Roberts and Andrew G. Watson, eds. London: The Bibliographical Society, 1990.

Jones, J. Gwynfor. *The Welsh Gentry 1536-1640: Images of Status, Honour and Authority.* Cardiff: University of Wales Press, 1998.

Kendall, Alan. *Robert Dudley: Earl of Leicester.* London: Cassell, 1980

Larsen, Thorleif. "The Early Years of George Peele, Dramatist, 1558-1588." in *Transactions of the Royal Society of Canada*, 22 (1928), 271-318.

Lewis, C.S. *English Literature in the Sixteenth Century, excluding drama.* Oxford: Clarendon Press, 1954.

Lloyd, David. *State-worthies, or the Statesmen and Favourites of England from the Reformation to the Revolution [1679].* London: printed for J. Robson, 1766.

Lucas, Caroline. *Writing for Women: the example of Woman as Reader in Elizabethan Romance.* Milton Keynes: Open University Press, 1989.

Maguire, Laurie. E. *Shakespearean suspect texts.* Cambridge: Cambridge University Press, 1996.

Marlowe, Christopher. *Doctor Faustus and other plays.* David Bevington and Eric Rasmussen, eds. Oxford: Oxford University Press, 1998.

May, Steven W. *The Elizabethan Courtier Poets: The Poems and Their Contexts.* Columbia and London: University of Missouri Press, 1991.

MacCaffrey, Wallace T. *Elizabeth I: War and Politics 1588-1603.* Princeton, NJ: Princeton University Press, 1992.

McCormick, Mary Martin. "A Critical edition of Abraham Fraunce's 'The Sheapheardes Logike' and 'Twoe General Discourses'". dissertation. St. Louis University, 1968.

McGinn, Donald J. *John Penry and the Marprelate Controversy.* New Brunswick, NJ: Rutgers University Press, 1966.

McMillin, Scott. 'Casting for Pembroke's Men: The Henry VI Quartos and The Taming of A Shrew', *SQ* 23 (1972), 141-159.

McMillin, Scott and Sally-Beth MacLean. *The Queen's Men and their Plays.* Cambridge: Cambridge University Press, 1998.

Michell, John. *Who wrote Shakespeare?* London: Thames and Hudson, 1996.

Murray, John Tucker. *English Dramatic Companies 1558-1642.* New York: Russell & Russell, 1963.

Nashe, Thomas. "Preface to Robert Greene's Menaphon" in *The English Stage: Attack and Defense 1577-1730.* Arthur Freeman, ed. New York & London: Garland Publishing, Inc., 1973.

Nashe, Thomas. *The Works of Thomas Nashe.* Ronald B. McKerrow, ed. volume 1. London : A. H. Bullen [etc.], 1904-10.

Nicholl, Charles. *A Cup of news: the life of Thomas Nashe.* London and Boston: Routledge & Kegan Paul, 1984.

North, Douglass C. & Robert Paul Thomas. *The Rise of the western world: a new economic history.* Cambridge: Cambridge University Press, 1973. repr. 1996.

Osborn, James M. *Young Philip Sidney 1572-1577.* New Haven and London: Yale University Press, 1972.

Parmenius, Stephen. T*he New Found Land of Stephen Parmenius: the Life and Writings of a Hungarian Poet, Drowned on a Voyage From Newfoundland, 1583.* David Beers Quinn and Neil M. Chesire, eds. & transls. Toronto: University of Toronto Press, 1972.

Patronage in the Renaissance, Gary Fitch Lytle and Stephen Orgel, eds. Princeton: Princeton University Press, 1981.

Patterson, Annabel. *Censorship and Interpretation: the conditions of writing and reading in early modern England.* Madison, WI: University of Wisconsin Press, 1984.

Peck, D.C. "Raleigh, Sidney, Oxford, and the Catholics, 1579." N&Q25 (1978) 427-31.

Perry, Mary. *The Word of a prince.* Woodbridge, Suffolk: Boydell Press, 1990; pb. repr. 1999.

Pettifer, Adrian. *English castles: a guide by counties.* Woodbridge, Suffolk: Boydell Press, 1995.

Picard, Liza. *Elizabeth's London: everyday life in Elizabethan London.* London: Weidenfeld & Nicolson, 2003.

Pritchard, R.E. *Shakespeare's England: life in Elizabethan & Jacobean times.* Phoenix Mill, Gloucestershire: Sutton Publishing, 1999.

Prouty, Charles Tyler. *The Contention and Shakespeare's 2 Henry VI: a comparative study.* New Haven: Yale University Press, 1954.

Rebholz, R.A. *The Life of Fulke Greville, first Lord Brooke.* Oxford: Clarendon Press, 1971.

Rees, Joan. *Samuel Daniel: a Critical and Biographical Study.* Liverpool: Liverpool University Press, 1964.

The Revels History of Drama in English, Leech and Craik, gen. eds. *Volume III* 1576-1613, J. Leeds Barroll et al, eds. London: Methuen, 1975.

Roob, Alexander. *Alchemy & Mysticism: the Hermetic Museum.* Köln: Taschen, 1997.

Rollins, Hyder E. & Herschel Baker. *The Renaissance in England: non-dramatic prose and verse of the sixteenth century.* Prospect Heights, Ill., 1954; 1992 reissue.

Rosenberg, Eleanor. *Leicester, Patron of Letters.* New York: Columbia University Press, 1955.

Sargent, Ralph M. *The Life and Lyrics of Sir Edward Dyer.* Oxford: Clarendon Press, 1968.

Schoenbaum, S. *William Shakespeare, a Documentary Life.* Oxford: Clarendon Press, 1975.

Shakespeare, William. *The Complete works of Shakespeare.* Hardin Craig, ed. Glenview, Ill. Scott, Foresman and Company, 1961.

Shakespeare, William. *King Henry VI, part 1.* intro. and ed. by Edward Burns. London: Arden Shakespeare, 2000.

Shapiro, Michael. *Children of the Revels.* New York: Columbia University Press, 1977.

Sheavyn, Phoebe. *The Literary Profession in the Elizabethan Age,* Manchester: University Press, 1909.

Sidney, Mary. *Historical Guide to Penshurst Place.* Tunbridge Wells: Goulden & Curry, 1931.

Sidney, Philip. *The Sidneys of Penshurst.* London: S.H. Bousfield & Co., 1901.

Skeel, C.A.J. *The Council in the Marches of Wales: A study in Local Government during the Sixteenth and Seventeenth Centuries.* London: H. Rees, 1904.

Smith, Alan G.R. *The Emergence of a nation state: the commonwealth of England 1529-1660.* New York: Longman, 1984.

Somerset, Anne. *Ladies in waiting: from the Tudors to the present day.* London: Phoenix Press, 1984.

Spurgeon, Caroline F.E. *Shakespeare's Imagery and What it Tells Us.* Cambridge: University Press, 1935.

Stone, Lawrence. *The Crisis of the Aristocracy, 1558-1641.* Oxford: Clarendon Press, 1965.

Strayer, Joseph R. *On the Medieval Origins of the Modern State.* Princeton, NJ: Princeton University Press, 1970.

Tasso, Torquato. *Aminta.* Malcolm Hayward, transl. Indiana: University of Pennsylvania, 1997.

Taufer, Alison. *Holinshed's Chronicles.* New York: Twain Publishers, 1999.

Taylor, Michael. *Henry VI, part 1.* Oxford: Oxford University Press, 2003.

Thomas, W.S.K. *Tudor Wales.* Llandysul, Wales: Gomer Press, 1983.

Trevelyan, G.M. *English social history.* Harmondsworth: Penguin Books, 2000.

Tyrwhitt, Thomas. in *The dramatick writings of Will. Shakspere : with the notes of all the various commentators, printed complete from the best editions of Sam. Johnson and Geo. Steevens.* London : Printed for, and under the direction of, John Bell, 1788.

Urry, William. *Christopher Marlowe and Canterbury.* London: Faber and Faber, 1988.

van Dorsten, Jan A. *Poets, Patrons, and Professors: Sir Philip Sidney, Daniel Rogers, and the Leiden Humanists.* Leiden: Leiden University Press, 1962.

van Dorsten, J.A.. *The Radical Arts: the first decade of an Elizabethan renaissance.* Leiden: Leiden University Press, 1970.

Varn, Lynette Kuran. "The Might in Marlowe's Line: a Linguistic Examination". PhD dissertation. University of South Carolina, 1981.

Vickers, Brian. *Shakespeare, co-author.* Oxford: Oxford University Press, 2002.

Warwick, Frances Evelyn Maynard Greville. *Warwick Castle and its Earls, from Saxon times to the present day.* London: Hutchison & Co., 1903.

Wentersdorf, Karl P. 'The Origin and Personnel of the Pembroke Company' in *Theatre Research International,* v.5 no.1 Winter 1979-80: 45-68.

Wildman, W.B. *A Short History of Sherborne from 705 A.D.* Sherborne: F. Bennett, 1896.

Williams, Glanmore. *Recovery, reorientation, and reformation: Wales, c.1415 – 1642.* Oxford: Clarendon Press, 1987.

Williams, Neville. *All the Queen's Men.* London: Cardinal, 1974.

Wilson, F.P. *Marlowe and the early Shakespeare.* Oxford: Clarendon Press, 1953.

Wilson, Mona. *Sir Philip Sidney.* London: Rupert Hart-Davis, 1950.

Women and literature in Britain, 1500-1700. Helen Wilcox, ed. Cambridge: Cambridge University Press, 1996.

Worden, Blair. *The Sound of virtue: Philip Sidney's Arcadia and Elizabethan politics.* New Haven & London: Yale University Press, 1996.

The Works of Thomas Kyd. Frederick S. Boas, ed. Oxford: Clarendon Press, 1962.

Yates, Frances A. *John Florio: the Life of an Italian in Shakespeare's England*. New York: Octagon Books, 1968.

PRIMARY SOURCES

All titles are given in modern English. Those seeking the original should use 16th and 17th century spellings of these titles.

Anonymous. *The First part of the Contention betwixt the two famous Houses of York and Lancaster, with the death of the good Duke Humphrey*. London: printed by Thomas Creed for Thomas Millington, 1594.

Anonymous. *A Pleasant conceited history called The Taming of a Shrew*. London: Peter Short [for] Cuthbert Burbie, 1594.

Anonymous. *The True Tragedy of Richard Duke of York, and the death of good King Henry the Sixth*. London: P[eter] S[hort] for Thomas Millington, 1595.

Ascham, Roger. *The Schoolmaster*. Edward Arber, ed. Westminster: A. Constable and Co. Ltd., 1903.

The Geneva Bible, a facsimile copy of the 1560 edition. With an introduction by Lloyd E. Berry. Madison: University of Wisconsin Press, 1969.

Breton, Nicholas. *Britton's Bowre of Delights, 1591*. Hyder Edward Rollins, ed. New York: Russell & Russell, [1968].

Breton, Nicholas. *The honourable entertainment given to the Queen's Majesty, in progress, at Elvetham in Hampshire*. 2nd ed. London: John Wolfe, 1591.

Breton, Nicholas. *The Pilgrimage to Paradise, joined with the Countess of Pembroke's love*. Oxford: Joseph Barnes, 1592.

Camden, William. *The History of the most Reverend and Victorious Princess Elizabeth...composed by Way of Annals*. London: Benjamin Fisher, 1630.

Churchyard, Thomas. *The Epitaph of Sir Philip Sidney Knight, lately Lord Governor of Flushing.* London: printed by George Robinson for Thomas Cadman, [1587].

Daniel, Samuel. *A Defence of Rhyme: Against a Pamphlet entitled: Observations in the Art of English Poesy.* London: printed by V.S. for Edward Blount, 1603.

Daniel, Samuel. *Delia. Containing certain Sonnets: with the complaint of Rosamond.* London: printed by J.C. for Simon Waterson, 1592.

Daniel, Samuel. *Musophilus.* London: printes by P.S. for Simon Waterson, 1599.

Fenton, Geoffrey. *Certain tragical discourses written out of French and Latin.* London: Thomas Marsh, 1567.

Fraunce, Abraham. *The Lamentations of Amyntas for the death of Phillis.* London: printed by John Wolfe for Thomas Gubbin, 1587.

Fraunce, Abraham. *The Arcadian rhetoric: or the precepts of rhetoric made plain by examples, Greek, Latin, English, Italian, French, Spanish.* London: printed by Thomas Orwin, 1588.

Fraunce, Abraham. *The Lawyer's logic, exemplifying the precepts of logic by the practice of the common law.* London: printed by William How, 1588.

Fraunce, Abraham. *The Countess of Pembroke's Ivychurch.* London: printed by Thomas Orwin for William Ponsonby, 1591.

Fraunce, Abraham. *The Countess of Pembroke's Emmanuel. Containing the Nativity, Passion, Burial, and Resurrection of Christ : together with certain Psalms of David.* All in English Hexameters. London: printed for William Ponsonby, 1591.

Gascoigne, George and others. *The Princely Pleasures at the Court at Kenilworth.* in *The complete works of George Gascoigne,* volume 2. John W. Cunliffe, ed. Cambridge: Cambridge University Press, 1910.

The plays & poems of Robert Greene. Ed. with intro. and notes, by J. Churton Collins. Freeport, N.Y., Books for Libraries Press [1970]. Greene, Robert. *Menaphon: Camilla's alrum to slumbering Euphues, in his melancholy Cell at Silexedra.* London: printed by T[homas] O[rwin] for Sampson Clarke, 1589.

Greene, Robert. *Menaphon: Camilla's alarm to slumbering Euphues in his melancholy cell at Silexedra.* Edited with introduction and notes by Brenda Cantar. Ottawa : Dovehouse Editions, 1996.

Greene, Robert. *A disputation, between a he conny-catcher, and a she conny-catcher.* London: By A. I[effes] for T. G[ubbin], 1592.

[Greene, Robert.] *The Defence of Conny-catching or A Confutation of Those two injurious Pamphlets published by R.G. against the practitioners of many Nimble-witted and mystical Sciences. By Cuthbert Cunny-catcher, Licentiate in Whittington College.* [London, 1592.]

Greene, Robert. *A Quip for an Upstart Courtier.* London: John Wolfe, 1592.

Greene, Robert, *The Black Book's Messenger.* London: John Danter, 1592.

Greene, Robert [and Henry Chettle]. *Greene's groatsworth of wit: bought with a million of repentance (1592).* D. Allen Carroll, ed. Binghampton, New York: Medieval & Renaissance texts and studies, 1994. also G.B. Harrison, ed. London: Bodley Head, 1923. and, London: as imprinted for William Wright, 1592.

Greville, Fulke, Lord Brooke. *Certain Learned and Elegant Works.* London: printed by E[lizabeth] P[urslowe] for Henry Seyle, 1633.

Harington, Sir John. *Nugae Antiquae.* London: printed for W. Fredericks at Bath, 1769.

Harvey, Richard. A *Theological Discourse of The Lamb of God and His Enemies.* London: imprinted by John Windet for W[illiam] P[onsonby], 1590.

Harvey, Richard. *Plain Percevall, the peace-maker of England.*

[London]: printed [for G. Seton, 1590].

Hentzner, Paul. *Travels in England During the Reign of Queen Elizabeth.* Nuremberg, 1612; Richard Bentley, transl. London, 1797. HTML rendering by Steve Thomas, 2004. http://etext.library.adelaide.edu.au/h/hentzner-travels/

Holinshed, Raphael. *The Chronicles of England, Scotland and Ireland.* London: J. Jonson, et al, 1807-8.

Leicester's Commonwealth: The Copy of a Letter Written by a Master of Art of Cambridge (1584) and Related Documents. D.C. Peck, ed. Athens: Ohio University Press, 1985.

Lyly, John. *Euphues: The Anatomy of Wit.* London: Gabriel Cawood, 1578.

Meres, Francis. *Palladis Tamia.* London: P[eter] Short for Cuthbert Burbie, 1598.

Painter, William. *The Palace of Pleasure.* introd. by Hamish Miles. London : Cresset Press, 1929.

Petrarch, Francisco. *Il canzoniere; e, I trionfi.* Rome: Salerno, 1993.

Puttenham, George. *The Art of English Poesy.* Electronic Text Center, University of Virginia Library. http://etext.lib.virginia.edu/toc/modeng/public/PutPoes.html

Queen's Majesty's entertainment at Woodstock, 1575. from the unique fragment of the edition of 1585, including the Tale of Hemetes the Hermit, and a comedy in verse, probably by George Gascoigne. Oxford, Reprinted by H. Daniel and H. Hart, 1903 & 1910.

Shakespeare, William. *Mr. William Shakespeare's comedies, histories, & tragedies.* London: Isaac Jaggard and Ed. Blount, 1623. fac. pub. New York: Applause, 1995.

Sidney, Sir Henry. *A Viceroy's vindication? : Sir Henry Sidney's memoir of service in Ireland 1556-1578.* Ciaran Brady, ed. Cork:

Cork University Press, 2002.

Sidney, Mary, Countess of Pembroke. *The Triumph of Death and other Unpublished and Uncollected Poems by Mary Sidney, Countess of Pembroke (1561-1621).* G.F. Waller, ed. Salzburg: Institut für Englische Sprache und Literatur, Universität Salzburg, 1977.

Sidney, Mary, Countess of Pembroke. *The Collected works of Mary Sidney Herbert Countess of Pembroke.* Margaret P. Hannay, Noel J. Kinnamon and Michael G. Brennan, eds. Oxford: Clarendon Press, 1998.

Sidney, Sir Philip. *Defence of Poesie, Astrophil and Stella and other writings.* Elizabeth Porges Watson, ed. London: J.M. Dent, 1997.

Sidney, Philip. *Miscellaneous Prose of Sir Philip Sidney.* Katherine Duncan-Jones and Jan van Dorsten, eds. Oxford: Carendon Press, 1973.

Sidney, Sir Philip. *The Countess of Pembroke's Arcadia.* Maurice Evans, ed. Harmondsworth, Middlesex: Penguin, 1977.

Sidney, Sir Philip. *The old Arcadia.* Katherine Duncan-Jones, ed. Oxford: Oxford University Press, 1999.

Sidney, Sir Philip. *The Poems of Sir Philip Sidney.* W.A. Ringler, ed. Oxford: OUP, 1962.

Sir P.S. His Astrophel and Stella. London: printed for Thomas Newman, 1591.

Sir P.S. His Astrophel and Stella. London: printed for Matthew Lownes, 1591.

Sir P.S. His Astrophel and Stella. London: printed for Thomas Newman, 1592.

Spenser, Edmund. *The Shorter Poems.* Richard A. McCabe, ed. Harmondsworth: Penguin, 1999.

Spenser, Edmund. *The Works of Edmund Spenser.* Ware, Hertfordshire:

Wordsworth Editions, 1995.

Stow, John. *A Survey of London.* London: printed by Elizabeth Purslow, 1633.

Webbe, William. *Discourse of English Poetry.* London: John Charlewood for Robert Walley, 1586.

INDEX

A

actors 5, 18–23, 43–44, 46, 48, 57, 99–100
  touring 18, 22, 43, 44, 53, 99–100, 119, 156
Admiral's Men 22–23, 43, 46–47, 57, 61, 146
Aesop's Fables 67, 71, 72
alchemy *vi*, 72, 81, 87–88, 126, 146
Allen, Thomas 29
Alleyn, Edward 23, 42, 47, 57, 61, 99
Amaranthus (soubriquet) 82
Amaryllis (soubriquet) 81–82
Aminta 33
Amoris Lachrimae 42, 69
A Notable Discovery of Cozenage 112
A Poetical Rhapsody 147
Arcadia 24, 28–29, 30, 31, 32–33, 35, 80, 102, 144–145, 146, 157
Archilosus (soubriquet) 86
Arden, Mary 3
Aretino 105
Ascham, Roger
  The Schoolmaster 134
astrology *vi*, 21, 29, 81
Astrophel (soubriquet) 32, 64, 65, 68, 83, 88
Astrophel and Stella 32, 64, 65, 76, 79
Aubrey, John 24, 81, 132, 139

B

Bacon, Francis 53, 128, 157
bear and ragged staff (emblem) 18, 42, 107, 133
Beauchamp Court 14, 15
Belleau, Rémy 35
Bible vii
  Genevan edition 36, 37, 131
Black Book's Messenger, The 113
blank verse 39, 41, 49–50, 51, 54–55, 56, 58, 62, 70, 95, 96
Book of Martyrs 131

Book of the Courtier 84
Brayne, Eleanor 22, 60
Bretchgirdle, John 5
BRETON, NICHOLAS 42, 45, 61, 64, 66, 68, 69, 70, 74, 75,
77, 83–90, 101–102, 111, 115, 120, 126, 137, 146, 154, 155

and Mary Sidney 42, 68, 69–70, 74, 84–90, 101–102, 111, 115,
120, 126, 137, 146, 154, 155

works
Britton's Bower of Delights 42, 66
Amoris Lachrimae 42, 69
*Pilgrimage to Paradise, The, joined with the
Countess of Pembroke's love* 83–90

Britannia 14, 32
broadcasting 21, 43
press 21, 43, 53, 67, 83, 85
pulpit 7, 21, 43
stage 19, 43–44, 53, 56, 57, 145, 146
Bryskett, Lodowick 132
Burbage, Cuthbert 22, 60
Burbage, James *iv*, 12, 17–20, 21–24, 30, 42–43, 47,
60–61, 75, 115
Burbage, Richard (actor) 22, 23, 60–61, 75
burrs (soubriquet) 115
Busby, John 100–101, 111

C

Cambridge (university) 32, 48, 49, 53, 54, 58, 110, 114, 157
Camden, William
Britannia 14, 32
Campion, Thomas 65
Carey, Sir Henry, Lord Chamberlain 21, 22
Case, John Dr. 84, 88
Castiglione, Baldassare
Book of the Courtier 84
Catholicism *vi*, 4, 10, 26–27, 52, 58, 109
Cecil, William, Lord Burghley, Lord Tresurer 73, 108
censorship 100, 116

Certain Tragical Discourses 134–135
Charlecote, Warwickshire 15
Chaucer, Geoffrey *i*, 26, 27, 60
Chettle, Henry 47, 54, 113, 156
  Greene's Groatsworth of Wit 47–48, 112–118, 120–121
children's companies 21, 53, 146
Christ Church (Oxford) 84
Church of England *vi*, 52, 54, 81, 100, 105, 109, 110, 111
Churchyard, Thomas 32, 80
  Epitaph of Sir Philip Sidney Knight 32
Clarendon House, Wilts. 28, 30
class, social *iii, iv, vii*, 6, 12, 14, 24, 25, 41, 43, 44, 61, 112
Clifford, Rosamond 80
Cobbler of Canterbury 60, 70
Colin Clout (soubriquet) 77, 81, 104
Colin Clout's Come Home Again 41, 77–83
Combe, John 2
Comedy of Errors, The 121, 143, 145, 156
Complaints 30, 42, 83
Complaint of Rosamond, The 80
conny catchers 112–113, 116, 127, 172
Cook Robert, Clarenceux King-of-Arms 8
copyright 67, 73
Corialanus 133
Corydon (soubriquet) 79
Council of Wales 12, 15–16, 96, 129
Countess of Pembroke's Arcadia (1590) 24, 30, 32, 33, 35, 80, 144
Countess of Pembroke's Arcadia (1593) 144-5, 146, 157
Countess of Pembroke's Emmanuel 76, 88
Countess of Pembroke's Ivychurch 82
Countess of Pembroke's Love 83, 86–90
Court of High Commission 110
Covell, William *ii*
Croydon (London) 100
Cuddy (character) 147

D

D'Avenant, Sir William 14
Daniel, Samuel 64–65, 79–80, 145, 157
  Delia 79
  Musophilus 80
dark lady (character) ii, 28–30, 32, 64, 86
David
  Psalms 32, 36–37, 41, 76
Davison, Francis
  A Poetical Rhapsody 147
Dee, John 21
De Illorum Daemonum 111
Delia 79
Devereux, Penelope 28–29, 64
  as *dark lady* ii, 28–30, 64, 86
  as *Philoclea* 28
  as *Stella* 28, 86
Devereux, Robert, Earl of Essex 157
Devereux, Sir Walter, Earl of Essex 29, 108
  as *Forester* 108
de Vere, Edward, Earl of Oxford 26–27, 53, 65, 73, 133, 146, 157
Dialectica 32
Diana (soubriquet) 30, 34, 86, 106
Dowgate (London) 112, 116
dropsy 112
Du Bartas, Guillaume de Salluste 35
Dudley, Ambrose, Earl of Warwick 4, 5, 6, 7, 8, 13, 17, 29, 42, 43, 129, 133, 135, 136, 137
Dudley, John, Duke of Northumberland 4, 129
Dudley, Katherine, Countess of Huntingdon 135, 136
Dudley, Lady Mary 31, 41, 129, 132, 134, 135, 137
Dudley, Robert, Earl of Leicester 4, 7, 8, 10, 14, 15, 17, 18, 19, 20, 21, 22, 23, 27, 31, 42, 43, 47, 52, 73, 78, 83, 104, 107, 109, 110, 111, 129, 131, 133, 135, 136, 137, 147
  and Warwickshire 10, 14, 15
  and extreme Protestantism 17, 52, 131
  and John Whitgift 73

and Martin Marprelate controversy 111
and Sir Walter Ralegh 78
as *Bear* 106–110, 147
as literary patron 133
as Master of the Horse 4, 107, 129
as paterfamilias 24, 43
chancellor of Oxford University 83
Kenilworth royal visit (1575) 7, 14, 19, 24
Netherlands expedition (1585) 31, 47
romance with Elizabeth I 7, 14, 78, 129, 132–133, 135–136
theatrical patronage 18, 20, 21, 22, 23, 27

Dugdale, Sir Walter 1–2
Dyer, Sir Edward 26
Dymoke, Sir Edward 79, 96
Dyos, Roger 5

E

Earl of Pembroke's Men. *See* Pembroke's Men
Edward VI 5, 129, 141
ELIZABETH I vi, 4, 5, 7-8, 14-5, 19, 21, 24, 25, 26, 27, 29, 30, 33, 34, 43, 52, 53, 58, 59, 73, 78, 79, 81, 83, 106, 107, 108, 109, 111, 119, 120, 125, 128, 129, 130, 131, 132, 133, 135, 136, 137, 138, 141, 142, 143, 144, 145, 146, 147-9
and Edward de Vere 53
and Ambrose Dudley 4
and Katherine Dudley 136
and Mary Dudley 132, 137
and Robert Dudley 108, 129, 132, 135–136, 138
and Fulke Greville 12, 14–15, 25
and Henry Herbert 33, 43
and Christopher Marlowe 58, 59
and Mary, Queen of Scots 108
and Thomas Nashe 58, 76, 111, 147–149
and Sir Walter Ralegh 30, 78, 81
and Sir Henry Sidney 129, 130, 131, 141
and Mary Sidney 14, 24, 29, 43, 73, 119–120, 128, 130, 132, 138, 141, 142–143, 144, 147–149

and Sir Philip Sidney 14–15, 26, 27, 34, 79
and Edmund Spenser 78–79
as *Astrea* 147, 148
as *Cynthia* 78
as *Diana* 30, 34, 86, 106
as *Faerie Queen* 78, 102
as *Gloriana* 79
as *Lion* 107, 109
French wedding proposal 26
governing style *vi*, 8, 21, 52, 53, 109
Privy Council orders 8, 59, 98, 107
processional visits 119–120, 128, 147
theatrical patronage 5, 21, 43, 53, 57, 146–147
English Civil War (15th C.) 61, 80, 99, 117, 121
Epitaph of Sir Philip Sidney Knight 32
Exchange (London) 76

F

Faerie Queen, The 78, 102
Fenton, Geoffrey 134
  Certain Tragical Discourses 134–135
'First Folio' (1623) contents recto, 1, 2, 11, 13, 127
First Part of the Contention betwixt the two famous Houses
  of York and Lancaster, The 61–63, 66, 70, 91–95, 122
Florio, John 79
  and Samuel Daniel 79
Fox (soubriquet) 109–111
Foxe, John
  Book of Martyrs 131
France 26, 27, 62, 99, 108, 131, 133, 136, 157
FRAUNCE, ABRAHAM 32–35, 37, 39, 68, 74, 76, 77, 79, 82,
  88, 96, 101, 141, 143, 146

  and the Council of Wales 79, 96
  and Ramus 32
  as *Corydon* 79
  as defender of Mary Sidney 74, 76–77, 146
  as tutor to Mary Sidney 34–35, 141, 143

education 32
patronage 32–33
works
The Arcadian Rhetoric 35
The Countess of Pembroke's Emmanuel 76, 88
The Countess of Pembroke's Ivychurch 82
The Lamentations of Amyntas 33–34, 81–82, 101
The Lawyer's Logic 33, 35, 141

Frobisher, Martin 8
fustian *vii*, 13

G

Gager, William 84, 85
Gammage, Barbara 78
Garnier, Robert 39, 57
  Marc Antoine 39–41, 57, 144
Gascoigne, George 84, 137
Gilbert, Adrian 81
Gileta of Narbonne 133
Globe (playhouse) 17, 20
Gloriana (soubriquet) 79
Golding, Arthur 133, 135
  Metamorphosis 133
Gosson, Stephen 19–20, 27, 46
  The School of Abuse 19–20, 27
Gough, John 130
Gravesend barge (soubriquet) 60, 70, 100
GREENE, ROBERT *ii, iv, v,* 15, 47–49, 50, 51, 52, 54, 55, 57, 59, 62, 65, 70–71, 92, 95, 97, 112–119, 121, 122, 126, 146, 154, 156

  and *The Cobbler of Canterbury* 60
  and *The First Part of the Contention* 62–63
  and Thomas Kyd 49–51, 54–57, 61
  and Christopher Marlowe 49–52, 54, 59, 60, 61, 113–114
  and Thomas Nashe 54–55, 57–58, 61
  and Pembroke's Men 47, 113–118

and William Shakspere 97, 118, 127, 154
as Pasquil (pseudonym) 52, 54
works
  Alphonsus King of Aragon 50
  A Notable Discovery of Cozenage 106
  Greene's Groatsworth of Wit 112–118, 120–121
    To his quondam acquaintance 113–118
  Menaphon 54, 55, 60, 61, 65, 71, 165, 172
  Penelope's Web 49
  Perimedes, the Blacksmith 50, 59–60, 113
  Quip for an upstart courtier 114, 116
  The Black Book's Messenger 113, 172
  The Repentance of a Conny-catcher 113

Greene's Groatsworth of Wit 48–49, 113–119, 120–121
GREVILLE, FULKE 12–16, 24–26, 30, 32, 79, 80, 96–97, 137, 144
  and Elizabeth I 14–15, 25
  and Samuel Daniel 79–80
  and Sir William D'Avenant 14
  and Robert Dudley 14
  and Ben Jonson *ii*, 13
  and Sir Thomas Lucy 15–16, 96
  and William Shakespeare 12
  and William Shakspere 12, 13, 14, 15, 96-7
  and Mary Sidney 14, 16, 24, 30, 96–97, 137, 144
  and Sir Philip Sidney 13, 16, 24, 25, 26
  as *Shakspeare's Master* *iv*, 12–13, 96–97
  as M.P. for co. Warwick 15
  as Clerk, Council of Wales 15

Greville, Fulke, Sir 14
Grey, Lady Jane 4, 129

H

Harington, Sir John
  Nugae Antiquae 81

Harvey, Gabriel *ii*, 114, 121, 157
Harvey, Dr. Richard 53, 114
Hastings, Henry, Earl of Huntingdon 135, 136
Henslowe, Philip 23, 99, 100
Herbert, Henry, Earl of Pembroke 15, 16, 24, 25, 29, 33, 43, 63, 75, 105, 138, 140
  as Lord President of Wales 15, 63, 67
Herbert, Sir William, 1st Earl of Pembroke 141, 142
Herbert, William *ii*, 29, 80
History of Error 143
Holinshed's Chronicles 31, 61, 130
Homer 35
Horace 35
Howard, Charles Lord Admiral 22–23

I

Inns of Court 32, 95
Isam, Mrs. 112, 121
Italy 64, 79, 132, 133
Ivychurch 82

J

James I 12
Jane I 129
Jewel, Simon (actor) 118, 120
Joan of Arc 99
Johannes factotum (soubriquet) 118
Jonson, Ben *ii*, 1, 11, 13
  role in First Folio 13
Jupiter and Saturn, conjunction of 21
Juvenal (soubriquet) 114

K

Kenilworth royal visit (1575) 7, 14, 19, 24, 109, 135, 136
Kent (shire) 24, 99, 135, 141
King's Lynn (town) 99
Knollys, Lettice Countess of Essex 108

KYD, THOMAS *iv*, 23, 45, 46, 48, 49, 50, 52, 54, 55–57, 58, 59, 61, 65, 75, 120, 121, 146, 156

and Christopher Marlowe 48, 49, 52, 58, 65
and *The First Part of the Contention* 61–62
and Robert Greene 49–51, 54–57, 61
and 'The Play of Rome' 49, 50, 51
and *The Taming of a Shrew* 65, 119
and *The True Tragedy of Richard, Duke of York* 99

L

Laura (character) 39
Leicester, Earl of. *See* Dudley, Robert, Earl of Leicester
Leicester's Hospital 110
Leicester's Men 18–22, 27, 143
Linceus (soubriquet) 110
Lodge, Thomas
  as Pasquil 54
Lord's Room (playhouse) 19–20, 44
Lucrece i, 133
Lucy, Sir Thomas 10, 12, 14, 15, 16, 79, 96, 118, 128
  as permanent member of Council of Wales 15
Lycambes (soubriquet) 86
Lyly, John 53, 146

M

Marc Antoine 39, 57
Marin (character) 78
MARLOWE, CHRISTOPHER *iv*, 23, 41, 45, 46, 47, 48, 49, 50–51, 57–58, 60–62, 65, 70, 99, 113–114, 117, 121, 128, 144, 146, 156, 157

and *The First Part of the Contention* 61–62
and Robert Greene 48, 49–51, 59–60, 113–114
and *Tarlton's news out of Purgatory* 59
and Thomas Kyd 48, 49, 51, 58–59, 65
and Thomas Nashe 48, 54–55, 58–59, 65, 70, 100, 113
and *The Taming of a Shrew* 65–66, 119

    and 'The Play of Rome' 51
    and *The True Tragedy of Richard, Duke of York* 99
    as *Gravesend barge* 70, 100
    works
      Tamburlaine 41, 46, 49, 50, 51, 59
      The Tragical History of Dido, Queen of Carthage 58
      Doctor Faustus 51–52, 57
Martin Marprelate controversy 53–54, 73, 110–111, 146, 149
Martin Marprelate (pseudonym)
  as *Chameleon* 110
Mary (mother of Jesus) 146
Mary Magdalene 146
Mary I 4, 129
Mary Queen of Scots 108
Master of the Revels 21
Menaphon 54, 55, 60, 61, 65, 71
Metamorphosis 133
Mira (soubriquet) 26, 30
Mirror for Magistrates 80
Maria, Mistress 132
Molineux, Edmund 31, 130
Morton (criminal) 113
Myra (soubriquet) 26

N

NASHE, THOMAS *ii, iv, v*, 45, 47, 48, 51, 53–59, 60–74, 76, 79, 83, 84, 85, 87–88, 94, 95, 96, 99–111, 113, 114–117, 120, 146–149, 156, 157

  and Admiral's Men 57
  and Edward Alleyn 57
  and Nicholas Breton 66, 69–70, 83, 85–86
  and *The First Part of the Contention* 63, 94
  and *Henry VI* 99
  and Robert Greene 54–55, 57–58, 61, 71, 112, 113, 114–115
  and Thomas Kyd 54–57, 57–59, 61, 65–66
  and Christopher Marlowe 54–55, 57–59, 61, 65–66, 70

and George Peele 61, 71–72
and Pembroke's Men 48, 61, 63, 64, 72, 75, 146–149
and Mary Sidney 64, 65, 68–69, 70, 72, 74, 87–88, 111, 114, 147–149
and Sir Philip Sidney 65, 66–67, 68, 101–103
and John Whitgift 73
as *Archilosus* 86
as *Aretino* 105
as *Juvenal* 114
as *Pasquil* 54, 58, 63
as *Pierce* v, 99, 100, 103, 104, 106, 111, 114, 147, 149
as *Piers* 100, 147–149

works
  Anatomy of Absurdity 58, 59
  Somewhat to read for them that list 65–74
  To the Gentlemen Students of Both Universities 54–59
  The Tragical History of Dido, Queen of Carthage 58
  Pierce Penniless his Supplication to the Devil 99–111, 115, 147
    tale of a Battledore 107–111

neo-Platonism vi, 72, 77, 81, 87–88, 90, 126, 146
Netherlands 22, 31, 32, 34, 42, 47, 86, 109
Newman, Thomas 65, 73, 76, 79, 145
Nugae Antiquae 81

O

Oriel College (Oxford) 83
Othello 134
Ovid 35, 133, 161
  Metamorphosis 133
Oxford (university) 5, 54, 83, 85, 88
  Oxford university press 83

P

Pasquil (pseudonym) 54, 58, 63
Peele, George iv, 23, 45, 46–47, 48, 61, 62–63, 71–72, 84, 85, 92, 99, 113, 115, 117, 121, 146, 156

Pembroke, Countess of. *See* Sidney, Mary Countess of Pembroke
Pembroke, Earl of. *See* Herbert, Henry, Earl of Pembroke
Pembroke's Men *iv*, 11, 12, 15, 16, 43, 44, 45, 46, 48, 54, 60, 61, 72, 91, 99, 113–121, 126, 146–147, 156, 157
  repertoire
    The Taming of a Shrew 65, 119
    The First Part of the Contention betwixt the two famous Houses of York and Lancaster 61–63, 66, 70, 91–95, 122
    The True Tragedy of Richard Duke of York 117, 122–125, 127
Penry, John 110
Penshurst (manor) 135, 141–142
Petrarch 35, 38–39, 41, 144
  Triumph of Death 38–39
pheon (arms) 142
Phillis (character) 33–34, 39
Philoclea (character) 28
phoenix (emblem) 17, 72, 87, 88, 90, 155, 157, 158
  phoenix nest 90, 157
Pictorius, Georgius
  De Illorum Daemonum 111
Pierce (soubriquet) *v*, 99, 100, 103, 104, 106, 111, 114, 147, 149
Piers (soubriquet) 100, 147, 148, 149
Pilgrimage to Paradise, The, joined with the Countess of Pembroke's love 83–90
'Play of Rome' 49, 50, 51
players. *See* actors
playhouses *iv*, 12, 17, 18, 19, 20, 22, 23, 44, 46, 97, 98, 99, 115, 116, 143
  economics of 12, 19–20
  physical design
    galleries 19
    Lord's Room 19, 20, 44
  Rose playhouse 23, 45, 46, 48, 98, 99
  Theatre playhouse *iv*, 12, 17, 19, 20, 22, 27, 41, 46, 47, 48, 49, 57, 70, 116, 143
A Poetical Rhapsody 147
Ponsonby, William 24

Presbyterianism 53, 109–110
Price, Henry 84
Protestantism 4–5, 10, 17, 26, 36, 53, 85, 131, 135
punctuation, value of *v–vi*
Puritanism 19, 20, 27, 53, 85, 106

Q

Queen's Men 5, 18, 21-2, 43, 50, 53, 57, 99, 146

R

Ralegh, Sir Walter 30, 77–78, 79, 81, 157
  and Adrian Gilbert 81
  and Edmund Spenser 30, 77, 78
  and Queen Elizabeth 77–78
  and Mary Sidney 78, 81, 157
Ramsbury (manor) 119, 120, 125, 128, 146, 147
Ramus, Pietrus (Ramée, Pierre de la)
  Dialectica 32
Repentance of a Conny-catcher 113
Richard III 121, 156
Roberto (character) 47–48
Rose (playhouse) 23, 43, 45, 46, 48, 98, 99
Ruins of Time, The 30–31, 32, 38, 41, 68
Russell, Anne, Countess of Warwick 8, 29, 133, 135, 137

S

Sappho 68–69
Saturn and Jupiter, conjunction of 21
Saxton, Christopher 130
Schoolmaster, The 134
School of Abuse 19, 27
Senecanism 18, 39, 41, 54, 55, 56–57

SHAKESPEARE, WILLIAM (THE POET) *i–v, vi*, 1–3,
  10, 11, 12, 13, 14, 17, 22, 29, 33, 35, 65, 74, 91–95, 97, 113,
  122–125, 127, 128, 131, 132, 135, 138–141, 143, 144, 145,

149–154, 156–159
and Fulke Greville 13–14, 96–97
and Mary Sidney 128, 129–135, 138–141, 142, 143, 145, 149–154, 156–159
rewriting Pembroke scripts 91–95, 122–125, 144, 145

works
Comedy of Errors 121, 143, 145, 156
'First Folio' (1623) 1, 2, 13, 127
2 Henry VI 62, 91–95
3 Henry VI 62, 122–125
Henry VIII 17
Love's Labours Lost 145
Othello 134
The Phoenix and the Turtle i
The Rape of Lucrece i
Richard III 121, 156
Shakespeare's Sonnets i, 29
Timon of Athens 133
Titus Andronicus 122, 156, 157
The Two Gentlemen of Verona 145
Venus & Adonis i, 157

Shakspere, John 3–9, 10, 14, 118
SHAKSPERE, WILLIAM (THE ACTOR) iv, 1–3, 9–12, 15–16, 17, 95–97, 113, 116–118, 127, 128, 129, 154

acting career 95–96
and James Burbage 17
and Fulke Greville 12–14, 15, 16, 96–97
and Mary Sidney 14, 15–16, 96–97, 116–118, 119, 126, 128, 129, 149–154
as *Johannes fac totum* 118
butcher's apprenticship 10, 12, 16
children 9
funerary poems 2, 128
monuments, Holy Trinity Church 2, 3
horse attendant 95

poaching 10
siblings 6

Shepherd's Calendar 27, 32, 147
Shepherd of the ocean (soubriquet) 78, 81
Sherborne Castle (manor) 81
Shoreditch (London) 12, 17, 23, 48, 112, 116, 118, 143
Shrewsbury 14, 32
Sidney, Sir Henry 15, 24, 31, 33, 129–132, 134, 140, 141
  Lord Deputy of Ireland 130, 139
  Lord President of Wales 63, 67, 129
SIDNEY, MARY COUNTESS OF PEMBROKE *iv, v,*
    14–15, 24–25, 26, 28–30, 31, 32, 34, 35–37, 38, 39, 41,
    42–43, 44, 57, 63–64, 65, 66, 67, 68–69, 70, 72, 73, 75,
    76–77, 78, 79, 80, 81, 82, 83, 84–90, 96, 103–104, 105, 119,
    128, 129–155

  and Nicholas Breton 42, 68, 69–70, 74, 84–86, 86–90, 101–102,
    111, 115, 120, 126, 137, 146, 154, 155
  and Samuel Daniel 64, 66, 79–80, 145, 157
  and Abraham Fraunce 32, 33–34, 34, 35, 37, 74, 76–77, 81–82,
    88, 96, 101, 141, 146
  and Fulke Greville 14, 15, 16, 24, 30, 79–80, 96–97, 137, 144
  and Thomas Nashe 64–65, 66, 67, 68–69, 70, 72, 73, 74, 76, 87,
    105, 111, 114, 147–149
  and Sir Walter Ralegh 78, 81, 157
  and Sir Philip Sidney 14–15, 16, 24, 25–30, 31, 32, 33–34,
    36–37, 38, 42, 64, 77, 81, 82, 86, 88–90, 149–151
  and Edmund Spenser 30–31, 32, 38, 41, 68, 74, 78, 79, 83,
    103–104
  as *Amaryllis* 81–82
  as *Marin* 78, 81
  as *Minerva* 68
  as *Mira* 26, 30
  as *Myra* 26
  as *Pallas* 73
  as *Thenot* 147-9
  as *Urania* 82–83
  as *Verlame* 32

children 80
siblings 31

works

To the Angel Spirit of the most excellent Sir Philip Sidney 149–154
Antonius 39–41, 57
A Dialogue between two shepherds 147–9
Psalms 32, 36–37, 41, 76
Triumph of Death 38–39

SIDNEY, SIR PHILIP 13, 14–15, 24, 26–30, 32, 33, 34, 38, 42, 64, 66, 67, 77, 79, 81, 82, 84, 86, 88–90, 101, 103, 115, 135, 136, 143, 149, 150, 162, 163

and Fulke Greville 14–15
as *Amaranthus* 82
as *Amyntas* 33–34, 81–82, 101, 102
as *Apollo* 66, 68–69
as *Astrophel* 65, 68, 83, 85, 88
as *Phoebus* 68
as *Pyrocles* 28

works

Arcadia (1580) 24, 28-9, 30, 31-2, 33, 35, 102, 144
Astrophel and Stella 32, 64, 65, 79
Countess of Pembroke's Arcadia (1590) 24, 30, 32, 33, 35, 80, 144
Countess of Pembroke's Arcadia (1593) 144-5, 146, 157
Sir P.S. His Astrophel and Stella 65, 79

Sidney, Sir William 141
Sir P.S. His Astrophel and Stella 65, 79
Southampton (town) 99
Southbank (London) 17, 23, 47

SPENSER, EDMUND 27, 30–31, 32, 38, 41, 42, 68, 74, 77–83, 94, 101, 102–105, 115, 145, 147

and Mary Sidney 30–31, 32, 38, 41, 42, 68, 74, 77, 78, 81, 82, 82–83, 103–104, 145, 147

works

Complaints 30
The Ruins of Time 30–31, 32, 38, 41, 68

The Tears of the Muses 83
Colin Clout's Come Home Again 41, 77–83
The Faerie Queene 78, 102–103
Stationers' Company 42, 59, 67, 73, 111, 113
Staunton, Judith 9
Stella (soubriquet) 28, 86
Strange's Men 23, 43, 99
Sylvia (character) 33

T

tale of a Battledore 107–111
The Taming of a Shrew 65, 119
Tasso, Torquato 33, 35
　Aminta 33, 82
Theatre (playhouse) *iv*, 12, 17, 19–20, 22, 27, 41, 46–47, 48, 49, 57, 66–67, 70, 116, 143
Thenot (soubriquet) 147–149
Throckmorton, Sir Nicholas 108
Tilney, Edmund 21
Timon of Athens 133–134
The True Tragedy of Richard Duke of York 99, 117, 122–125, 127

U

Urania (soubriquet) 83, 104
Urbina, Duchess of 84

V

Venus 30, 73, 157
Verlame 32
Virgil 35, 58

W

Waldegrave, Robert 111
Wales 15, 24, 25, 33, 79, 129, 130, 138–139, 141
Walsingham, Sir Francis 21
Warwick, Earls of. *See* Dudley, Ambrose and Dudley, John
Warwick (shire) 1, 4, 5, 8, 10, 14, 15, 110, 124, 129

Watson, Thomas 33, 82
Weever, John *ii*
Westminster 7, 10, 26, 95, 105, 143, 144
Whitgift, John, Archbishop of Canterbury 73, 100, 110
  as *Linceus* 110
Willobie, Henry *ii*
Wilton 24–25, 26, 28, 29, 30, 33, 34, 80, 81, 82, 89, 132, 139, 141, 143–144, 157
Worcester's Men 5

Z

Zutphen, Neth. 31

ISBN 1425107397